Marcia B. Siegel

MARCIA B. SIEGEL was born in New York
City, where she now lives, and graduated
from Connecticut College. She is currently
dance critic for the *Soho Weekly News* in
New York and for the *Hudson Review* and
writes on dance for a wide variety of
publications. Ms. Siegel is also active
across the country as a visiting critic and
teacher. Marcia Siegel's first book, *At the
Vanishing Point* (1972), won high critical
praise. She has also written *Please Run on
the Playground* (1975), a report on the
movement-in-the-schools training program, for the Connecticut Commission on
the Arts. She is currently at work on a
thematic history of American dance, to be
published by Houghton Mifflin Company,
for which she received a John Simon
Guggenheim Memorial Fellowship.

WATCHING
THE
DANCE
GO BY

Also by Marcia B. Siegel

*At the Vanishing Point: A Critic
Looks at Dance*

Watching the Dance Go By

Marcia B. Siegel

Illustrated with Photographs

HOUGHTON MIFFLIN COMPANY BOSTON
1977

Most of the pieces in this book appeared in slightly different
form in *The American Poetry Review*, *Ballet Review*, *The Boston
Globe*, *Boston Herald American*, *Dance Magazine*, *Eddy*, *The Hudson Review*,
The Soho Weekly News, and *Los Angeles Times*. They have been
reprinted here with permission.

Herbert Migdoll's photograph of *Sue's Leg* is reproduced here
courtesy of "Dance in America," a television series produced by
WNET/13,
New York, under grants from Exxon Corporation, the National Endowment for the Arts and the Corporation for Public Broadcasting.

Library of Congress Cataloging in Publication Data

Siegel, Marcia B
  Watching the dance go by.

  Includes index.
  1. Dancing — United States — Reviews. I. Title.
GV1623.S54   793.3'2   76-58029
ISBN 0-395-25173-7

Printed in the United States of America

V 10 9 8 7 6 5 4 3 2 1

Contents

Illustrations

following page 184

Don Quixote pas de deux (Petipa/Minkus). Gelsey Kirkland and Mikhail Baryshnikov.

Le Baiser de la Fée (Neumeier/Stravinsky). Daniel Levins, Bonnie Mathis, and William Carter of American Ballet Theater.

Don Quixote, Act III (Balanchine/Nabokov). Suzanne Farrell and Richard Hoskinson with New York City Ballet.

La Sylphide (Bournonville/Loewenskijold). Natalia Makarova, Karena Brock, and Ivan Nagy with American Ballet Theater.

The Big City (Jooss/Tansman). Jan Hanniford and William Whitener with City Center Joffrey Ballet.

"Mistake Waltz" from *The Concert* (Robbins/Chopin). New York City Ballet.

Stravinsky Violin Concerto (Balanchine/Stravinsky). Kay Mazzo with New York City Ballet.

Appalachian Spring (Graham/Copland). left: David Hatch Walker; right: Tim Wengerd and Diane Gray with Martha Graham Company.

Here and Now with Watchers (Hawkins/Dlugoszewski). Erick Hawkins and Nada Reagan.

Rebus (Cunningham/Behrman). Merce Cunningham and company.

Piano Peace (McIntyre/Williams). Dianne McIntyre.

Nijinsky, Clown of God (Béjart/Henry). Ballet of the XXth Century.

Quarry (Monk). Meredith Monk and *The House*.

Sticks (Brown). Trisha Brown and company.

Sue's Leg (Tharp/Waller). Rose Marie Wright, Tom Rawe, Twyla Tharp, and Ken Rinker.

Lazy Madge (Dunn). Above: Diane Frank, Daniel Press, and Douglas Dunn; below: Jennifer Mascall and Dunn.

Introduction

DANCING MUST BE the most exhilarating and terrifying of all professions, so short is a dancer's allotted span of work. Lifetimes pass in a season, five years can frame a generation. For the two or ten or fifteen years of his peak performing career, a dancer compresses all the skill, the ambition, and the anxiety of existence into a few half-hours a week. We see this. We understand that no dance performance can be exactly repeated or preserved. No wonder dance has a special appeal in an age of programmed, laundered, reliably glib entertainment.

In the past five years, dance has come into its own as a major cultural medium, something the dance field and all its well-wishers have long awaited. But the course of acceptance took some unforeseen turns. This coming-of-age coincided with the adoption of government subsidies as a way of life for cultural organizations. All during its development in America, dance survived as an independent — it had no institutions, no agencies, no big benefactors except those it attracted by the force of its imagery. There was nothing to coast on, nothing to live up to, no one to please but the artists who brought it into being. The achievement of those first decades was brilliant. Then — just as the first creative dynasty was beginning to thin out — came subsidy.

At first subsidy seemed to be a wonderful Oz, offering rewards for the deserving, security for the homeless, and access to a once-indifferent public. Then, after an initial period of openhanded uncertainty, the major fund-granting agencies began to deal out dollars more carefully. What most artists had feared was direct government control of artistic content. Although that didn't occur, something else did. Arts funding unobtrusively linked itself into the industry of arts consumerism. Subsidy became increasingly dependent on the size of a company's budget and of the audience the company serves. The seldom-acknowledged connections among the popular appeal of a repertory, the company's ability to sell tickets, the priorities for dispensing of taxpayers' dollars came out in the open, to be adopted as matters for appraisal and recommendation by certain critics who felt their own jobs to be a vital element in the industry's success.

Subsidy did not stimulate new artists, it encouraged safe ones. Novelty was more important than innovation. The star system flourished. In addition to putting our large ballet and dance companies into an almost unassailably prominent position in the public view, government funding has created a middle echelon of management and production organizations at every level of dance activity. Rather than deal directly with individual choreographers and companies, government prefers to contribute to festivals, touring programs, and other centralized producing or booking entities, which in turn choose the dance to be presented. This system also tends to favor the most popular companies, which are not necessarily the most creative ones.

I am not against public subsidy for dance, nor against making some dance experience available for every kind of taste. I'm certainly not against dance being popular. But somehow, it seems to me subsidy has gotten off on the wrong foot. More emphasis could have been given to creative work; that is, a larger share of the appropriations could have been set aside for choreography and for testing new work under informal conditions. Dance companies could have been granted direct operating subsidies and allowed to determine their own futures, rather than annual appropriations, often tied to short-term performance and production plans. In scarcely more than a decade, dance subsidy in America has become a means of giving dancers work and putting dance performance in front of the public. The business of fostering artistic excellence, of discovering new forms, and of expanding the public's receptivity to the art experience — these have continued to fall on the individual artist, subsidized or not.

I had thought of public support for the arts as a sort of First

Amendment gift. Like a free press, public arts ought to serve the most interests — dance ought to exist for the broadest possible range of audiences, but all dance should not try to please some hypothetical common denominator. We need many dance companies that represent many points of view, not a few companies and producers who have no point of view. But this new egalitarianism is not merely a function of the bureaucratic process. One of the most persistent residual attitudes from the revolutionary 1960s is that of antielitism. Long after the last decade's political idealism, radical life-styles, and militant devotion to change had given way to the materialistic, skill-oriented, buttoned-up 1970s, people still quietly believe you shouldn't trust the artist.

You can trust the star because the star is manipulable — is in the audience's power. But the creator, the innovator, is unpredictable; he or she can't be easily managed or led, can't be counted on to bring forth what everyone will like. The artist is undemocratic. The very existence of artists refutes the belief that all persons can do all things in an open society. The separateness of the artist — his superior gifts — should be cherished, not distrusted. No George Balanchine or Martha Graham or Merce Cunningham or Twyla Tharp could have survived in an antielitist America. Our initial toleration for the artist-outlaw, miserly and indifferent though we may have been, is what permitted our dance to reach its present state of excellence. Without that freedom, we probably would have been stuck from the beginning with empty, slick imitations of traditional European opera house ballet.

I think the dregs of the sexual revolution may have imposed another burden on the arts. New York is full of would-be swingers and the entertainments that cater to their pent-up eroticism; and it's fallen to the arts, especially dance, to project the fantasies we can't act out. There's no use pretending that dance doesn't turn people on; it always has. What's new is the extremity of violence, aggression, and ugliness cast as sexual encounter that audiences will accept. Dance can so easily take abstract forms; we can always think we're applauding the technical skill of the dancers or the intensity of their performance, and not the anomie, the ruthless exploitation, the sexual despair. Perhaps we see that too, and secretly, subconsciously, thrill to it, even long for it.

One of the hardest problems in criticism is finding how to tell what we see, without glossing over the moral implications. Young writers and audiences want to know why it isn't all right just to enjoy something that appeals to their senses, engages their love of physicality. Why do some critics want to spoil their pleasure by demanding more from the experience? Why must we expose the maggots under the gold lamé? I think the fact that dance has no institutionalized history imposes extra responsibilities on its critics. We are its reporters and sometimes its interpreters, but we are also its memory, its conscience. By that I don't mean that critics have the best memories, or possess any unusual moral qualities. I mean that they are professional observers, and that what they tell us is our only systematic account of an ongoing history.

Since we're living in a time of a rapidly growing audience and a need to satisfy many entertainment tastes, we're more than ever in need of critics who can make fine distinctions. The present dance audience has very little anchorage in the past. People looking at dance for the first time have no background in which to situate their own preferences, they have no concept of who the Bachs and Beethovens of dance were, or what they did, or why the dancer's legs turn out or the arms move as they do. Many of us have hoped for an expanding of people's interests, a crossing-over of the audience between ballet, modern dance, and experimental dance. But we have not, I think, anticipated a situation where all dance was considered the same thing, required to serve the same purpose, evaluated on the same grounds.

Probably the most important phenomenon of the past five years is the blurring of dance's former lines of demarcation. It's not just that modern dancers take ballet class or that ballet choreographers design movements that are unclassical or earthbound. As I was gathering photographs for this book, I was struck by how freely dance is sharing its resources. Ballet companies do modern dance choreography, dancers visit around as guest artists, choreographers with companies of their own make new dances for other companies. Within the modern dance field, once the stronghold of individual styles, companies are performing the works of more than one choreographer, and sometimes the choreographers don't even represent the same branch of modern dance.

Dancing today is remarkable for its technical excellence and for its ready adaptability to classical, modern, or abstract themes. But I find a certain erosion going on everywhere, a smoothing out of differences, a subtle neglect of detail. I don't think José Limón choreography should look like Martha Graham choreography, or that Graham should look like ballet. The dancer's body is his instrument, and if you tune all instruments to sound the same, you'll get only part of the music — the thematic development maybe, but not the texture. Of course there are valid reasons for this homogenization. The pioneers are gone, most of them, and their missionary dedication has been replaced with a more practical, competent professionalism: choreography must be created to highlight a season, to feature dancers, to attract reviewers, not to unearth mysteries. Dancers can do everything from a contraction to a split jump, and they want to display their skill; it seems unfair to them not to be allowed to point their feet and look beautiful.

One can't object to this, except for one thing. When a dance style begins to change, once the weightiness or the accent or the particular roundedness of gesture begins to lose its definition, history starts to slip away from us. Our dance heritage is not adequately recorded on film, nor have our dance styles been sufficiently analyzed or documented, for some future generation to go back and retrieve what doesn't suit our taste in 1976. Other art forms can be recovered; if we ignored Charles Ives or Scott Joplin in their lifetimes, at least we can honor them now. There's a certain arrogance in the way dancers are constantly mucking about with their own posterity.

The distance between excellence and genius is often very small, but I think at the moment we see it, we recognize it. A dance critic tries to halt certain moments as they fly across a matrix of time. I believe that the better I can do my job — the more completely and accurately I can represent this fascinating winged creature — the more I can help dance to have a history. I wish people cared more about what critics see than about what they think. Seeing is a very selective, individual, and concrete process, and it means more to me than opinion. Nancy Goldner, Arlene Croce, and Deborah Jowitt can all see different things than I did in a dance we all liked. This speaks not only of the associations and values that make those colleagues interesting to me, but of the resonating power of the dance itself. Like any real artwork, a dance can reach out to people in many ways, move us differently at different times. We sell it short by thinking we can fix it once and forever in some pigeonhole of consensus or individual judgment. Each separate dance experience carries its own unique and momentary life, but to consider *only* that singular evening's lifetime, it seems to me, is to deny evolution, to deny civilization.

Selfishly, I write, as much of the time as I can, about what really interests me. Though my writings may contribute to history, this book is not a thorough history of these five years. Each of us watching the dance go by in New York sees a different dance. Perhaps 2000 dance performances take place in a year, but even if we had a much narrower choice, none of us would perceive the same constellation of events. My dance is a version of a scene, one of many versions. I finish every season thinking I haven't dug deeply enough into the diversity of what I see, I've lingered too long over my loves, haven't made enough opportunities to discuss interesting choreography that isn't new, omitted to write about some dancers because what they dance is trivial. Similarly, what I've selected to put in this book, out of all I've written, is not broadly representative or always fully explained. I've tried rather to give a sense of the flow and interaction of a world viewed from one place, my place — even though that place shifts a little bit too, from time to time.

Except for minor repairs, the articles in this collection appear as they were written. I think that is part of their value. They do fix a time, a viewpoint — what I saw when it went past. So this is my history as well as a fragment of dance's. The limits of both seem important to preserve. I may reconsider dances many times, but what I observe can occur only once. I don't care to re-create my past observations or states of mind. Later, at the ends of seasons, the ends of books, I can see where my lapses are and resolve to do better next time, but I can never be where I was because the dance is incomplete, and so is the wonder.

Marcia B. Siegel

September 1976

WATCHING
THE
DANCE
GO BY

One Thousand Roses

JUST BEFORE the National Ballet of Canada's final performance in New York last August, a friend who monitors the intricate behavior of the balletomane subculture told me that Rudolf Nureyev was going to receive a thousand roses from his fans. Once I knew it was going to happen, of course, I had to stay around to see how it would be engineered. The well-organized demonstrators had spotted themselves all over the front of the Metropolitan Opera House audience, and they heaved their identical scarlet bouquets across the orchestra pit with judicious timing, so that the deluge would be impressive but not too brief. At first Nureyev started gathering the flowers, as if he didn't know the task would eventually require a small truck, but a few minutes into the presentation I noticed a photographer walk onto the stage from the wings and start taking pictures of the crowd.

Summer — usually the time of year when dancers and dance audiences head for the hills — has developed into a heavily starred, status-laden extra season in recent years. Two theaters at Lincoln Center this year were running dance almost continuously through June, July, and most of August. The Met barely squeezed in a few weeks of opera between the Royal Ballet with Nureyev, the Moiseyev, and the Canadians with Nureyev. The New York City Ballet was succeeded at the New York State Theater by six weeks of American Ballet Theater and two more weeks of Alvin Ailey for good measure — it was Ailey's third New York engagement of the '73–'74 season.

Whoever was filling up all those seats for all those weeks, there must have been a lot of people we don't especially identify as the dance audience. Although opera is scratching around for new audiences, dance is beginning to emerge as big box-office entertainment. There are probably all kinds of reasons for this. Obviously, dance as a theatrical experience is still a novelty to most people, and the ballet repertory is neither as limited nor as familiar as the standard opera rep. But I think some of the reasons are tied to who we are now as a society — to a wish for sexual liberation and a great deal of sexual doubt, and to the increasingly frustrated desire for personal expression. Those precarious four-inch platform shoes that so many New Yorkers were teetering around on last summer are not merely some weird gimmick of the designers. They're a direct throwback to the Greek kothornoi, the shoes worn by actors to make them look more majestic.

The New York dance public wants stars. Eats up stars. Sometimes it invents stars where there are none, sees a star where there isn't one any longer. Something in the basic nature of ballet has always favored the star system — ballet was first danced by a king after all, Louis XIV — and until the twentieth century it was almost exclusively concerned with creating star roles and surrounding them with appropriate spectacle. Even in modern times, when choreography began to be considered an art, when the corps had to look as though it belonged to the ballet and the stars had to do steps that were reasonably similar at each performance, there have been very few real ensemble ballets.

Eliot Feld, Jerome Robbins, and Twyla Tharp are almost the only working choreographers whose ballets don't revolve around the presence of one or two principal performers — and none of them can be considered a strict classicist. They are capable of making us see the whole stage organism working and changing in its interrelated patterns; they can make a group of dancers balance, or even overbalance, a single soloist; and they can interest us for long periods of time in a stage action from which the principals are absent. Most of the prominent "modern" ballet choreographers, Kenneth MacMillan, Rudi Van Dantzig, John Neumeier, Gerald Arpino, John Butler, and the late John Cranko, have worked with a much more traditional, hierarchical stage focus, which may be one reason for their huge popularity in the opera houses of Europe and North America.

Ovations have grown extravagant and kinky in New York dance. Sometimes you'd swear the hordes are yelling their contempt instead of their approval. They act as if they're being cheated when the Alvin Ailey company doesn't comply with their demand for an encore of *Revelations*. The exploding flash bulb has become so common during dance performances now that the tonier houses actually make an announcement explaining how dangerous it is for the dancer to get that blast of light in his eyes. This summer someone reportedly lobbed a plastic bag of eggs at Natalia Makarova during a bow, and I saw several dancers get belted in the stomach with flowers.

It's all reminiscent somehow of the Kennedy era. Except I think what the mob wanted so desperately with the Kennedys was to believe they were common men. Now the crowd wants to believe in itself as star. A few years ago Alvin Ailey made a dance about the mutual turn-on and drag-down that stars and audiences exert over each other. It was suggested by the life of Janis Joplin and it starred ballerina Lynn Seymour, and was called *Flowers*.

This insatiable public loves its stars when they play stars and scorns them when they expose any weakness. Cynthia Gregory, that most knowing of dancers, exploits her fabulous technique, mocks the audience, and at the same time revels in their screams of adoration. Bruce Marks, whose theatrical wisdom and security make him an invaluable partner for Gregory, returned to Ballet Theater this summer looking as if he hadn't been dancing enough these last few years in Denmark, and the audience wouldn't give him the time to get back in form. Young Fernando Bujones, all brilliant technique and insufferable conceit, is being rushed to fame, as if the audience can't wait for his head to catch up with his body.

Ballet Theater has always capitalized on its stars, and the company has a magic propensity for coming up with a new phenomenon just when its own fortunes seem to be plunging the steepest. This summer, with its fiscal policies and personnel under attack by the New York State Council on the Arts, the company was supposedly thinking of curtailing its season, or maybe even throwing in the towel altogether, depending on which rumormonger you listened to. Suddenly there was Baryshnikov, and the roller coaster headed upward again.

ABT snapped up the Russian prodigy just after he defected in Canada, early in the summer, and presented him for his U.S. debut partnering its other lapsed-Soviet superstar, Natalia Makarova. Since her arrival here in 1970, Makarova has displayed a very publicizable temperament, cultivated a healthy coterie of fans, and incidentally danced very well indeed on several occasions. But she was becoming stale news, and this summer they touted her in a new role, as director of a revival of the last act of the old Petipa classic, *La Bayadère*. She did a fine job with it too, extracting a certain alert stylishness from ABT's somnolent corps de ballet.

Baryshnikov danced four sensational performances with Makarova — one *Giselle*, two *Bayadères*, and the *Don Quixote* pas de deux. Given the feverish conditions of this debut, I can be sure only of his virtuosity and how he achieves some of it. His power is in his legs and his unusually flexible back, which give him thrust and speed, accuracy and elevation. He can do more beats, more complicated footwork, faster turns than any male dancer I've ever seen. Some of his most dazzling steps result from his ability to change the position of his legs or upper torso right in the middle of a jump or a turn. He's not a large man, yet onstage he gives you the impression of covering vast distances; he has the athlete's ability to continue sending his force and speed all the way out from the energy source to the very ends of his legs and beyond, into space; the illusion of motion extends the actuality of it.

But Baryshnikov is no mere powerhouse. He places his muscular strength and coordination in the service of artistry. His line is precisely drawn — clear, classical, where he wants it to be. He always looks cool and collected, there's no harshness in the transitions, no abrupt slowdowns or speedups, just perfect control. Arlene Croce described Baryshnikov as some kind of futuristic superdancer, who has extended the classical vocabulary beyond what ordinary dancers can now do. I think it may be his technical achievement rather than his aesthetic beauty that wowed our audience of technocrats.

No other art offers us man arrayed in such splendid form. The dancer's accomplishment is a perceivable skill, an excellence, like the workings of any fine mechanism. Even a mediocre dancer undergoes rigorous training, has a body that must be in top condition, and must master a high degree of discipline, detail, and precision. Some of the audience's favorite "stars" are terrible artists — wooden of expression, rigid or sloppy or disproportionate of line — but they have technique, and one thing this computer age worships is technique. I wouldn't be surprised if, once the flames die down, Nixon's abdication enters the mythology as having resulted from a failure of technique.

Ballet training has been infiltrating the modern dance field for years, and you can see almost as many arabesques and pirouettes in some modern dance performances as at the ballet. Perhaps there is a natural progression in art from the individual innovator or revolutionary to the establishment of rules, systems, academies, and in this process what was personal to the artist becomes impersonal tool and methodology. In dance we've seen this happen in our own time with Martha Graham. We've seen it happen even quicker, and paid less attention to it, when a ballet or a modern dance of particular style gets out from under its creator's thumb. There seems to be an inexorable force — the force of all those years of habit and classes perhaps, pushing the dancer's body without volition into its accustomed shapes — warning the muscles not to do anything that feels different.

In today's ballet market, only a choreographer with the hard-nosed prestige of a Jerome Robbins can insist on casting and coaching his ballets each season as they are done by various companies. More often, a few months after a piece enters the repertory, it starts to melt around the edges, get a tiny bit distended here, a bit shrunken there. If it's a pleasant ballet, it can still be successful, and nobody notices that it's lost its style.

We had a striking view of this process last June when Eliot Feld's new company produced *Intermezzo* and *At Midnight*, two works that had been slogging along for years looking like all the other staples in the Ballet Theater repertory. Feld's early works have always made a hit with audiences; they're beautifully crafted, musical, and even a few notches less inane than the average ballet. Those are the qualities that come through even in a rotten production. But now that the ballets have returned to something close to their original state, Feld's distinction as a choreographer is once again apparent. His own dancers are so articulate in space, making clear differences between the space that is close to the body and that which is far away. They show you when a movement is three-dimensional — spiraling, enclosing — and it often is; not linear the way it came to look. They stress the ongoingness of the dance, and also that the action is self-contained. Something is happening, really, among the dancers; not being fabricated for the benefit of us out in the audience.

Feld's work since 1971 has been a disappointment to me, because he seems to be denying most of the things that made him truly creative with the ballet medium. Rather he seems to have been searching for restrictive forms, as if he would like to fashion a new kind of academicism before his descendants and imitators do it to him. His two new works, *Sephardic Song* and *Tzaddik*, both have a kind of spareness — almost stinginess — of material, a narrowness of focus, a single-minded anxiety that we should get the point. I'm sorry he is limiting his invention so severely now, but I found that some ballets I had thought too thin and repetitive looked all right in this new context. I hate to settle for simplicity when I know the man is capable of depth, but Feld is refreshing after the overelaborate, overdecorated, overdanced 1974 ballets everywhere else.

Topping the season for gross, convoluted production values and a total absence of choreographic individuality was John Neumeier's *Baiser de la Fée*, premièred by Ballet Theater in mid-July. Neumeier, an American who's been working in Germany for the past few years, is the new darling of the opera house crowd. We saw his *Don Juan*, a Nureyev set piece heavy with psychological portent and light on danced information, during the National Ballet of Canada's first visit to the Met in May. *Baiser* is even more ambitious. A young man about to be married to a sweet hometown girl dances with his vision of ideal mature love (I guess). The vision (fairy) is first a singer, then a dancer. The young man has two doubles, an older man and a little boy. There is a troupe of fairies dressed in white ballet tunics, and they alternate numbers with Tyrolean-costumed wedding guests. Scenery rumbles in and out on wagons. The ballet ends and ends and ends while the bride rearranges her dress and the groom pursues his vision into a forest of scrims.

In place of classical virtuosity Neumeier specializes in a vocabulary of acrobatic lifts by Hollywoodized couples yearning at each other. The men hardly dance at all; they're mostly breaking their backs hoisting the women into esoteric poses. The women trip around in orderly squadrons, doing academic maneuvers and oblivious to any content of Stravinsky's music except its beat.

This is the climate of indulgence and hyperactivity in which dance is flourishing today. Small wonder the audience hasn't the patience to learn finesse and style, or to discriminate between high camp and high art. Even in Denmark, where the technique and choreography of the great Romantic ballet master August Bournonville have been preserved as a national treasure, the subtle, delicate Bournonville style is gradually eroding as the gaudier affects of contemporary ballet win audience approval. Only constant vigilance and coaching can keep this nuance of classical dancing from dissolving into the standard ballet rhetoric.

Erik Bruhn, who's now retired from dancing, has been a devoted protector of the Bournonville style, and he undoubtedly had a great deal to do with the understated way the Canadians played *La Sylphide* on that last night of the summer. Nureyev, with his ego restrained and his dancing excesses curbed, looked more like the great dancer he used to be than the great star he now plays. Bruhn was making his debut in the mime role of Madge the witch, and you could feel, around the corners of his malevolence, that he was keeping a wary eye on his exuberant colleague.

But when it got around to the last ballet of the evening, José Limón's *The Moor's Pavane*, Nureyev had it all to himself, or grabbed it. *The Moor's Pavane*, based on "Othello," was an almost perfect achievement of modern dance, a beautiful balance of music, movement, and acting. Limón, and later his dancers after his death, set the dance on a number of ballet companies, where it receives varying treatment. Usually its theater values are exploited and the powerful, expressive movement is only sketched in.

The Nureyev version reduced Limón's choreography and his movement style to some barely familiar floor patterns. In an altered costume — a get-up with a dark red robe slashed above the hipbones to provide the audience with a provocative view of fuchsia tights encasing the celebrated legs and crotch — the star pranced and stumbled, emoted and tossed his hair and gnashed his teeth, and failed to do the steps. The three other dancers in this stately dance-drama wandered pale and ineffectual in his wake.

I know the fans had bought all those roses, and had to present them, deserved or not. But the ovation was as heartfelt as if they'd seen wonders. They might as well have endowed a barber shop.

Winter 1974–75

Steps in the Fog

Swan Lake is all steps. At least, more and more I'm beginning to perceive it that way. *Swan Lake* is not my favorite ballet, but increasingly the things that don't fascinate me about it are the pomp and pomposity, the hoked-up transformations and the manufactured fogs, the all-purpose crowds exuding a spurious air of celebration. The things that do are the steps.

We can't know, of course, if the steps we're seeing are the ballet's original steps, since Ivanov's second act was done in 1894 and the rest of the ballet premièred the following year. There are steps in the Royal Ballet's present *Swan Lake* that we don't see in Ballet Theater's, and different dancers do different steps according to their talents. What's so amazing is that even in the eccentric Bruhn and Balanchine versions *Swan Lake* always manages to look like the same ballet and even to maintain a choreographic image that is distinctive and consistent.

What I'm talking about is the way the ballet looks as a dance, rather than how it looks as a dramatic presentation, or how it proceeds as a sequence of floor patterns, scenes, or musical passages. Someone once enthused to Eliot Feld over a young dancer who appeared in one of his ballets with a company not his own. Wasn't she sweet, wasn't she charming? "She didn't do my steps," Feld replied. If the dance image isn't there, the dance isn't there either; when the National Ballet of Canada puts on *The Moor's Pavane* as a theater piece, changing or merely disregarding the steps José Limón choreographed, they're saying how superior their company is to the work they're exploiting.

But something about the way *Swan Lake* was made preserves its integrity through changing productions, concepts, and casts. I think it has to do with the integration of the dance steps and dramatic gestures. Only recently, while thinking about *Swan Lake*, I've realized just how separate these two elements usually are in ballet.

Ballet steps are really *steps* — they're done by the feet and the lower body. The arms, head, and upper torso are tacked on to achieve a harmonious line or a contrasting one, to create the stresses of approach or withdrawal, of turning away from the movement or fully participating in it, as the dancer goes from one step to another.

Miming in ballet — at least the formal gesture language that goes back almost as far as the classical vocabulary of steps — is done almost entirely by the upper body. Most often we see mime in old ballets as standing-still conversations, like the one in the first act of *Swan Lake*, where the Queen Mother gives the Prince his birthday present and admonishes him that it's time to stop carousing and settle down with a wife.

Like any language, this mime is symbolic; its meaning frequently isn't even suggested by its form, and compared to the active use of the whole body that we see in dancing, it isn't terribly interesting. I can understand if kinetically tuned-in American audiences have less patience for these static mime passages, and in fact some of the most famous ones — Giselle's mother's prediction of death and Wili-dom, for instance — have been deleted from American productions. (Joan Lawson's excellent book "Mime, The Theory and Practice of Expressive Gesture" not only translates the gestures, but tells in detail how they're executed.)

In *Swan Lake* the attitudes of the upper body that accompany the dance steps, instead of following the standard positions and port de bras, are often variations of specific mime gestures. The birdlike look of the arabesques is not derived only from the arabesque, which is used in virtually all ballets and for innumerable purposes. What makes the women look birdlike is the opening of the chest and spreading back of the arms — the mime-language for bird. Odette and the swans often jump into a position with one arm shielding the face and the other wrapped around the center of the body — the mime expression for hiding.

We all think of the corps of swans in swirling flocks, running around the stage flapping their arms up and down. But one of their most beautiful movements is not literal at all: the one where they jump straight up in the air, lifting their forearms on either side of the head and pulling them straight down along the body. This oddly effective figure — something I've never seen in any other ballet — is evidently an elaboration of the mime expression for tears.

Throughout the ballet the swans and the Swan Queen make references to and variations on the mime for prisoner — arms extended downward with clenched hands crossed at the wrists — or resignation — the same thing with unfolded hands; and its opposite — uncrossing the hands and opening the arms to signify rescuing or setting free. The Prince embraces Odette from behind in the pas de deux, holding her by the wrists and releasing her arms from their symbolic bondage; and later he supports her in a series of pirouettes that she finishes by bending backward away from him and flinging her arms wide.

The third act pas de deux, the Black Swan, is a typical nineteenth-century virtuoso display, and the steps aren't especially changed or inflected — except during the interlude where Odile deliberately reminds the Prince of Odette by reproducing her arm motions. And in one astonishing action, which I noticed for the first time when Makarova did it this summer — maybe she invented it — Odile falls backward into the Prince's arms, just as Odette did, except that the Black Swan adds bird arms to the fall, spreading and slowly pressing the hands out from bent wrists.

Makarova was dancing wonderfully well this summer. I saw her *Swan Lake* at the end of Ballet Theater's Lincoln Center season, and Cynthia Gregory's at the beginning. Both ballerinas looked especially beautiful to me; both made impressive Swan Queens of quite different temperaments and technical approaches.

In terms of stature and bearing alone, Gregory is regal, imposing. She's tall, with a vertical tendency in her body that seems to elongate her long neck and limbs. Everything about her announces firmness and security. Among all the swan-women she's the obvious leader. You wonder how Rothbart could have gotten her under his spell in the first place, and you feel she must be paying the price for some terrible flaw, perhaps the maliciousness that is revealed in the character of Odile.

As Odile Gregory is cold, almost stern. She seems determined to overwhelm the Prince with the precision of her feet, the magnificence of her balances, the speed of her turns. The entire third act pas de deux mounts steadily in excitement: she's turned on by the increasingly difficult steps and her own mastery of them, and the Prince is aroused by her, by the way she dances and by the pleasure she shows. Bruce Marks, who returned to Ballet Theater this year after several seasons with the Royal Danish Ballet, works up a feverish passion during this scene. The hotter he gets, the cooler Gregory gets, until the audience is screaming.

Makarova is small and sensuous, mercurial where Gregory is like a rock. She's not the swans' leader at all, but perhaps their adopted sister who needs to be protected. When she begs the hunters not to shoot, you almost feel the flock has put her up to it because she looks so frail and pathetic. In the third act she's the femme fatale, the girl who has men falling at her feet without her lifting a finger, and who can do unimaginable tricks out of pure self-confidence. Fooling the Prince into forgetting his real love is a lark to her, not a challenge as it is with Gregory. When she succeeds, you feel she's pulled off a great, gala escapade rather than a conspiracy.

Like Gregory, Makarova plays around with tempos. But while Gregory may stretch time almost to the breaking point, she seldom distorts the basic beat. Her dancing makes continual little accelerations and decelerations, so it gives the appearance of being balanced or measured and at the same time very much alive. Makarova really forces the beat. Her second act variation was so slow, and stayed so slow, that you almost gave up hope of her ever moving normally again. In the adagio she stretched and curved along the slowest possible thread of energy, as if she wanted to cast an indelible impression of changing body parts. Ivan Nagy, the adoring Prince, so soon to be trumped by these very same shapes, took in her languid line as if all 6000 eyes in the theater belonged to him.

The Ballet Theater *Swan Lake* is very little more than a vehicle for star performers now. I don't remember if it ever was anything else, but at least some of its gaucher details didn't irritate me as much as they do now. Rothbart's castle breaking in half at last, like a tube of dairy-case biscuits, and sinking into the floorboards. The perfumed fake-smoke that fills the palace — and the theater — and makes the Prince's birthday party look like a Beowulfian orgy.

Ballet Theater appears to have given up entirely on the crowds. The company's sole gesture toward naturalism is to give all the tall men aristocrats' parts in the first act and make all the shorter men peasants. The trouble with this is that in this company the smaller men are the more elegant. Warren Conover and Kenneth Hughes just don't look right stomping around the maypole.

I used to find it amusing to watch what the peasants were doing out back, around the wine casks, but now they just seem to be kidding around. So I pick out one dancer — Ruth Mayer seems to know what she's doing there, and she shows me that when the Prince hands out ribbons, they're not just something to wave during the dance but favors that she'll always treasure.

The aristocrats are insipid, as if they've been told to take good care of their costumes. In the third act, the six princesses who compete for the Prince's hand all bring their entourages, those pseudo-Spaniards and other national types who are to provide the entertainment. But later, during the pas de deux, when all the courtiers and guests have converted themselves into background, I've noticed that the dancer-escorts are getting much too familiar with the princesses.

There are possibilities for action that's in character, and sometimes a dancer seizes them. In the first act, Maria Youskevitch plays a noblewoman who gets paired up with the Prince for the farewell dance of the party. She's sort of a plain girl and never expected him to notice her. She talks to him animatedly, smiles too much. Marks, whose Prince is bored and a little pained by official niceties, almost ignores her but she smiles even more anxiously. Nagy, who's well bred and agreeable, treats her so politely that she almost hopes . . . But the toast is drunk and the guests turn to leave. Youskevitch hesitates an instant, sees he's forgotten her, lifts her chin, and sweeps out as if she hasn't just received the most crushing snub of her life.

October 1974

Birth of a Galaxy

WINNIPEG — Ordinary ballet stars blaze up and burn out regularly these days. Gelsey Kirkland and Mikhail Baryshnikov are going to be a galaxy.

The new whiz kids made their debut and out-of-town tryout

here in Canada as guests of one of the continent's oldest ballet companies, the Royal Winnipeg.

Looking at the first two of their six scheduled *Don Quixote* pas de deux was a little like going along on somebody's honeymoon. Whatever becomes of the partnership, it is fascinating now, if a bit nerve-racking, to watch these two superb dancers overcoming their reservations and hesitancies about each other, getting in synchrony, learning when to take over and when to give the stage to each other.

Despite their different backgrounds — Baryshnikov was trained in the Leningrad Kirov and Kirkland in the New York City Ballet — they are potentially an ideal team. Baryshnikov is a fabulous technician, and so is Kirkland. They both excel in the fine details of classicism — precision in footwork, musicality, elegance of line, and a certain cool dance intelligence compounded of security, imagination, and daring that allows the great performers to decide how they're going to do something while they're doing it. Cynthia Gregory has this quality. Patricia McBride. Christine Sarry. Maybe that's it among American ballerinas right now.

Besides her dancing excellence, Kirkland seems a match for Baryshnikov temperamentally. They're both very reticent dancers — they don't play up to the audience or do any unnecessary salesmanship. They pay attention to each other and to what they're doing mostly. But inside of them both is a kind of rage that will suddenly launch them into the most dangerous gambles, impossible leaps, precarious balances, delays of the inevitable.

I was prepared for Baryshnikov to be astonishing, but Kirkland equaled him. In a way, hers was the greater achievement; the publicity touts Baryshnikov, plays her as an unknown Cinderella, yet she's as virtuosic as he is. The second night in particular she lit on one toe endlessly, swept into faultless turns in arabesque as if she had complete confidence in his being there to bring her out of them.

I suspect Baryshnikov has a tendency to be too serious, and Kirkland's playful streak relieves that heaviness. Her delicacy complements his driving strength. Her exceptional control covers for his moments of recklessness.

One of the special excitements of the first two performances — and it may turn out to be a distinguishing feature of the team — was the dancers' ability to make smooth, very quick transitions. You hardly realize they're doing something phenomenal till they've done it. When Kirkland takes her balance from his support, you don't see her wobbling and centering herself, she just hangs. Baryshnikov changes his leg positions in midair, throws his torso out of alignment, stops just when he's going fastest, and sends no telegrams about it.

The extraordinary things that were going on escaped much of the Winnipeg audience. On the second night, primed perhaps by their two newspaper critics, they roused themselves from polite welcome into something like an ovation. But during the dance, people around me regarded with composure things that were making me gasp.

In ballet, Winnipeg is a company town, and the company is complacent. People told me the RWB has the second largest subscription list in North America or the Western Hemisphere or something, as if that guaranteed its cultural validity. The audience approves its locals, applauds any unusual quantity of motion, like pique turns. Despite the RWB's thirty-five-year tenure, its audience seems to be back where dance isn't an acceptable entertainment for men, isn't a turn-on for kids, and isn't viewed with much sophistication or continuity by anybody.

The dances I saw on the program with Kirkland and Baryshnikov were decent if unexceptional choreography, and the company seems well trained and cleanly rehearsed. But its delivery is uniformly bland — everyone smiles ingratiatingly all the time except when they're being soulful or distraught. The dancers almost never look at their partners at the same time their partners are looking at them. I don't know if this denotes boredom or inexperience.

In a way, Winnipeg's tepid atmosphere was a good place for Kirkland/Baryshnikov to dunk its toe in. They certainly couldn't do any wrong here. And the cheers will be hurtling into them soon enough.

October 10, 1974

Starsmoke

EVERYTHING ELSE may have gone to smash, but 1974 will exit with plenty of stardust on its heels. Maybe that's the most appropriate way to go.

American Ballet Theater inaugurated the winter season of its thirty-fifth anniversary year at City Center with a sackful of star vehicles and some real stars to dance them. For the first two weeks there is a big story ballet at every performance, plus a couple of repertory items — an Ashton, a MacMillan, a Robbins — in memory of past successes. All this, with Nureyev and his Friends installed down the street doing what stars do to top themselves: four star ballets in four different styles at each performance. I shudder to think what they'll dream up to usher in 1976.

What keeps the whole thing from being a press agent's dodge is extraordinary dancers, and Ballet Theater has a pretty good corner on those at the moment. Up to this writing I've seen Natalia Makarova kick off the season's round of *Coppélias*, with Ted Kivitt, and the second night Gelsey Kirkland and Mikhail Baryshnikov made their New York debut in the same piece.

After these first two *Coppélias*, I was thinking how little there is in this ballet besides the stars. Except for eons of colorless corps dances, mazurkas, czardases, friends' dances, and two small solos in the last act, no one dances but Swanilda and Franz. There's a lot of character comedy, some of it dumb, and some of it hammy, and too little of it good enough to watch again and again, the way you can watch Chaplin or Jerome Robbins' *The Concert*, for instance.

I know people who think the plot of *Coppélia* teaches great moral truths, but I can't see it. In the Ballet Theater version two boisterous kids play a trick on a harmless eccentric old man. The heroine has a moment of remorse after she's punctured his illusions, but then nobody gives him a second thought. They buy off his indignation with a bag of money, which is promptly extorted from him by the priest. He gets over this disappointment as quickly as he forgot his despair that his Coppélia doll wasn't a real girl. ABT's Buddy Balough plays Dr. Coppélius as ineffectual, myopic, dizzy. His magic is clearly in his own addled head and his anger dissipates itself in small vague fits of motion. If anything, he's almost lovable. Baiting him is like razzing a cripple. Not a very nice lesson for the kids in the audience.

As for the stars, these two pairs were satisfying in different ways. Makarova is a wonderful comedian. She takes the stage in *Coppélia* with great gusto, drives to the hilt of every joke, and both Kivitt and Balough play effectively to that energy. You can't quite believe she's all that scared when she and her pre-Lib girlfriends sneak into Dr. Coppélius' workshop — all that huge hanging back and knees knocking together in supposed terror. But later, when she's pretending to be his beloved doll come to life, she's again the resourceful mischief-maker we know her to be.

Along about the third act I begin to tire of her mannerisms, the finger poking coyly into the mouth, the petulant shrugging shoulders. And I wonder why, especially with Makarova's gift for acting, the Swanilda who finally marries Franz has to turn into a swooning Hollywood romantic instead of keeping some credible amount of her former starch.

Coppélia is Gelsey Kirkland's first effort in one of these big story ballet classics. Amazingly, she carried it as if she'd been born to, even though most of the hoopla revolves around Baryshnikov. They're delightful together flirting and feuding in the first act, and she can almost match him for fabulous dancing. The great third act pas de deux is more dancing than acting as they do it.

Kirkland is a more controlled, concentrated dancer than Makarova. She doesn't look as if she personally is having a great time doing the ballet, but she *does* the ballet more fully — gives herself to the role and to the steps. Her long second act encounter with Dr. Coppélius, where she has to imitate a mechanical doll, gradually come to life, dance to his command, and try to figure out how to get herself and Franz out of the place, was beautifully clear and sustained.

Baryshnikov proved intelligent in his acting and prodigious in his dancing. This is one time when all the blurbs are true — you have never seen dancing like this; it simply hasn't been done. I wish we weren't living in a time when tricks are so much in demand. These are the kind of stars you can celebrate with quietly.

January 2, 1975

Siegel's Notebook

JANUARY 3, 1975 — Nagy is one of the few ABT principals who looks right doing Bournonville. His beats are clear and his jumps curve up into the air and down. He opens his upper body as well as his arms in those famous jumps to the audience. Nagy's quality of reticence, his modesty, is naturally suited to Bournonville. What energy he keeps in reserve can go into gradual changes of line and tempo.

I like more things about Makarova this season than ever, though she never completely convinces me. Her *La Sylphide* had less mugging and more good dancing than anything I've seen her do in ages. The first instant when she's dying is superb — all of a sudden, with her wings gone, she's a creature of the ground, an alien element for her. I hadn't even been thinking of her as particularly unearthly before, only very quick and light. Then in this moment she changed herself without doing much. Her movement became laborious, as if she were pushing through something viscous, something that was choking her.

But then she added the melodramatic touch of blindness — she couldn't see Nagy, though she could feel him kneeling before her. Her eyes stared tragically out into space. Another tear-jerking death scene.

JANUARY 4, 1975 — Sylphide is not a natural part for Gregory. I don't know why exactly — perhaps a combination of her seriousness and the solidity of her dancing. In *Coppélia* these qualities are not a detriment. In fact, this season I found her the most satisfying of all three Swanildas I saw — Kirkland and Makarova were the other two. Without being giddy or coy, she's humorous, intelligent, and basically responsible — which is why you don't get that jarring feeling others give, that it's a completely different, grown-up person who suddenly appears in the last act.

But the Sylphide is another thing. This girl-creature has to be "feminine" in all the charming old-fashioned ways. She likes to play, flirt, tease, but not in the calculated way a Swanilda does. The later romantics gave their heroines a certain amount of shrewdness if not intelligence. But Bournonville was showing not only a woman without guile but a spirit, a symbol of everything mortals are not. We have to believe the Sylphide really loves James, that she isn't deliberately provoking him, and that she has no idea of remorse about luring him away from his real life. She's mercurial, amoral. Maybe loving him is the hidden element of humanness coming out in her (as she uncovers the spirituality in him), but it isn't complete, it's like an organ or a limb that hasn't evolved yet. Gregory isn't a dancer who can create one-dimensional characters; normally that's one thing I love about her. But here I don't want her to be so real.

Makarova's dying moment the other night was beautifully symbolic. It told you not only what had happened to her but what happens when man tries to capture his fantasies. They can't live in his world any more than he can in theirs.

*

JANUARY 5, 1975 — Kirkland's Sylphide wasn't anything like what I had expected her to do. She didn't exploit the possibilities for fey humor at all and so was much less like Makarova than in her *Coppélia*. Her comic sense is quick and wry, as she showed in her marvelous *Fille Mal Gardée*, but here she takes the character from the sadness of the very first solo. There's a lot of grieving in this *Sylphide*, as if James reveals to her something she didn't know she lacked.

This isn't anything deep or rational, but it seems to subdue her all the time a little bit. Her changes of mood are — Kirkland-like — never abrupt, so you get less of a feeling of willfulness and calculation.

When she's dying she gropes in the air for the impalpable substance that's always held her up before. When James grabs her hand she's jolted by the very materialness of him. She looks down at him once, then off to where she'd like to fly, then, taking off the ring and dropping it into his hands, dies.

These three performances of Kirkland's have taken my breath away. The range of what she's been able to do, with almost no previous experience doing it, is unbelievable. I don't think I've ever seen a Sylphide who better embodied the romantic ballerina idea. It's partly her terrific lightness, fluidity, and delicacy, but also her restraint. She doesn't dance it as a *role*, she dances it transformed and committed.

If anything has been as amazing as Kirkland, it's Baryshnikov's versatility. How many dancers can not only make themselves into different characters for different roles, but also reinterpret drastically the same role with different partners, as he did with Makarova and Kirkland in *Fille?* Like Kirkland, he takes a role seriously, he doesn't seem to be commenting on it or embroidering on it when doing it. His *Sylphide* bows were still sad, though the ovation went on long after the death scene.

Ballet Theater bows are almost as long and elaborate as ballets.

JANUARY 6, 1975 — I suppose one had to come down sometime, and the two *Giselles* yesterday were it. Both were extravagant, in different ways, one straining to get some response out of a tepid audience, the other to keep a ravening one from hysteria.

Gregory was injured and couldn't do the matinee, so D'Antuono and Denard played to two thirds of a house. There isn't anything to say about D'Antuono — she has her fans. I am not one. Denard almost matches her for neutrality of expression, except he never even gives any fake warmth. He has taken to posing on half-toe for a long time, just like a ballerina. David Gilbert's tempos were so funereal that it would have taken more than the one person who was really dancing them (van Hamel as Myrtha) to dissipate the torpor.

Makarova-Baryshnikov's *Giselle*, their only one of the season, was the hottest ticket in town. The audience vulgar, rubbernecking at celebrities, ready to scream at anything. Some of these Ballet Theater audiences will applaud any person who is caught with both feet off the ground. The performance was one of those superartificial ones, everything calculated to be exquisite and affecting and to prevent any unseemly demonstrations from spattering its glassy finish. It felt desperately held back to me, but perhaps being in the sixth row magnified some things.

Baryshnikov looked stern and almost forbidding. That seems to be his way of controlling the audience in serious ballets.

JANUARY 12, 1975 — ABT's thirty-fifth anniversary gala was as interesting for what it left out as for what it included. For all their professed family feeling and institutional warmth, these people are curiously ungenerous at a time when they could afford to thank everybody.

The gala made Ballet Theater look like my image of what it must have been in the 1940s — an amalgam of Russian ballet and whatever was most successful in contemporary ballet at that time. I got this nagging feeling that nothing has happened to the company since those wonderful days de Mille was eulogizing — that the dancers we saw doing the works are only the latest reinforcements in an endless, faceless army of people whose job is to keep on reenacting the image. The original greats were there — Tudor, Kaye, Laing, Youskevitch, Robbins, etc. — but almost no one in between them and the pres-

ent dancers. People who made a difference to me in the sixties
— Feld, Sarry, Marks, Verso, Smuin, Lander, Serrano, Fer-
nandez — were not there, were not mentioned. Not even
Fracci was mentioned!

Maybe a ballet company, like a modern dance company, is
strongest at its inception, when all the creative talent that's
been needing to come together finally finds an outlet.

It was wonderful to see the old greats on stage, doing some
things so well. Youskevitch, Eglevsky, Douglas, and Young
partnering Gregory in the Rose Adagio — somehow representing Man, all ages of Man paying court to youth and beauty and
mastery. De Mille and Lazowski clowning in *Three Virgins
and a Devil*. The intensity of Nora Kaye and Hugh Laing in
the opening of *Pillar of Fire*. Sono Osato's mannered seductiveness as Rosaline in *Romeo and Juliet*. Why do American
ballet companies never use the power of older dancers?

Of course, the dancers can't see themselves as mature either.
Though they're mortally afraid of film, dancers want to preserve the moment of glory even more desperately than the rest
of us. Sometimes it almost seems suicidal to me — once they
hit their greatness, nothing after that seems much of an
achievement. What a waste.

Then there's Bruhn. Retired — yet dancing magnificently
with Gregory in *Miss Julie*. I don't think I've ever seen such a
powerful, totally theatrical presence on a stage. Nureyev —
even Baryshnikov — they're always conscious of the audience,
of giving a performance. Bruhn becomes the role — devours
and absorbs it, and is devoured by it.

JANUARY 19, 1976 — Makarova's face, during the bows of
MacMillan's *Concerto*, to Nagy: "Well, if the audience is silly
enough to go for this, we'll bow all night."

I guess one reason the audience loves Makarova is that she's
so irrepressible. She can't resist including us in her private
thoughts about what she's doing. It's like a second ballet going
on, a second dialogue between us — you can just see the
wheels going round in her head: "Now I'm going to pull a joke
— it's corny but don't you think it's fun? — Here's where I do
my fast jetés across the footlights, are you watching? Yes.

Now I finish with a balance. Perfect. Longer still. And fly into the wings. Now in this part we have to be serious because it's even harder." There's an intimacy about this, and it's related to the almost lascivious way the Ballet Theater audience looks at celebrities in its midst.

Makarova's *Fille* is a collection of gambits — she plays for every opportunity to have fun. And it all works, except it doesn't add up to any conceivable whole character. But in their second *Fille*, Baryshnikov succeeded in restraining her a bit — she even took her second act variation seriously. Really serious, not playing-at-serious.

Watching Baryshnikov during these three weeks has been an inspiration. To see him trying, learning, growing. His face is never still — his expression changes constantly, and sometimes — as when he watched Kirkland's variation in their second *Coppélia* — his own personal pleasure is unnervingly beautiful — far more convincing than any acted-out emotion could be.

I wonder why the openness of Baryshnikov pleases me so much while that of Makarova puts me off. Perhaps because it always seems Baryshnikov is trying to deal with the ballet seriously, while Makarova is always a little above it.

In *Fille*, his last performance of the season, his variations were the most relaxed, happy dancing I've seen him do. As if he felt at home finally with this audience and this dancing. Not that he's ever lacked confidence but you felt him weighted down with his own fame, and with all the things that are new to him right now, and with the convulsions of the audience that seem to disconcert him. At last he seemed, that time, to have gotten it all under control. To have convinced us we didn't need to scream every minute in order to show we like him. And that was the most extraordinary dancing of all.

Spring 1975

Sic Transit Cynthia Gelsey

AMERICAN BALLET THEATER opened its winter season last week at the Uris. The star system made its majestic, flimflamming noises. Careers rose and fell. Sublime performances were given in a stage landscape about as inspiring as eastern Colorado. The ballet was *Giselle*, the heavies were Gelsey Kirkland and Mikhail Baryshnikov, and the men in the audience wore velvet.

Giselle is a pretty interesting ballet as the old-timers go. About thirty-five years older than *Swan Lake* and the great Russian classics, it is worlds away aesthetically, as different, say, as *Fancy Free* is from *Petrouchka*. A few years are a long time in ballet.

Giselle is concentrated where *Swan Lake* is extended. The main roles in *Giselle* are character studies; the main role in *Swan Lake* is a device for displaying the ballerina's virtuosity. Both acts of *Giselle* are pervaded with the mysteries of life and death, of class and honor, portents and punishments; in *Swan Lake* these same human involvements only serve to touch off the plot or provide a reason for spectacular stage events to occur.

It seems to me a great ballet company, if it's strong enough to have both these works in its repertory, ought to be able to show the audience how they differ. Nobody in Ballet Theater seems to care a bit about this, and the dancers, left to their own resources, behave the same way in both. Like the toneless lighting, scenery, and costumes they perform in, they seem to exist only so the stars won't have to dance on a bare stage. Kirkland and Baryshnikov are so good they almost made you believe this moving wallpaper behind them was alive. But it remained a brown, boring, unbudgeable mass. Even Martine van Hamel, an imposing Queen of the Wilis, somehow faded into the general murk.

Kirkland's approach to the role at this performance was through some inner music. Her energy, her whole vitality changed as the story unfolded. By taking her opening dance and much of the first act quite fast and bouncy she creates a sense of youth and daring as the commoner who's courted by a nobleman.

When she goes mad from the shock of learning he's tricked her and already has a fiancée, she doesn't so much go off her head as further into it. People have been warning her all her life that her high spirits will get her into trouble and that some special curse hangs over her; now, on the brink of death, she seems to hear these mysterious spirits whose world she's about to join.

In the second act, now a Wili but still lingering in the real world, she moves very slowly, deliberately, without a trace of impetuousness. She's playing for time, trying to keep Albrecht alive until dawn ends the avenging power of the Wilis. But you also feel that after she accomplishes this great act of forgiveness, Kirkland will be a creature, a shade, for whom time doesn't matter, for whom haste is unnecessary, and who has nothing to be expectant about.

Baryshnikov's Albrecht is not so much a bounder as a victim of his own infatuation. This Giselle who's caught his eye has turned out to be more than just another back-street romance for him, and when his fiancée shows up he's not just embarrassed, he's panicky, trapped. After Giselle saves him from being danced to death by the Wilis, I'm not sure he wants to go on living without her.

The dancing of these two was not only spectacular but beautiful. There were Baryshnikov's high jumps, his amazing brisés with his torso slowly arching backward and, later, fast ones all doubled over; he even did some triple tours en l'air, I think, though I wasn't counting. And Kirkland, unfolding her leg into a développé and smoothly reversing it into its descending path, without stopping to show us how long she was balancing on pointe; her flexible feet; her weightless fairy jumps.

Musically the performance was a shambles. I'm losing my

tolerance for the routinely terrible way our pit orchestras sound, Ballet Theater's especially, but when you have dancers as musical and thoughtful as Baryshnikov and Kirkland, the orchestra's failure to support them is an outrage. Conductor Akira Endo may not have had enough rehearsal time to work out some of the odd tempo changes they were trying for, or enough authority to hold his own beat. But, also, the partnership of these fabulous dancers seems slightly less in tune than it was a year ago. There were instants of uncertainty between them, and Baryshnikov actually upstaged Kirkland a couple of times. Whatever is disturbing their accord may or may not be the work of the same merciless hand of fame that gave us Cynthia Gregory and is trying to remove her too soon.

Gregory, like Kirkland, was no instant phenomenon. She had danced in the company, done leading roles, and was on the spot with her grand physical presence, her strong technique, and her quick stage intelligence just when ABT had gotten about all the mileage it could out of the alleged feud between Carla Fracci and Natalia Makarova. Some of the most worshipful ovations — and the most vulgar — were thrown for Gregory in the last few summers at the New York State Theater. Her dance power seemed invincible then; she looked as though she knew just how to turn on the audience — she used them and needed them at the same time.

But of course, the public started to turn elsewhere, nudged by the management. New faces came up, new stars. This season Ballet Theater will be offering guest performances from everyone but circus midgets, and I probably shouldn't give it the idea. Maybe Gregory's confidence began to slip, maybe she got tired of the glory game, maybe a thousand things. Rumors have been circulating for several months that she wanted to make a change, and it was announced on opening night that she won't be dancing with ABT this season.

Whether she will be back, or has quit the company, or has quit dancing are questions no one has answered to my satisfaction. Everyone who participates in the star system is to blame for this tragedy, if it is indeed as drastic as some of the fame mongers are saying. I am not about to take sides, since I don't know what the sides are.

A dancer is entitled to be disillusioned with the very same system by which she attained her success. She's entitled to go away and think, and I hope Gregory will. She's also entitled to our courtesy, and our permission to come back. I hope the press and the flacks won't blow this thing up to the epic proportions that drove Suzanne Farrell to Maurice Béjart a few years ago, when her temperamental differences with the New York City Ballet might have been patched up quickly if everyone had kept quiet. The fact that Cynthia Gregory is a star and a commodity shouldn't make us forget that she's also an artist. One thing is replaceable. The other isn't.

January 1, 1976

Panned Off

THERE'S BEEN so much inflammatory rhetoric about the Panovs that it may never be possible to look at their dancing as dancing. Their debut last week in Philadelphia's huge hockey dome, the Spectrum, was fraught with politics, with the years of agitating to spring them from Russia, with their alleged exploitation by American impresarios, with the claims of genius that have been made to justify their martyrdom. I don't know if any artist could live up to all that, but there's probably no way they can be convincingly disparaged either, at this point.

The Panovs did four divertissements, alternating numbers with the Baltimore Symphony Orchestra under the direction of Robert Zeller. All of the dances, even the ones with familiar titles, were choreographed or arranged or adapted by Valery Panov, so it was difficult to tell if the distortions I saw were deliberate eccentricities or just not great dancing.

They seem oddly matched as a pair. Galina Panov is the more classical in line, with supple feet and a high leg extension for her small, muscular body. Valery Panov seemed more comfortable in the semiclown roles of Petrouchka and Harlequin, doing fast pirouettes and twisted jumps where the position of his arms or the alignment of his upper body wasn't important. His performing dynamic is characterized by a lot of explosive force — he throws himself into things. It's the impact of his statement that you receive, rather than the refinement of line or the height of the jump. Ms. Panov's quality was harder to determine; she seemed undone by the enormity of the situation. Who wouldn't be, having to dance the Sugar Plum Fairy under sweeping orange and pink floodlights for an immense crowd of restless sports fans and concerned citizens interested in the liberation of Soviet Jewry.

For every disappointment the Panovs handed me, I had to allow mitigating circumstances. If Valery Panov looked like the same oafish character in four very different roles, I was sitting a block away and he was projecting twice as far. If their timing in the pas de deux misfired, maybe they haven't had enough practice since their confinement in Russia. Whatever extravagant hype preceded them, the outrageous proportions of the arena nullified any real achievement.

I thought the image was kind of sad. Here were two people who've been cast as symbols of cosmic issues — the clash of ideologies and the survival of cultures — and every actuality of the event told us how insignificant and ineffectual two mere dancers are.

The Philadelphia Spectrum is the home of the Philadelphia Flyers hockey team, the Philadelphia 76ers basketball team, the Ice Capades, the Roller Games, and, if its promoters get their wish, the future scene of "unprecedented horizons in the field of entertainment." What better way to certify the era of dance as mass spectacle than to present the principals in a cause célèbre for 10,000 partisans. This event was for showing off — an affirmation of a deed well done. The *idea* of the Panovs made the occasion, not anything they did that night.

But perhaps there really is a way for dance to cash in on the mass-entertainment boom. The mammoth Spectrum with its computerized light, heat, and sound, its sixteen box offices, and its scientifically controlled traffic patterns — the place emptied out quicker than the Metropolitan Opera House — was about as alien an atmosphere as I've ever watched dance in. Once I got into its plastic ambiance, though, I really dug the sound of the Baltimore Symphony, electrified by seventy-five mikes and belting out Respighi's "Pines of Rome." Composers like Berlioz and Strauss and Giovanni Gabrieli were no slouches when it came to flashy coloristic effects, and they probably wouldn't disapprove of being plugged into the present generation's ears.

So what the Panovs couldn't bring off, maybe some *Swan Lake* with a corps of 100 could, or a reconstruction of Laban's movement choirs, or a replica of a Louis XIV court spectacle. Sooner or later somebody's bound to figure out how to amplify the dancers.

February 13, 1975

Nutcracker

TO SOME PEOPLE *The Nutcracker* is a disease or a curse. To some it's just another holiday chore. To thousands of screaming kids it's the event of the year. I guess the only people without preconceived notions about *The Nutcracker* are four years old.

Jeffrey, who escorted me to the New York City Ballet's annual Christmas marathon, is four years old. Although he has lived a rich full life, he had never seen *The Nutcracker* before. In fact, he had never seen a ballet. For all the pains taken to enchant him, Jeff viewed the proceedings with the noncommittal pragmatism of his age.

He followed the narrative party scene with which the ballet opens, and made decent sense of it. When the children jumped up and down in front of the Christmas tree, he wondered whether they were trying to pull the ornaments off. This seemed a reasonable interpretation of what the children were doing — a perfunctory representation of "we're excited," imagined by a grown-up and never enacted by a real child.

Similarly, Jeff missed entirely the breaking of the toy nutcracker, because there was nothing visibly broken about it, and any kid knows you have to do something much more creative to break the average toy than drop it on the floor.

He was not impressed by the scenic transformations that are supposed to give this ballet its magic. His version of the scene where all the proportions change, where Marie (Carlyn Rosenberg) falls asleep and dreams of a giant Christmas tree and child-size toy soldiers battling mammoth mice, was that the tree "flew up in the air."

During the intermission, when a friend took us backstage, he discovered that the snowstorm was really made of paper — he probably had suspected this all along — and wanted to know if he was obliged to keep the handful of it that a stagehand magnanimously bestowed on him. I personally love the snowstorm, with the blue white Snowflakes dancing under the huge pillowy evergreens, but maybe only a grown-up can get lost in such a complicated illusion.

In the second act, Jeff wisely interested himself in Violette Verdy's Dance of the Sugar Plum Fairy, the first real ballerina-dancing of the afternoon; the pantomime of the Little Prince, young Christopher d'Amboise, who already displays the charm and assurance of his famous father; and the finale, in which all the candy characters come back and dance very briefly.

Jeff liked the ballet most when a lot of people were running around the stage in different directions. At other times he rested. He thought there was more than enough for him to do, and once during a long dance by people all in the same costumes, he told me in exasperation: "I want to turn that show off!" Later he announced that he preferred concerts to ballets because there was more music in them. Of course, he could change his mind by the time he's five.

But the afternoon was a success. I realized ballet as a human endeavor had been completely vindicated as the curtain went up for the first time. Gazing at the painted drop with the snow-covered, sparkly rooftops and the angel lighting up a star in the sky above them, Jeff whispered to me: "I didn't know it would be like this!" Anything that is news to a four-year-old is something our society needs. Badly.

January 10, 1972

Sleeping Beauty

THE THING I sometimes wonder about fairy-tale ballets is whether they're for children or grown-ups. Rudolf Nureyev's *Sleeping Beauty*, being presented at the Metropolitan Opera House by the Canadian National Ballet, is definitely for grown-ups.

I don't mean it's a salacious remake or anything like that, I mean it gives the appearance of a fantasy without requiring any imagination. Perhaps that's a definition of escapist art.

There's nothing at all surprising about this production — everything is built on materials we already know. The audience applauds when the Prince and the Lilac Fairy ride to the enchanted castle in a remote-controlled boat, through a forest of scrims going up and down and some machine-made fog. To see through illusion and applaud how it was made is the act of a realist, not an innocent.

This production is very elaborate, and very dark. Nicholas Georgiadis' sets and costumes are rich with patina, like metals and fabrics taken from an ancient burial vault. The royal court of the first and last acts is set in about Louis XIV's time, and you can see why ballet didn't get past its infancy until later — what with all those brocades and dainty slippers and long, heavy wigs.

Nureyev has set a surprising amount of dance for the people who are encumbered this way, and it's all hard to see — you can't tell what the women's feet are doing; the men look squatty under those horrible wigs; the design of the dance gets fractured by all the other decoration around it.

This kind of spectacle was the forte of Marius Petipa, who originated the Russian classical style Nureyev loves so well. Petipa had an ingenious gift for clearing away everything superfluous to the dancing of the moment. Except where he's been most faithful to Petipa, in the last act divertissement and second act pas de deux when the Prince and Princess meet in a dream, Nureyev's production looks more like a picture-book page shifting around.

His rechoreography for the ensembles and many of the solos has a fussy, too-difficult look, a feeling of overloading the music. His own solos, particularly the first one, are pushed beyond virtuosity into some arcane realm of the superfeat. He does extravagant things with his feet that you can't even follow. He makes sweeping circular runs with interpolations of straight-legged brushes back and forth, the kind dancers do in class to tune up their hip sockets. It's an indulgence, a dessert, but it never becomes kooky or unclassical.

Nureyev's Princess Aurora the night I attended was Karen Kain, a tall, strong girl who hurls herself into space with reckless courage. When she comes galloping on for her first scene, the famous Rose Adagio, you admire her great vitality and spirit — she's the kind of beauty who's impressive when she's awake, not asleep.

The company, which I haven't seen before, gave the old story a sense of action without much drama. Events proceeded headlong, one after the other without letup or tension, and except in Ms. Kain I missed any sense for character.

My favorite scene was the Prince entering the castle to waken Aurora from her hundred-year sleep. With sunlight spilling down the stairs behind him, he descends into the dank hall and runs from one inert figure to another until he finds her. It was the first time the ballet breathed.

May 4, 1973

Cranko's Curse

THERE'S NO TELLING what John Cranko would have done if he'd lived. Having started the trend back to opera house ballet, he might have veered off on some other tack — as the Stuttgart Ballet now seems about to do anyway, under the leadership of Glen Tetley. But Cranko's box-office brain child lived after him, frozen in all its obsolescent success.

At least two major companies were showing opera house ballet here this spring, the National of Canada and the Royal of Britain, and it's probably not coincidental that both, like Cranko's Stuttgart, came here under the aegis of the Hurok organization. No one knew better than Hurok how to spot a box-office hit, or doctor one into existence. I wasn't really surprised to read in a program article by former Hurok press chief Martin Feinstein that it was canny Sol who laid the evening-length ballet on Americans, in 1949, when he "insisted" that the Royal initiate its first U.S. season with *Sleeping Beauty*.

Sleeping Beauty and its companion ballets *Swan Lake*, *Nutcracker*, and the rest of what we think of as the classics were the products of the nineteenth-century opera houses, and they passed quite naturally to the Royal and several other modern institutions. In Europe, ballet and opera were a logical pair for practical and social reasons as well as artistic ones, and the major state companies of Europe today are still allied in spirit if not in fact with policies that favor the star system, sumptuous productions, an emphasis on virtuosity and style, an avoidance of experimentation, and an attitude that the audience is an aristocratic gathering whose taste for entertainment must be served.

In modern times classical opera house ballets have grown into symbols. Diaghilev fell back on the classics during his recurring choreographer shortages, but he understood that he was putting on an idea as well as a ballet. He acceded to his traditionalist colleagues, led by Benois, who urged a *Giselle* for the Ballets Russes' second Paris season (1910), at least in part because it had a big role for Nijinsky. And when the company was in financial straits after World War I, he hoped *Sleeping Beauty* would prove "a ballet that would run forever." In fact, *Beauty* ran for 105 consecutive performances with four alternating ballerinas, but failed to pull Diaghilev out of debt. Some of his associates thought he had betrayed his own modernist philosophy, though the conservative critic Arnold Haskell considered this production an "ultra modern experiment."

When the Royal Ballet (then the Sadler's Wells) reestablished itself in Covent Garden in 1946, it chose *Beauty* as its first production, a daring extravagance that gave infinite satisfaction to the public in those days of postwar austerity. Again, when American Ballet Theater was recovering from the latest of its chronic financial reverses, the company entered a period of international star-studded opera house ballets with *La Sylphide* (1964), and in 1967 staged the first full-length *Swan Lake* by a major American company.

And if staging the classics has often been used to prove a point, not staging them has been a kind of trademark with other companies, notably the New York City Ballet. That company has made almost a credo out of not looking like an opera house company. All its dancers are listed in alphabetical order regardless of rank or seniority. Costumes and sets are anathema to the Balanchinian sensibility, and when a classic is done, it usually has some peculiarities grafted onto the old scenario. NYCB audiences are anticipating this summer's announced *Coppélia* with a mixture of delight, incredulity and awe, and in some cases horror.

Whatever their public relations value, these old works are almost the only vehicles we have for preserving ballet history; they're the only way we get to see dancers do certain styles and conventions, and for that reason I'm glad they still exist.

Cranko supplemented the old classics in his repertory with "new" classics. He found stories that hadn't been used for ballets before, often from literature. These stories appealed to the romantic taste but substituted "psychological" problems for the intervention of the supernatural, upon which most of the original classics had relied to instigate and then resolve the plot. Cranko heroes swashbuckled their way through richly appointed drawing rooms filled with tempestuous women, and after a duel, a disgrace, and several athletic pas de deux, the plot would be satisfyingly wrapped up — or skewered together.

I don't know which of the elements made the Cranko operatic ballets so popular — whether it was the expensive décors and costumes, the spectacular dancing, or the quantities of nineteenth-century angst with which they were laced. Besides, they were long — full-length ballets usually — which impressed the cultural snobs in the audience. They had consecutive story lines that were easy to follow. And they were linked to the "great" — meaning officially approved and already understood — music and literature of the past.

Yet Cranko choreographed a lot of naturalistic violence into his pieces; the pas de deux especially were rough, grasping, "sexy" as compared to the gentler, more suggestive duets of tradition. So without having to stretch its aesthetic criteria in the slightest, the audience can see in Cranko "major" work that has tinges of modern-day freedom.

Post-Cranko opera house ballet is an odd blend of realism and artifice. Historical characters are beginning to supplant fictional ones. Kenneth MacMillan's *Anastasia* told the story — partly as a schizophrenic multimedia fantasy — of the last days of the Russian monarchy; and John Neumeier has recently produced a treatise on the composers Giacomo Meyerbeer and Robert Schumann.

This trend may further break down the already tenuous distinction between the onstage dancer and his offstage publicity-mongered personality. With some hysterical ballet fans, the star need not dance well or create a believable role, he just has to be there in the flesh. As Bobby Kennedy or Cinque he will presumably seem even more one of our own.

Even the more realistic opera house ballets are padded and extended beyond the believable range of the story. Mac-Millan's *Romeo and Juliet*, given this spring by the Royal Ballet, is loaded with pretexts that we would accept nowhere else. In Act I, the Prince of Verona interrupts a street brawl between the Montagues and Capulets. Furious, he stops the fight. At his command, all the dead bodies are dragged to the center of the stage like sides of beef and piled artistically behind him. In the bedroom scene, as Romeo looks out the window at the approaching dawn, Juliet leaps out of bed and runs frantically to the *other* side of the stage to prevent him from leaving. When she takes the sleeping potion later, she summons enough energy before passing out to fall exquisitely on her back on the bed, instead of on the floor.

If Juliet had fallen on the floor, her six friends, entering to escort her to her wedding with Paris, would immediately think she was dead and lose their chance to do their little wedding dance around the bed. And if she simply collapsed on the bed after taking the dope, she wouldn't get to do her agony solo. This kind of ballet is caught between the accommodations it must make for artistic effect and its pledge not to strain the modern audience's credibility.

If MacMillan's new *Manon* is merely a spectacle, it's drab and ordinary, and if it's about human relationships, it's an insult. L'Abbé Prévost's eighteenth-century story of Manon Lescaut tells something about a woman's predicament during a time of social change. The lovers, Manon and Des Grieux, are ruled and finally destroyed by the conflicting demands of passion, morality, and manners. MacMillan shows the woman as a victim — not even a victim, an object, a piece of currency for which men gamble, scheme, and fight each other. Manon is completely passive or completely cooperative as the case demands: she seems to have no personal feelings toward her suitors. The men have no scruples or self-control. MacMillan is just as obtuse about the hero's feelings as about the heroine's. Constantly the opera house mentality asserts itself over the necessity of reasonable motivation or sequence, so even if the dancers had some point of view about the characters they play, it would be impossible to sustain through the long cadenzas of virtuoso-descriptive dancing.

John Neumeier's *Don Juan*, performed by the National Ballet of Canada, is even less integrated. Though it seems to be a study of Don Juan's personality — well, some spoken words by Max Frisch seem to be that — the ballet is actually a series of pantomimic episodes in which the Don acts callously toward innumerable women.

Don Juan is patently a vehicle for Nureyev. Given a challenge, Nureyev can be an interesting actor, and he has the intelligence to look at the legendary Don Juan's character in a new way. But Neumeier has made the role a figurehead — most of the time the Don merely observes the other dancers, including a surrogate Don, his servant, as they act out love scenes and other incidents in the form of a party entertainment.

Nothing is clear about the ballet, neither what is happening nor why it is happening, nor even sometimes who is doing what to whom. A synopsis provided in the program doesn't help very much. What we can distinguish about Don Juan is that not women but playing with women turns him on. Neumeier seems to suggest that the Don is nothing but your common everyday narcissist, and that the ideal he's been chasing all along is really death.

The audience perceives this idea only through the verbal accessories that are supplied and through the fact that he dances himself to death with the elusive Lady in White in the final scene. *Don Juan* is a spectacle, a costume-ball mise en scène where, aside from the inevitable and interchangeable strenuous duets and solos, the only dancing seems to consist of a chorus doing chassés and wrist flips back and forth in the distance — looking exactly like something incidental from "Don Giovanni."

July 1974

The Royal Ballet's Great
Identity Swap

THERE PROBABLY WASN'T any less variety of style or subject matter in the Royal Ballet's repertory of 1970 than there is now, but thinking over what I saw of the season just ended at the Metropolitan Opera House I'm not as clear as I used to be about what the company does. I think it's undergoing an identity crisis.

Nineteen seventy marked the premature retirement of the company's director and chief choreographer, Frederick Ashton, for reasons that were never completely convincing to me. Kenneth MacMillan assumed command, and in the ensuing two years he dropped a number of Ashton ballets — which used to form the backbone of the repertory — and brought in considerable new choreographic blood. If the Royal Ballet's touring repertory is an accurate gauge of its overall policy, the old Royal Ballet we've known as the supreme classical instrument of the world is gone. This is a transitional period, possibly leading to a more exciting, theatrical company. But it strikes me we already have enough of those — I wonder if the Royal's transformation will be worth what it's sacrificed.

Temperamentally I've never been entirely sympathetic to the grand old ballet tradition. I don't have any special reverence for the old-fashioned story ballets and I don't spend my life looking for the perfect arabesque. But you couldn't help appreciating the Royal's pristine magnificence. Purity of execution; a concern with detail in period, place, and story; and a willingness to trust dancers — these were the things that the Royal Ballet did so much better than other traditional companies.

They were Ashton's preoccupations, I think, as company director as much as in his choreography. Alongside a tendency

to be stuffy that I can do without, Ashton has remarkable witti-
ness and a gift for creating character that I miss very much
now. Ashton's ballets collectively, whether in comic or period
genre, narrative, abstract, or classical style, have serene assurance and good taste. They're built for display without ostenta-
tion, appreciation rather than experiment. I don't know if anyone is doing the old Ashton ballets in England now, but if
Britain's official company doesn't preserve the works of its first
choreographer, who is going to? And will the same thing happen to the works of our own, much more independent, non-
official George Balanchine in a few years?

Some Ashton does remain in the RB's repertory, notably *The
Dream*, a delightful one-act version of "A Midsummer Night's
Dream," which seems to me the ideal fairy-tale ballet because
it's got all the important things in it and none of the tedium.
Unlike the motley string of divertissements, dances, narrative
scenes, and spectacle that make up your usual fairy tale, *The
Dream* has a cohesive choreographic idea. Following Mendels-
sohn's familiar music, Ashton has given the whole ballet a very
fast pace, with each set of characters using speed in a different
way. Titania and the corps of fairies streak over the ground
with tiny, delicate steps. Puck and Oberon swoop around
boldly. Bottom and the rustics do a gawky, cloglike dance, as if
performing makes them self-conscious and they'd like to get it
over with. The mortal lovers caught in Puck's misguided magic
are always running headlong after each other or away from
each other.

The ballet keeps up this driving swiftness until after the tan-
gled plot has been straightened out; then suddenly Ashton ends
it with a slow, absolutely unflustered pas de deux for Oberon
and Titania. It's a beautiful comment on all the foolishness
that has gone before and on the quiet nobility of the fairy mon-
archs. I saw Jennifer Penney and David Wall do the leads,
and, though Penney couldn't calm down enough to make this
contrast work, they were both excellent in the first part of the
ballet.

Jerome Robbins' *Dances at a Gathering* has been acquired
since the RB was last here, but unfortunately it was only scheduled three times during the six-week run. The English dancers

do it very differently from the Americans for whom it was made. Robbins follows no formal continuity or structure in the ballet, and his steps don't adhere to classical patterns either. Everything that happens in the piece is unexpected; it almost looks improvised.

What the RB dancers don't do is make easy transitions between steps and "everyday" movement, between what's supposed to look set and what's supposed to look casual. Rudolf Nureyev, opening the ballet in the part created by Edward Villella, establishes this stylistic point. Where Villella strolled on, surveyed the dancing-space, and fooled around with a few steps as if they'd just come into his head, Nureyev enters ready to dance. He dances. In between he saunters, as a ballet dancer saunters, which isn't the way you and I would do it.

But that just makes *Dances* a slightly different ballet, no less interesting once you see that it's going to be a performance instead of an illusion of naturalness with danced commentary. I liked Nureyev in it, and Anthony Dowell, Michael Coleman, and Lynn Seymour, but Monica Mason was outstanding. She seemed to catch on to the drive of the ballet, the dashing, gotta-dance energy of an early duet with Coleman, the tugging at the shape of the music in a solo created for Violette Verdy, the times when the arms just swing and when they are choreographed. I wish I could have seen more of Mason in challenging ballets. Or any ballets.

Kenneth MacMillan's full-length *Anastasia*, seen here for the first time, surprised me by not being half as bad as most reports said it was. It's a realistic narrative of the last days of Tsar Nicholas II of Russia and the young princess who supposedly escaped when the royal family was executed by revolutionists in 1917. For a traditional story ballet *Anastasia* is handsomely furnished, with the requisite showy dancing, period detail, a well-designed ballroom scene. I found the first two acts no less interesting than, say, *Swan Lake* — although it betrays its modernity by substituting a squad of soldiers for the female corps de ballet.

As dance, *Anastasia* is far superior to anything John Cranko has done in the same vein. MacMillan begins to show a sense for character, an ability to give the appropriate movement precedence over the purely eye-catching one. He usually gets beguiled back into the old tricks, but the insight is there. I particularly liked a tender little Russian dance that Anastasia does in the first act with her mother, the Tsarina (Lesley Collier and Georgina Parkinson when I saw it). Dances of affection between two women are rare enough; this one also managed to convey two distinct personalities. Later MacMillan has an older woman (Gerd Larsen) join in, followed by Anastasia's three sisters, and it becomes just a number.

Despite its heavy realism — people diving off a pier in the background of the first act, which takes place at a resort; disgruntled peasants muttering around the soup kitchen at the gates of the Tsar's palace — *Anastasia* risks some innovation and generally succeeds. The set for all three acts, designed by Barry Kay, is dominated by a huge spiral frame with gauze stretched over it. Suspended symbolically over the action, it could be the inside structure of a shell, or the whirlpool of events that were to suck this way of life down to oblivion. In the last act — choreographically the weakest — the traumatized Anastasia relives the destruction of her family and the set serves as a screen for projections of actual films, a huge, inescapable cylinder of ghastly memories.

MacMillan has chosen to accompany this act with an orchestral/concrète score of the neurosis-and-agony school by Bohuslav Martinů, which is shocking and effective after the first two acts of Tchaikovsky. Old ladies started walking out of the theater immediately, of course, but that just proves the point.

June 18, 1972

The New Romantics

As the highlight of its fall season the Joffrey Ballet gave Frederick Ashton's *The Dream* a lovely production, its first by an American company. The 1964 work, based on "A Midsummer Night's Dream," merely tells Shakespeare's story of the wise and foolish fairies and the moonstruck mortals. Two years earlier George Balanchine had expanded the story and turned it to the service of ballet by adding a second act wedding scene in the tradition of the grand old nineteenth-century ballets. The Balanchine *Dream* offers the dancers and audience a divertissement with a classical pas de deux, which would have been difficult to fit into the story illusion of the first act. Ashton doesn't allow himself any surrogate dance personages, so all his characters have to dance *and* tell the story. As a consequence, I think he's made one of the most expressive story ballets in the repertory.

For the Joffrey, David Walker designed the romantic forest set and the costumes — gauzy confections for Titania and Oberon's court and Victorian finery for the mortals — and Tom Skelton has ingeniously lit the stage so that the mortals move always in a warm glow and the fairies in a spray of silver. When the fairies first run across the stage, pausing in Sylphide-like attitudes to listen, and then skittering off again, you realize how foreign all this is to the Joffrey. The long Taglioni skirts are unusual; the Joffrey girls ordinarily wear no skirts over their tights, or filmy little nothings that show off the whole length of the leg. But this is also the company's first attempt in a long time to deal with the whole old-ballet convention, the classical gestures, the use of the corps de ballet to create choral backgrounds and bridges for the main action, and the classical idea of dance as movement that can represent feelings, relationships, even happenings without literally doing them or imitating them.

Ashton's ballet is not without literal mime or naturalistic acting. Larry Grenier as Bottom, awakening from his enchantment and scratching his head in befuddlement and shock at the idea that he may have turned into an ass and been loved by the Queen of the Fairies, gave one of the finest character scenes I've ever seen. But the ballet's distinction lies more in the nonliteral storytelling that is found in the dancing alone.

The piece begins on the run and keeps up its allegro pace right to the final scene. But the fast tempo of the fairies is smooth, airborne, in contrast to the mortals' agitated chases and graspings, their huge efforts to entrap or escape from one another. Ashton's choreography shows us two sets of characters, one unruffled, above the fray, the other confused, taking everything too seriously, accident-prone.

The final pas de deux is more than just a love duet between the reconciled Titania and Oberon. Ashton has been showing us an Oberon of great stillness and command, also of anger and compassion, and a Titania who's so high-spirited she's almost flighty, who's temperamental but warm-hearted. In this beautiful dance, the choreographer slows down the tempo to a lullaby, until at the end the lovers retire together after the night's mischief. Oberon steadies and calms the excitable Titania. As he supports and finally cradles her, her movement gradually becomes smaller and less animated, she gives up her impulse to fly and yields to his unhurried persuasions. This is a pas de deux that shows us the character of the two dancers as much as it shows us that they can dance.

I think Ashton's best work is grounded in the dance image, just as in a different way Balanchine's is. He's not primarily making a dramatic point with *The Dream*; he's saying this is one kind of thing you can do with dancing. If you can't see Ashton this way, if the dancers don't show him to you this way, his ballets can be trivial, dull, academic, or vaguely disappointing. *Façade* (1931), for instance, which returned to the Joffrey repertory after a lapse of a few seasons, is a pastiche of popular and theater dance styles, but the Joffrey plays it as if the dancing were just a pretext for jokes. The Royal Ballet gives this work quite reservedly, so you see that there's more to it than comedy.

The Dream is just beyond the Joffrey dancers' capacities. They do fairly well with the acting work, but when it comes to Ashton's steps — his complicated enchaînements, exacting turns and balances, fluid changes of speed and direction, a precise though sometimes distorted line — they are in trouble, and the acting disappears altogether. They lose all character and become dancers working at steps.

Francesca Corkle, the company's strongest dancer technically, was given only a single matinee to try Titania, and she wasn't able to bring much assurance to the acting demands of the role. The other Titania was Rebecca Wright, the company's resident soubrette and ingénue, paired with Burton Taylor. Both Taylor and Glenn White, who partnered Corkle, are handsome, and Taylor has a noble line that makes him look like a king. But Taylor, White, and Wright couldn't meet the choreographic rigors of their roles. Russell Sultzbach was cast as Puck because he is red-haired and puckish, I suppose, and because the audience loves him, but his concept of both the role and the dancing seemed to come from Road Runner out of Loony Tunes.

The sentimentalizing of *The Dream* is symptomatic of the Joffrey Ballet's whole outlook and emphasis. This company has always made a point of its appeal to contemporary taste. It developed an enthusiastic young audience in the late-sixties– early-seventies with a series of genre pieces based on various popular fancies: the psychology of dreams, fear of the Bomb, mixed-media, occultism, love-peace-n-rock, and it still announces with some pride that critics think Gerald Arpino's *Trinity* is "the best rock ballet ever created," as if there were a distinction in that. Having exhausted the fairly shallow possibilities of these ideas, the company began dipping into the ballet repertory of the past; that is, of the twentieth century, which is about as much of a past as ballet can muster. It has acquired the Ashton, several Massine works, Limón, Jooss, a *Petrouchka*, names worthy of preservation, which in dance means live performance.

Concurrently with its youth pitch, then, the Joffrey presents itself as a museum, a company with a sense of history. I have trouble reconciling these two aesthetic points of view even if the audience doesn't, but there does seem to be a logic in it. Escapism, superficiality, showiness have always been components of ballet, and these elements seem to submerge or drift up to the surface in direct proportion to the strength of the choreographic talent around. In the Joffrey's case, the attitudes of escapism have become so pervasive that they throw a sickly cast over even good choreography.

The audience's tepid reaction to George Balanchine's *Square Dance* put the whole fall season into perspective. *Square Dance*, the only Balanchine work in the Joffrey's active repertory, usually gets a couple of insufficiently rehearsed performances a season. It is the most classical ballet the company now carries, the most concentrated on dance values. It gives the dancers, and especially the ballerina, Francesca Corkle, their best chance to show off the classical vocabulary. Yet the audience appears to think it's a bad ballet about a square dance.

The Joffrey is topic-oriented. Everybody comes to see the dancing, of course, to experience the vicarious thrill of motion and mastery, to look at the marvelous bodies, the theatricality. The fact that it's dance is taken for granted as something wonderful, a zippier, more exciting way to see a story told. But it seems so undifferentiated — the *kind* of dance, the quality, the appropriateness of it doesn't seem to matter.

So they gave us this fall yet another revival of José Limón's *The Moor's Pavane*, performed for its top layer only. Limón's original role, the Othello, has now come to be the property of a black man if the company doing the dance has one. Christian Holder is black, physically big, and charismatic, but he made hash out of Limón's choreography. The other dancers achieved the shape and intensity of the choreography with somewhat more success, but they never got it to look like a modern dance.

The pop audience accepts size in place of power, dramatic conflict for choreographic style or definition. *The Moor's Pavane* is first-rate storytelling, but it must have weight, amplitude in space, incisively controlled and balanced tensions among the four characters in order to be Limón. With each successive Limón revival, I see these essential dynamics slipping away, and I get very pessimistic about modern dance repertory. If Limón, Humphrey, Graham, and the others created ultimately to provide fodder for entertaining ballet, the modern dance hasn't amounted to anything.

Limón was a romantic, and his dances retain a certain verisimilitude, even in stylistically weak versions, because his basic vision was so grand. He conceived his characters and developed his movement heroically. I can see why they work as ballets. The new romantics want the feeling of a period, a place, an idea, a human incident; they want to be able to recognize the theme right away, feel at home with it, amble along with it pleasantly.

Or, as in the case of Robert Joffrey's own new ballet, *Remembrances*, wallow in it. *Remembrances* is based on Wagner's "Wesendonck Lieder" and other music associated with a lost love of the composer's youth, Mathilde Wesendonck. Not one but three protagonists are introduced: Donna Roll, "She, who sings"; Jan Hanniford, "She, who remembers"; and Francesca Corkle, who dances and has no name. All this Martha Grahaming suggests the women are aspects of the same character, but Roll sings and acts out the words most expressively, Corkle dances beautifully without any particular indication of character, and Hanniford glides back and forth between them to no apparent purpose.

I guess *Remembrances* is supposed to be an evocation of unfulfilled love. It goes on for a very long time. Corkle dances with various partners, mainly Jonathan Watts; other couples go in and out; nothing develops and nothing changes. The ballet is dark and luxurious, a mood, an atmosphere. Maybe it's meant as a soothing accompaniment for the audience's reveries.

There is so much surface attractiveness to the Joffrey repertory that it's easy to see Twyla Tharp's ballets as just more pop. Clive Barnes, defending some sort of faith or other, savagely attacked Tharp and those who prize her as being either disrespectful or ignorant of true classicism. The most charitable way I can interpret Barnes's insensitivity to Tharp is that he has some preconceived, unyielding idea of what is allowed in the name of "classic ballet." Of course, the Joffrey is not a "classic" company by any means, and if we followed Barnes to a logical end we would have to exclude Balanchine, Robbins, and Barnes's one-time favorite, Gerald Arpino, all of whom have played with music and movement the same way he accuses Tharp of doing. I wonder what work Barnes would consider a true-blue "classic ballet" today, or if there are any. In any case, he has been the chief advocate of pop dance in this country, so it's difficult to understand why he can't accept Tharp as enthusiastically as he did Arpino and many other pop choreographers.

It seems to me Tharp is both a pop artist *and* a classicist, if we must give her labels. But she is first of all an original; she makes her own terms, and her hand is so sure that those terms are compelling even when we don't know precisely what they are. *Deuce Coupe*, her wonderful pop ballet of last spring, is what pop should be but never is. We think of pop art as being exploitative, made to order, salable, determinedly not serious. But here came Tharp, using all the pop paraphernalia — Beach Boys music, boogaloo and frug, live graffiti painters painting a backdrop, lickety-split jokes, more danced references to kid life in America than a barrel of *Trinitys* — and with this vocabulary appended to her own movement and classical ballet steps she said things that were serious, moving, sad; things maybe even profound about kids and about dancing and I guess about us too.

Pop ballets are usually created by fortyish guys working hard, out of nostalgia and a little envy, to identify with Youth; by people who are yearning to be in touch with their time only they can't find out what that is so they create what they would like it to be. I'll bet Twyla Tharp hasn't spent five minutes in the past year wondering where it's at or what to use for a theme so her next ballet will be contemporary. You can feel an energy of creation in her dances, an energy that is so concentrated it seems to have bored right into the earth and the vitals of the dancers, an energy that comes out, inevitably, alive and of this moment.

As Time Goes By, her new work, hasn't even got the trappings of pop — and maybe that's what got Barnes so steamed up. Its music is Haydn, the last two movements of the "Farewell Symphony," and its theme is dancing — as classicism's theme is dancing. Heresy rears its ugly head. Tharp uses the classical movement vocabulary with distortions, changes, interpolations. She plays around with our ideas of how a classical work should look. She mixes up the order of energies, starting fast and ending slow. She makes the stage space all bunched up and busy sometimes instead of clear and symmetrical. She feints around the edges of things that are supposed to be hammering you into your seat, and she evades climaxes that have been working out the same way for generations.

I don't think Americans understand classicism very well. They think it means anything old. Or anything *representing* anything old. They think it's anything that satisfies their longing for the safe, the secure, the already understood and explained. The Joffrey Ballet repertory is loaded with old-fashioned ballets — Ballet Russe de Monte Carlo ballets and movie-romance ballets and World War II jazzy America ballets and Arpino ballets in their various period guises, including Berkeley in the age of the flower children. Twyla Tharp is important to the Joffrey audience, not because she represents a now generation or adds a new item to the catalogue of styles. She's not even important because I and a lot of other critics say she is. Tharp is important because while everyone around her is enjoying a period of choreographic decline and even decadence, she is reversing the process. Or, as I overheard Valerie Bettis say one night after a performance of As Time Goes By, "It's nice to see someone who's busy about dance."

Spring 1974

Dance Anthology: 1972 Edition

AFTER SOME unsettled times, American Ballet Theater has now established an agreeable pattern of two New York seasons per year, six weeks at Lincoln Center in early summer and a winter month at the frumpy old City Center. Every time it's like having a favorite anthology come out in a new edition.

Antony Tudor's *Dark Elegies* (1937) belongs in any permanent collection of masterpieces. Ballet Theater is sparing to the point of stinginess with this great ballet, possibly because they're afraid the audience won't be able to take its somber mood. It was last done here for one performance in the summer of 1970, and this winter it was scheduled four times.

Set to Gustav Mahler's "Kindertotenlieder" ("Songs on the Death of Children"), it is a communal rite of grief contained and calmed. The setting is outdoors and Northern, and the dances are formal rather than ecstatic.

These people don't express their sorrow with passion, or abandon themselves to rage; they're mute and reserved. The shapes of the group and of the individual dancers' bodies are circles and straight lines, almost never twisted or spatially unclear. People reach out their arms to each other, they lift or support a crumpled form, but they don't embrace. They find solace in uprightness, not hysteria, even when they want to strike out at God's cruelty. I don't know of a contemporary choreographer who can match Tudor for conveying the character of a people purely in movement terms.

Dancers feel reverent about *Dark Elegies*, and it's always performed with great devotion. Bonnie Mathis, dancing the second Lament with Gayle Young, was especially beautiful. So was Sallie Wilson, who opens and closes the ballet with a hesitant procession of little jumps and dragging steps. Natalia Makarova, dancing in the work for the first time, seemed to me not to understand it. She danced very well, but she was acting out grief, rather than feeling the solemnity of the movement as the others do.

I had never seen *Rodeo* before, and I was delighted when its revival was announced. I was even more delighted when the piece proved to be a success on a very immediate level, not just one of those landmarks you dutifully have to respect but don't like very much. Agnes de Mille choreographed it thirty years ago, and by now everybody must know its Aaron Copland score and its Cinderella story about the Cowgirl who learns you can catch a fella better with a bow in your hair than a lariat in your fist.

I was prepared for the rather awful de Mille sentiments about love, sex roles, and the inescapable desolation of any female who hasn't got a date for the Saturday night dance. What was nice about *Rodeo* that I didn't expect was that the choreographer allowed her reformed tomboy to stay in character as a Plain Jane instead of blossoming out in gorgeous curly hair and a pink dress. The Cowgirl chooses not the handsome, uninteresting Head Wrangler but the altogether more suitable, homelier Champion Roper.

Christine Sarry made it all happen. I can't imagine anyone ever having done *Rodeo* better. Sarry is an absolute love of a dancer, comedian, partner, actress — she's alive, responsive, technically unflappable. Why she is not doing *Coppélia, La Fille Mal Gardée*, and a dozen other roles that Ballet Theater fills with vapid, merely competent dancers I do not understand.

She has a fine sense of dramatic balance; she never turns a role into a personal trip, but you always notice her at exactly the times you're supposed to. She's different with different partners, and she's acutely tuned in to the circumstances of the moment on stage, not just to the way she's learned to do the ballet. Sarry's Champion Ropers in the two performances I saw were a sweet, shy Terry Orr and the rougher, gawkier but likable William Carter.

The other big revival of this season was *La Fille Mal Gardée*, an old, old chestnut of a story ballet remounted, I guess, for the powerhouse stars of ABT: Carla Fracci, Natalia Makarova, Erik Bruhn, Ivan Nagy. (Bruhn was out from the beginning of the season due to illness — he later announced his retirement from dancing, though the dance world hopes it's not his final word. Also ill was Ted Kivitt, who had been scheduled for *Fille* too. Niels Kehlet of the Royal Danish Ballet replaced them in some performances.)

Fille is a two-act comic ballet, a couth, eighteenth-century precursor of the farmer's daughter joke. Lise, the daughter of the Widow Simone, loves Colin, a country lad, but her mother is determined to marry her off to the feeble-minded heir of a rich farmer. After a series of slapstick mistakes, Lise accidentally gets locked in the hayloft with Colin. Her purity thus compromised, she's now unfit for marriage with anyone else, to the lovers' relief.

Most of the characters in this ballet are freaky in the extreme: the Widow Simone is traditionally played by a man; Alain, the rich man's son, is a blithering idiot who likes to chase butterflies; the rich man himself is a waddling, red-nosed fool; there's a bunch of silly neighbors and superfluous friends; and even Lise and Colin act about twelve years old, except when they do a serious pas de deux. Ballet Theater's new production, designed in dollhouse pastels by Rolf Gerard, looks slightly demented in the comic scenes and almost entirely without style in the periods of pure dancing. It hasn't solved the problem of how to make all those standard peasant boys and girls look as if they belong with the crackpot main characters.

Carla Fracci's Lise seemed rather hard and calculating to me, like a nasty teen-ager. Makarova played her as a grimacing hooligan, kicking over the furniture and moving in a continual blur of nervous gestures. Nagy looked more relaxed than his usual princely self, but fondly bewildered by Makarova's nuttiness rather than an accomplice to it. John Prinz was funny and touching as the butterfly boy. He's usually cast in romantic and classic partnering roles; here he not only has to do lots of jumping, beats, turns in the air with one leg parallel to the ground, but he's not allowed to look handsome, and he has to use his comic intelligence as well. I thought he succeeded admirably.

February 6, 1972

American Heroine

THERE'S SOMETHING convincing to me about Agnes de Mille's ballets, a core of American truth underneath all that is disappointing. De Mille underchoreographs and overdramatizes. She's sentimental. She buys the whole American Dream and then wreaks punishment on her characters when it doesn't work out. But de Mille is essentially always making dance about growing up, and that seems to me a major concern, still, of American art.

De Mille's heroines don't fit in — they resist the roles that seem ordained for them in life. The ones that finally accept these roles live happily ever after, and the ones that don't get branded as outlaws or lunatics. They may end up as clichéd as when they began, but their struggle in between interests me. I think it's peculiarly American for adolescents to question the stability symbols that other cultures take for granted. For that matter, adolescents as a particular class of people with their own behavior patterns are a pretty American phenomenon.

And all the de Mille heroines I've seen are adolescent, the kid growing out of tomboyhood in *Rodeo*, the soon-to-be-spinster Lizzie Borden in *Fall River Legend*, the old-maid Southern recluse in *A Rose for Miss Emily*. They're all poised, or arrested, at that point before they have to take on the responsibilities of adult sexuality. In various ways they all perceive the world wrongly, because they perceive it as an ideal. They can't reconcile the inadequacies they feel with the perfection they'd like to attain.

Lizzie and Emily carry out what must be for both of them the single most positive act of their lives, by murdering the people they love and hate. This explosion of anger is followed by a retreat into numbed silence — neither one of them lives in the real world again. De Mille revised Lizzie Borden's story by sentencing her to death; in fact, Lizzie's own community permitted her to go free — probably they knew she'd exhausted all her resources and would never threaten anyone else.

The Cowgirl in *Rodeo* goes the other way. She sees in a moment of clarity that she can solve all her troubles by being a conventional girl. The minute she puts on a dress, the dream comes true. We can see the dream is false, that she had good reason to try to be different from the simpering dolls that the boys all chase after. But we can also see that this community has no room for nonconformists. She'll have to play the game or be a misfit.

This dilemma, this coming-of-age, is also at the heart of de Mille's new work, *Texas Fourth*, although I might not have seen that if the ballet hadn't been premièred on a program with *Rodeo* and *Fall River Legend*. *Texas Fourth* opens with a square dance, with Dennis Nahat playing a fiddle, dancing, and calling the set. This is the high point of the ballet's energy, which soon dissipates itself in almost random slices of American social dance styles, none as clearly or consistently choreographed as the first one, and none having any apparent relationship to the others.

Rebecca Wright and Eric Nesbitt seem to be central characters, energetic teen-agers in blazing white sneakers and bobby socks, who have an odd habit of rolling on the floor in a wrestler's clinch. This awkward device becomes a kind of theme that introduces a new set of dances or styles. There are moments that look — or sound, in an equally unfocused score that seems to have had three composers — vaguely like the Lindy, like the Charleston, like a waltz; there are drum majorettes and football cheerleaders, and a Dixieland band gets wheeled in and right out again on a platform covered with red, white, and blue bunting. There are some children dressed up for a parade. Someone does flips across the stage; Nahat twirls a baton and does undistinguished tours à la seconde at the same time; William Carter does a smidgen of a tap dance. There's a skeletal set suggesting a gas station and a roadhouse; it's wheeled in at some point and wheeled out at another point.

I have no idea what all this is supposed to be about, because the activity is so ill-defined. The dancers wear a series of costumes not really belonging to any particular period — the girls look sort of 1940-ish, the men are in all-purpose blue jeans — so I can't identify which dancers do which styles, or why they change costumes, or even why they run in and out. Later some people in vaguely nineteenth-century costumes appear; only one of them is given a name, Ghost of the Mother — whose mother anyway? The others dance together to "Streets of Laredo," run out, run in.

There must be some narrative in the background of *Texas Fourth* that the choreographer decided to omit. All I could make out was that Wright was having a dream of some sort, through which all these characters trooped. It may be her mother whose ghost Ruth Mayer plays, because after Nesbitt has thrown her to the ground innumerable times, and then danced around her with a combination of ballet and acrobatic steps, and beat his fists on his chest Tarzan-style about four times, Mayer comes and gives her a kiss or a blessing, and at last she flings her arms around Nesbitt, signifying, I surmise, that she can emerge from girlhood with the approval of her ancestors.

Texas Fourth opened on a gala evening that Ballet Theater devoted to Agnes de Mille, who's recovered from a serous illness that would have beaten anyone not as tough as she is. She accepted the Handel Medallion from Mayor Beame, assuring us in a voice with flags flying in it that she's still here by god. Her courage, her survival, is as good as fireworks. I can certainly celebrate that.

July 15, 1976

Feld Re-fielded

ELIOT FELD's early ballets left me dazed. I've lost my head about ballet on occasion: I swam euphorically through the Stravinsky Festival, I saw *Deuce Coupe* eight times in its first season. But when Feld's short-lived American Ballet Company was performing, for whole weeks at a time I seemed to be living his ballets myself. If I wasn't in the theater watching them, I was home writing about them; my mind reverberated with dancing, and the music played across my sleep.

But no matter how much I thought and said about Feld at the time, I was never quite satisfied that I'd unearthed what made him so important.

Feld always said he was a classicist, but people didn't want to believe him. His works were formal; you would be as interested in what the dance was going to do next as in what the dancers were going to do next. In his dance vocabulary, use of the stage, and the overall construction of a work, he was far less innovative than Twyla Tharp is now, for instance. But he was clever and his ballets looked different — just a little bit outside the categories. He was more than an individualist. You felt the great force of his will on the work, more than you felt his dedication to a tradition. We preferred to think of him as a romantic or a modernist than to admit him to the select company of classical giants.

I didn't know much about classicism then, and I didn't bother to get into the semantics where Feld was concerned. It seemed more important to record something about what he was actually doing. Now I see that, both in his choreography and in the way he directed his dancers, he was enriching a closed and often stale vocabulary. Season after season now, audiences confirm the solidity of those works. Without benefit of ballyhoo or stars, without pop props, Feld ballets fill audi-

ences with that sense of completeness and unhoped-for pleasure that a classic always does.

Feld invested the classical vocabulary with a sense of weight
and a fluent musicality. He wanted us to see every bit of space
the dancer was traveling through, not just the stopping or starting points. He considered space a three-dimensional possibility
rather than a breeder of only lines and planes. His dance gesture gave rise to character, not the other way around. These
seem far more important to me now than his inventiveness
with steps or the sunny, ingenuous smiles on the faces of his
dancers.

Harbinger (1967) is Feld's first and in some ways still his best
ballet. I'm constantly struck by its compositional depth; it's not
just a good upbeat opener, although in comparison with all the
dreary exercises I've seen before and since, it's a masterpiece in
that category. *Harbinger* is an intelligent ballet, and I confess I
love dance that has its wits together.

Feld begins with a pure and elemental movement theme, the
contrast between a tightly curled-up body and a stretched-out
body. Neither these nor any other body configurations are just
shapes to Feld. His dances looked unusually fluid and connected because the dancers weren't trying to hit a pose; a torso
closing up into a ball, like most of the gestural ideas in Feld,
can have both expressive and symbolic meaning, but it's also
the result of something or the initiation of something. It's
meant to be seen clearly, but so is the continuum of events to
which it belongs.

We see the solitary boy in the beginning of *Harbinger* repeatedly folding and extending his body; the reminder is fetal and
the choreographic reference seems to be to Balanchine's
Apollo. A youth poised on the brink of manhood, alternately
reaching out to life and retreating into himself. Six girls come
in, and the boy dances around them and in front of them but
never with them. They're like his daydreams. One by one
they slip away, then come back. When he's got them all docilely following his lead, he abruptly sinks down, and they hud-
dle over him protectively.

The fast duet (created by Feld and Christine Sarry) is such a
tour de force that I often sit through it barely breathing. It's

like trying to read while your plane is going through a thunder-storm. At last, though, I've been able to see this dance as more than a blast of speed and precision. It's a contest between two impulses. Sarry is always pulling away, trying to get out into space, while the man wants to contain her. Every time she reaches out, he grabs her and reins her in. She makes one last huge dive for freedom and he pulls her out of the air by clasping her around the middle. Almost reflexively, she doubles up. I think this two minutes of dancing is the story of *La Sylphide*, only in a different dance style.

Part three poses a self-absorbed couple against a group of seven other dancers. Without stressing the point at all, Feld shows us various possible combinations of people — the men and women pair off, but there's always one extra woman; people walk quietly around, touching hands and parting; at times the whole group packs together in one anonymous, solid clump that includes the now-separated lovers. By now Feld doesn't have to show you his folded-unfolded bodies literally; the same idea can be understood from the group massing together or spreading out into space.

Then there's a playful trio; both boys try to capture the girl, but at the last minute she steps out of the little nest they've made by curling themselves around her feet, and bounces away. In the finale all the movement themes from the first four sections recur, only they're not necessarily done by the same dancers, and it all happens at once. Then, in a cumula-tive series of synchronous patterns, Feld builds to a restatement of the duet's climax, and on three decelerating chords from the orchestra, all the men snatch all the girls out of the air and the curtain falls.

Maybe one of the things that defines the classical is its ability to be expressive without being entirely representational. Balan-chine has this gift, and so does Ashton. Feld's early ballets can almost always be seen as personal documents even when they seem to be only about dancing. And when they relate most overtly and graphically to the human condition, as in *At Mid-night* (1967), they don't lean entirely on mime and dramatic situations.

At Midnight, Feld's deepest and darkest ballet, is a meditation on the individual and the group. The premise is clearly set forth, in the first section of a man alone in the faceless world, and subsequently of a man and a woman without mates in a world of lovers. But in the two lovelorn solos, for instance, Feld is not merely pointing out that such a situation exists, as do many Pity the Outsider ballets. The woman alone possesses the entire stage, which is empty except for a couple in the down-right corner. The couple stay in place, always physically in contact and completely absorbed in each other. They change position very slowly and unemphatically, as if they had all the time in the world. Meanwhile the woman runs through the space, probing out into it, retreating from it, scooping up and spilling out great armfuls of it, wrenching into the air behind her with her elbows. She's constantly changing direction and level, and there's scarcely a moment when she isn't straining or tipping out of the vertical. It's not the pain on her face, but her restlessness and inability to hold on to anything solid that make her a sympathetic figure against the calm fixity of the couple.

In contrast, the man alone works against a stageful of couples. They glide quickly in and out of the space, lifting and embracing each other effortlessly, while the man scrambles and falters along a few straight paths among them. He seems caught in a rut, self-impeded, as he yanks and twists his arms and legs around his body.

I have to admit that part of what I'm telling you is remembered from 1969–1971. This winter's Ballet Theater productions of these two ballets, and of *Intermezzo* (1969), barely resembled the ballets that Feld choreographed and his company interpreted. In all of them lifts were botched or omitted, circular ideas got flattened into lines, steps that were meant to be fast and exact came out slurred. In none of them was a mood or intensity established. *Intermezzo* looked especially smudged and shapeless.

There are surface similarities between *Intermezzo* and various other ballroom ballets, but it was always very individual to me. I guess its main distinction is that it's so serious. Feld used none of the usual devices for ingratiating his dancers with the audience — no little anecdotes, competitions, changing of partners, and no dancing that's put there exclusively for show. His three couples dance for themselves, and I think the power of the ballet comes from seeing such spectacular movement pouring out of such a private ambiance.

Ballet Theater started tampering with *Intermezzo* when it first acquired the ballet in the summer of 1972. Parts were shifted around to build a star role for Cynthia Gregory, and later for stars-in-the-making. The humor got more pronounced and the virtuosity more noticeable. The balance, the sequentiality of the work was thrown all off, not only in terms of the way the dancing developed but in terms of the dancers as people. Each couple originally had its own particular quality, and you could see each one as belonging to the introspection and serenity of the atmosphere. Now one couple is there to get laughs, and one to drum up applause for the "star." Only Christine Sarry and David Coll, dancing the same parts Feld choreographed for them, give you any sense of what the ballet can be.

Much as I loved Feld, I don't want to see his works in this condition. Ex-Feld dancers Sarry, Coll, John Sowinski, and Daniel Levins understand the ballets, but Feld never did vehicles for one or two featured dancers. He saw a ballet as an ensemble, a community, even if a community dominated by his personal instincts. Ballet Theater's revivals are dominated by no central force, they present no sense of Feld's style and no appreciation of his value. This is a form of robbery, and Feld is not the only victim.

March 1974

Meanwhile, Away from the Hustle . . .

NEW YORK hasn't had a resident chamber ballet company since the Manhattan Festival Ballet caved in to economics about seven years ago. Now Eliot Feld seems to be making a new stab at it. Feld's choreographic career started off with such a hurrah, and his first company at Brooklyn Academy was so ambitious, I don't think anyone expected him to drop out of the rat race so soon. But I would imagine the demands of big ballet right now are not nice for a serious choreographer to contemplate. Feld threw a couple of efforts down the ravening maw of the ABT and Joffrey audiences before trading whatever advantage they offered him for the chance to play to his own three hundreds at the Public Theatre. In the Feld company's three seasons there since its founding in the spring of 1974 it has acquired a devoted audience. The dancers don't have to be anything but their unassuming selves to make an impact in this chummy downtown atmosphere. Feld's best ballets are about dancing, and among other things, the Feld company is teaching its audience to appreciate dancing for its own sake.

Perhaps even more important, Feld seems to be relaxing creatively under the care and protection he's getting from Joseph Papp and the Rockefeller Foundation. His two new ballets this season, *Mazurka* and *Excursions*, are better, I think, than anything he's done in a long time. There's no use lamenting the departed young romantic Feld, not as long as he's getting a chance to strengthen his present choreographic intentions.

Excursions, to Samuel Barber's 1945 piano suite of the same name, is a further edition of Feld's new classicism, more thoroughly worked out than some of his earlier dances in this style. With a very sparing use of movement material, he tries to catch an essence of a place or a period or a character. In *Excursions*, it's that particular view of America — half chauvinistic, half nostalgic — that American artists were picturing in the 1930s and '40s, when suddenly musicians and painters and dancers realized we didn't have to depend on Europe anymore for our cultural models. It's the "Americana" images created by Martha Graham and Aaron Copland and Virgil Thomson and Woody Guthrie and, yes, even Agnes de Mille that Feld evokes in *Excursions*.

Six dancers, led by a small human dynamo, Christine Sarry, skitter and romp and laze around the stage. They stretch and gaze off into the distance of a beautiful morning, and Sarry shakes her head vigorously, as if her face isn't broad enough to hold all the grin she has. Sarry runs and toe-steps very fast — having only seen it once, I can't tell you now when she's doing one thing or the other — while the music plays a tune with a perpetual-motion thing going on in the left hand.

Barber goes into a bluesy section that Sarry begins by rising on pointe and threading her way through the other dancers to get them into motion, a quote from Feld's *Intermezzo* that the audience immediately recognizes. The motif here is suggested by a swinging motion of the arms that, again, Feld transforms into ballet steps without your being quite aware of it. Sarry and Edmund LaFosse have a duet, then part.

The music embroiders on a cowboy tune like "The Streets of Laredo," and the dancers get all frisky and pretend to be wild horses, or cowboys breaking wild horses, or jest folks moseying and getting the kinks out of their bones. Just when you think they've used up all their energy — they all let out a whinnying snort of breath through their lips — the piano starts to play a hoedown, and they're off again on a shaking, thigh-slapping stampede that ends as they all pull up and lean in a clump toward the piano. There's a big collective exhale and a satisfied "Sheeeeutt!" from one of the men as the lights go out. You could hardly think of a more ingratiating way to end a dance among friends.

Excursions isn't entirely clear to me — maybe that's an indication Feld is changing. The dance is neither all mannerisms nor all form; it's a combination of the two that doesn't assert its own identity. The costumes, resembling practice clothes in pale pastels, are curiously at odds with the backdrop of awning stripes in primary colors spread across a white background.

Of course there's a lot of drive in the work, you can see that, and nobody can complain about a dance that has so much of wonderful Christine Sarry in it. But is *Excursions* only about dancers remembering that era now, the way *The Real McCoy* last season was about remembering the style of the Gershwin era? Or is it more than that?

I keep wondering what relation the dancers have to each other and to the movement Feld has so formally given them to do. The ballet is full of very personal gestures — men scratch their chests with both hands, people shake their heads in a seeming excess of high spirits, they fix their eyes on some yonder horizon — yet they do the gestures impersonally, all together in precise formations, like some corps de ballet of the prairie. It feels cramped to me, antithetical to the idealized wide open spaces where it came from.

As with *McCoy*, *Excursions* tries to extract the core of something that was a stylization to begin with. Feld isn't telling us how he feels about frontier America, but how he feels about Martha Graham's image of frontier America. And as with *McCoy*, I am more moved by the original.

Mazurka actually isn't all that different in conception. Feld makes a series of variations on the Petipa mazurka; you know, that same thing that you've been yawning through for years in the third act of *Swan Lake*. But he lets the dance have its way somehow. He doesn't try to confine it so tightly or project it so didactically.

The four couples dancing to Chopin piano music aren't really any more specific as characters than the dancers in *Excursions* — they don't tell a story or act out anything. But they seem more individual. *Excursions* is a group dance — Sarry, the soloist, is onstage throughout and the group is in attendance most of the time, echoing or framing or responding to her actions, nearly always in unison or some other unobtrusive configuration. *Mazurka* is a string of solos and duets interspersed with ensemble sections where, even though everyone may have the same idea, each couple will travel in a different direction, or move in canon, or distinguish themselves in some way from the others. Some of the dancers even seem to have particular identities, the way all the couples do in *Intermezzo*, identities that are suggested by the particular dancing they do, not by any superimposed acting gimmicks.

Feld's dance invention in *Mazurka* is stunning. What a pleasure to see someone taking the time to follow through on the implications of his own idea. Each section of the ballet elaborates on a different aspect of the mazurka pattern. There's Helen Douglas doing a solo based on the contrast of opening and closing body shapes. Later, in a duet with George Montalbano, she's lifted in the air, where the opening/closing idea is even more striking. Three men do a forceful dance where they start with a very big step but impede their own progress and throw the forward momentum into the ground by hitching up the back leg and sinking to one knee. Christine Sarry brings out the complementary, elevated side of this idea by suddenly springing into the air out of a chain of running steps. There are dances made on brushing steps, dances made on quick reversals of direction, dances involving exaggerated bending back of the torso, and dances built out of the skipping step that results from a distortion of the basic ¾ rhythm.

The partner work in *Mazurka* is gorgeous. You'd almost think it was tricky if it didn't come so organically out of the basic musical and movement material. Feld frequently has his couples work side by side, even in lifts, by slinging the dancers' arms around each other's shoulders and across their backs. As a kind of visual counterpart to the rubato in the music, where the middle note of the phrase lasts a little bit longer and the outer notes have to go faster to catch up, the women often go into the air in the middle of a step and are caught and carried by the men just long enough to extend their step unnaturally.

The ballet is fast and emphatic; the tempos and the rhythms are forced. Only toward the end does it get into the slower, darker aspects of the music, and at that point, for the first time, all the couples form one circle, as if there had to be a moment of communion to anchor all the individual variations and display.

Mazurka hasn't got the sense of continuous flow that you see in *Intermezzo*. Like the music, it's much more showy, more stagy. The phrase is shorter and comes to an end with a very definite pose or a very pronounced change of direction. Where the dancers are going in space, which way they're facing, whether they travel on a diagonal or go straight across the stage, all these things are more important than in *Intermezzo*, where the dance's rapture just seems to pour out wherever it can find room. Maybe the difference between these two ballets has something to do with the artist's process of growing up.

October 23, 1975

Stravinsky Lives! Notes from
a Diary

JUNE 18, 1972: Opening night. New York City Ballet's long-planned, unprecedented Stravinsky Festival. Thirty ballets, seven performances, all Stravinsky music. Will I survive? Will the company survive?

Performance is sold out. NY State Theater lobby crowded with beautiful and/or important people. There's a press table which is to become gathering place and wailing wall for the dozens of critics who hope to cover the event. Virginia Donaldson, NYCB's press agent, is looking grim; she faces a week of trying to cram too many people into too few seats and make them like it. She hands me my envelope with an apology, for the location and for the fact that she doesn't know yet whether I can come the rest of the week.

I open the envelope. It's worse than I expected. Row C in

the orchestra, on the side. After preliminaries — musical fan-
fares and welcomes, Stravinsky's Happy Birthday prelude (he
would have been ninety yesterday — Balanchine says he *is*
ninety) — they begin with Jerome Robbins' *Scherzo Fantastique*. Getting used to the angle and the proximity of my view,
I notice almost nothing, except that it's a brief pas de deux with
a three-boy chorus, and that Gelsey Kirkland is beautiful, and
perfect, even up this close.

Balanchine's first première is *Symphony in Three Movements*. I'm impressed with it, even knocked out sometimes.
Opening with a long diagonal, sixteen girls posed in white tank
suits, straining forward, arms flung up and out, as if they've
been launched into space and pinned there for a minute in
midflight.

The music is fast, keeping up a firm, unvarying beat, and the
movement is vigorous, even punchy, always reaching far out
into space. Big lunges, arm gestures, striding. There's a lot in
this piece that reminds me of Robbins — the jazzy, athletic
look of hip-thrusting walks with the opposite arm pushing out
into space.

Villella and Leland's duet — slower, odd. Hands are almost
always flat — they never seem to be able to get closer together
than the crooks of their elbows. But their concentration on
each other is oblique, inviting, detached enough to be almost
humorous.

The last movement resumes the athletic energy of the first,
ending with a Robbinsian pose, men crouching down front and
the women standing, arms extended — all facing the audience
boldly. Maybe this piece was designed for the Munich Olym-
pic games, where the company will perform later this summer.

Violin Concerto, also Balanchine's, is nicer but I like it somewhat less. More classical in design but with the inevitable surprises. It begins with each of the four soloists dancing with
four dancers of the opposite sex, then four of the same sex.
This is so well established that by the time Peter Martins comes
on alone for the eighth variation, it's a shock, you keep looking
for the four men. Then, just when you decide the pattern's
been broken and this one *is* going to be a solo, the men appear.

Contrasting duets by Karin von Aroldingen and Jean-Pierre

Bonnefous, Kay Mazzo and Martins. Ballet ends folkily, with lots of elbows, heel-walking, arms out with thumbs up. As a last surprise, you realize that in the whole ballet, where you've been made so aware of men and women, you haven't seen the eight corps girls and eight men dance together yet. When you realize it is in the last twelve bars or so of the ballet — that's the first time they partner up.

Firebird gets worse and worse. I suppose it was worth throwing out Balanchine's old, unpretentious version two years ago for the new fussy-arty Chagall version with the new Balanchine/Robbins self-important choreography — at least we got Gelsey Kirkland in a big ballerina part. Now Kirkland is replaced by von Aroldingen, wearing an atrocious new costume that's impossible to dance in and has decorations that come loose and fall on the stage in big, lethal chunks.

JUNE 20: *Symphony in E Flat*, Stravinsky's Opus 1, is Tchaikovskian, and John Clifford has choreographed it in a moody, romantic style. The ballet seems cleaner, more independently thought out than anything I've seen Clifford do. Kirkland is absolutely smashing in this. She seems to be running all the time, backward, forward, skipping, but always with that proud lift in the breastbone that tells you she's in command.

I've never liked *The Cage* (1951) — it may be daring and provocative but it's also ugly. Not only does Robbins portray a society of predatory females, he disfigures them physically, psychologically, every other way. Melissa Hayden looks like a wrestler in the vicious central role.

John Taras' *Concerto for Piano and Winds* is for fourteen men, but the movement is deliberately academic, the execution is so matter-of-fact that the achievement isn't exciting.

Up to this point I think it's been a pretty good evening — and then they do *Danses Concertantes*, and everything else recedes into the gray area of pastime. They say Balanchine has rechoreographed it because he couldn't remember the 1944 original, but could it ever have been any wittier, brighter, more musical? Here is the form, the good nature, the rhythmic intricacy that I missed in the other works tonight. It's a chamber-sized piece — unforced yet consistently surprising and individual and not the least bit modest. The dancers are like a small traveling troupe of players who make up new turns and combinations to amuse themselves. They don't bother to stress the standard big, flashy ballet things because they've done them so often.

JUNE 21: An evening of bits and pieces, but finishing up marvelously with Robbins' *Circus Polka*, the music commissioned in 1942 for elephants choreographed by Balanchine. Robbins' staging for forty-eight little girls from the School of American Ballet was charming and clever. Maybe the first children's dance I've ever seen that was as humorous as it was cute, and also worked choreographically. The audience demanded an encore.

Of the rest of the evening, I find Balanchine's *Divertimento from Le Baiser de la Fée* most interesting. Patricia McBride and Helgi Tomasson are superb as usual, but it's strange music — Balanchine invariably draws your attention to the music if you're paying any sort of attention at all. Stravinsky based it on Tchaikovsky themes — story of the ennobling, and fatal, gift of the muse to the artist. Below the melody is discord — restless harmony never resolving itself, fiendish rhythms and meters. All that is in the choreography, though the story isn't.

A corps of girls in peasant costumes is there at the beginning and end to provide a kind of reassurance — the stabilizing effect of unison and classicism. But the pas de deux. First all circling, turning, never finding center; then an adagio that keeps changing mood and direction until a momentary quiet; variations that are mysterious, don't beg for applause. Yet I feel I'm seeing steps I've never seen before, especially in Tomasson's low, circling, eccentrically timed leaps.

JUNE 22: Balanchine comes up with another stunning work, *Duo Concertant*. It's so simple, yet interesting and strange, the audience recognizes it immediately. After many bows for the performers, Balanchine comes out and gets a standing ovation and they have to turn the house lights on to stop it.

A piano and violin onstage — Gordon Boelzner and Lamar Alsop — Mazzo and Martins lean on the piano and listen to them play the entire first movement. As the second begins, the music seems to take hold of them and they dance together. Small, rhythmic gestures and steps, never straying very far from the spot where they started — like the music, which gives the violin a melody while the piano plays intervals of a fifth, steadily skimming up and down in a small tonal range. Part three is slow, almost romantic — the dancers listen, drift into slow lifts and carries, listen. Fourth part is fast, like a jig. Martins seems to say look at these little jumps and tilts and switchbacks I can do to that; Mazzo says me too. All four performers stop with a flourish and the audience, cheering, thinks it's over.

The light shutters down to a single dim spot on Alsop and he starts the very romantic last section. Another spot picks up Mazzo's arm, reaching out into blank space. Martins comes into the light, clasps her hand, kisses it. They do a brief, passionate duet — small spotlights follow them as they separate, draw together again. The feeling is almost surrealistic — this cutting off of all space so suddenly. The dancers seem disembodied, like the astral selves of those two dancers we were just watching, like some essential, intangible part of them that is alive only because of the music and as long as it lasts.

Taras' *Song of the Nightingale* isn't so well received after that, but I like the idea of it — an Oriental pageant done against black drapes with Rouben Ter-Arutunian's sumptuous yet simple costumes, white Kabuki-like make-up, towering head ornaments. Gelsey Kirkland is a marvelous, softly fluttering nightingale. But the ballet doesn't really work — too many lapses in the plot, too many encumbering problems with the costumes.

Evening ends with the *Rubies* ("Capriccio for Piano and Orchestra") section of *Jewels* (1967) — not one of my Balanchine favorites, but tonight I see so many odd and wonderful things in it. The way the ballet is built in a classical form, but not quite — the way the choreography picks up ballroom notions from the music and immediately makes off for new ground with them; the finale, riotous with circus allusions though it's like a Petipa finish too. McBride is coolly terrific in this and Villella is — Villella.

JUNE 23: Two superserious, overchoreographed pieces by the company's younger contingent, Richard Tanner's *Concerto for Two Solo Pianos* (1971) and Lorca Massine's *Ode*. The rest of the program is jokes — in-jokes, dirty jokes, dance jokes, vaudeville jokes. First, John Clifford all in purple as a Dead End Kid and Gloria Govrin in orange looking like Baby Snooks, upstaging, kicking, ambushing each other in Todd Bolender's *Piano-Rag Music*.

As the curtain is rising on Robbins' *Dumbarton Oaks*, a summer garden with tennis court, rattan chairs, lanterns suspended overhead, I react "Ashton" to the specificity of detail, and a few minutes later the corps comes on in 1920s tennis clothes and does a chorus line to a musical fugue. *Dumbarton Oaks* is a spoof of all potboiler ballets, so cleverly staged and attractively danced that you hardly notice it's a potboiler itself. There's no more plot than is necessary to get Allegra Kent and Anthony Blum onstage and making goo-goo eyes at each other. The dancing is fit for a Broadway show, laced with quotes from the ballet literature — Robbins' own *Fancy Free*, Balanchine's *Agon*, *Les Patineurs*, *Swan Lake*. In the finale the men wear tap shoes and the women short white gloves.

It's impossible to describe how well bred this all looks, how successful and pleasant it is, and how irritated it made me.

Pulcinella, the big production number of the festival, with the gaudy, floppy, bangly, fringy costumes, masks, disguises, wagon stages, props, and the thoroughly ratty, cluttered atmosphere belonging to the commedia dell'arte, designed by Eugene Berman.

Villella is a human pogo stick in the title role, supervising a barrelful of big and little sub-Pulcinellas who do the whole gamut of clown things from tumbling to sleight-of-hand to petty larceny. Violette Verdy is the Girl — first in beggar's rags, later in girl-clown costume — she's the only one who really gets to dance. Also notable is the duet for the co-choreographers, Balanchine and Robbins, as little old street beggars in tennis shoes, who beat each other up with their canes.

At the critics' party after the performance there are people from England, Germany, Austria, Holland, Denmark, Canada, France as well as numerous in and out of town U.S. writers. I'm growing pathetically fond of Virginia Donaldson as, each night, she bestows a seat on me, with a full view of the stage.

JUNE 24: Revival of Balanchine's *Orpheus* (1948), one of the festival highlights. Never having seen it before, I think what an insolent steal it must have seemed to modern dancers of its time, and how superior to modern dance the ballet fans must have regarded it.

Balanchine in his Martha Graham phase — symbolic props and sculptures by Noguchi — episodic, declamatory dancing — grandeur and tragedy in every move. But what separates *Orpheus* from Graham's Greek pieces is Graham's movement language. She wasn't just devising unusual shapes and body positions. Balanchine does that too, but his dancers continue to look balletic. Graham's dynamics came from the ground not the air; her rhythms sprang, you felt, out of eternal sources like breath, water flowing, the churning of molten rock ten miles down, not from such artificial and passing causes as a mere musical composition.

I like most the duet in which blindfolded Orpheus (Bonnefous) traverses the route out of hell with Eurydice (Hayden) clinging to his back, being so distracting and demanding that eventually he's driven to take that one fatal, forbidden look at her.

Orpheus flanked on this program by its companion Balanchine ballets *Apollo* (1928) and *Agon* (1957). What a brilliant sequence the three pieces make, as choreography and as idea. If Apollo presides over music and Orpheus creates it, the nameless dancers in *Agon* live it, use it, embellish and illuminate it.

JUNE 25: The last night. Balanchine, clutching a glass of vodka, invites entire audience to join in a toast — on the house — to the health of "Igor Fedorovitch friend-of-ours Stravinsky."

It's that kind of evening, that kind of festival. Friendly, ceremonial, more about living than dying. Balanchine's *Choral*

Variations on Vom Himmel Hoch is architectural, quiet, courtly dancing — more Bach than Stravinsky — more concerned with design than texture. Forty-six dancers including six soloists and twelve little girls. Big and beautiful, affirmative and completely un-maudlin.

Monumentum pro Gesualdo/Movements for Piano and Orchestra, choreographed by Balanchine in 1960 and 1963, is perhaps the greatest musical statement in the whole week, or maybe I know it best, or maybe it's just the superb performances of Gelsey Kirkland and Conrad Ludlow, Kay Mazzo and Jacques d'Amboise.

The *Gesualdo* is melting, soft, circular. Like the harmonic structure of the music it's constantly changing key, a little at a time — step by step the dancers move across the stage, through each other, into new formations. It's not complex or polyphonic, it doesn't have many ideas working against one another. Maybe one has to have sung *Gesualdo* madrigals to appreciate the sensuality of this dance.

Movements is serial music — orchestral sparks sprinkling out, sounds held until they break apart, odd rhythms. So is the dance of course. I have the feeling of movements too big for what they're accomplishing, of gestures and intentions not completed, or sidetracked. There's much wit here, in Mazzo finding herself in a midair contortion, in the efficient but not disinterested way d'Amboise handles her. But as always with Balanchine, the movement dictates the relationship, not the other way round.

Robbins' *Requiem Canticles*, the last ballet of the festival, is a pretentious collage of "serious" ideas from contemporary dance. Among the religious or anguish-prone works referred to are Balanchine's *Ivesiana*, Tudor's *Dark Elegies*, all of Anna Sokolow, Limón's *Missa Brevis*, Ailey's *Revelations*, even his own *Les Noces*.

Robbins is so gifted at arranging the ideas of others that you have to admire the effectiveness of the ballet. But as a climax to this incredible week of tribute and creativity, the piece is particularly inappropriate. It doesn't express Stravinsky and it doesn't express Robbins. All it expresses is the need for a showpiece. I prefer to remember the evening as it ended, with a glowing performance of the "Symphony of Psalms" by the Gregg Smith Singers.

July 9, 1972

Spunk and Senescence

THE NEW YORK CITY BALLET'S winter season, like a big Balanchine ballet, wound up covered with glory — by the skin of its teeth.

It wasn't one of the company's best seasons. A comic-opera strike by the dancers, who wanted somebody to guarantee that there would be no *orchestra* strike in midseason, canceled the entire first lap of the season. So ballet lovers lost the month of repertory with which they usually fortify themselves against the long *Nutcracker* debauch. The strike also shoved aside plans to celebrate the fortieth anniversary of Balanchine's arrival in America.

Opening night coincided with the first *Nutcracker,* and the machinery was still a little creaky and underrehearsed. Both Patricia McBride as the Sugar Plum Fairy and Gelsey Kirkland as Dew Drop appeared that night, perhaps as a token of propitiation. But before the company got back to repertory again in mid-January, McBride was out with an injury. Neither she nor Violette Verdy, who had been hurt before the opening, had recovered by the close of the season, and they were just the first of a series of casualties. By early February, the company was distributing a letter of explanation and apology on the nights when the most drastic program and casting changes had to be instituted.

After another interruption, for a week's run of *Don Quixote,* only six repertory performances remained. Over that last weekend, I saw three people fall down. So many ballets and dancers had been changed by that time that only the principal substitutions were announced, and the mavens gathered at intermissions to straighten out their records. Yes, that *was* Wilhelmina Frankfurt in *Movements for Piano and Orchestra*, and yes, Colleen Neary did substitute for Renee Estopinal in the corps of the third movement of *Symphony in C*, even though she had just substituted for Karin von Aroldingen in the lead of the first movement.

In the last three performances, you could have seen — I hope you did — the best that this tremendous company can offer. There isn't another organization in the world that can show you dancing in such an advanced state of intelligence. There was the rigorous classicism and grand scale of *Symphony in C*; the smaller, diverting classic, *Donizetti Variations*; the profound and mysterious meditation on classicism, *Serenade*; the contrasting modern miniatures, *Monumentum pro Gesualdo* and *Movements for Piano and Orchestra*. There were the duets *Afternoon of a Faun*, with its impressionistic theatricality, and *Duo Concertant*, classical but thrown-away at the same time.

There was the big, brassy *Stars and Stripes* — choreographed during what Lincoln Kirstein seems to consider the company's dancing-for-the-masses period — which is draped in patriotic clichés but flying Balanchine's irrepressible genius for composition at full staff. And there was Balanchine's latest and most baleful comment on popular taste, *Variations pour une Porte et un Soupir*.

I found *Variations* repulsive and funny and nastily attractive. It seemed to say something about where Balanchine's mind was when he made it, and that wasn't a pleasant place. The piece is a blatant send-up of all those duets between predatory females and impotent males, some of which are found even in the NYCB repertory. Everything about it partakes of the pop art sensibility — the chic costumes and make-up, the musique concrète score by Pierre Henry that accompanies John Clifford and Karin von Aroldingen as they twitch and throw hostile stares at each other. Von Aroldingen, the mistress of the trap, is herself entrapped and reduced to insignificance by an enormous swatch of black silk that's fastened to her waist and manipulated from backstage and spreads and billows into fantastically beautiful erotic shapes. Exploitative and sensational as the ballet's concept is, it does what it sets out to do more successfully than any of its models.

It's hard to avoid seeing a reference here to Maurice Béjart, who has made so many ballets like this, and in whose company Suzanne Farrell took refuge after leaving NYCB. Whether or not Balanchine intended to make a comment on the way his former favorite's gifts have been turned to increasingly vulgar, restricted uses in the Béjart company, I found the inference irresistible.

It seems to me the New York City Ballet is the phenomenon it is because virtually every commitment it makes is full-out. Balanchine pays as much attention to a potboiler as he does to a major opus, which is why his failures make us so uncomfortable and his successes give us so much joy. His attitudes come across, even though he may not intend to expose them, because he isn't working to conceal them. He probably doesn't consider them at all, but they must be close to the surface along with all the other resources he brings to the choreographic task. We don't expect a ballet company to be so straight with us. I often feel uneasy watching the company, almost voyeuristic, as if some stranger were telling me his life story.

Don Quixote has always given me this feeling. It's impossible not to identify the ballet's poet-hero, who's always pursuing an idealized and unattainable woman, with Balanchine. As far as I know, this is the only role Balanchine has performed in recent years, except for the beggars' duet at the première of *Pulcinella*, in which he squabbled with his co-choreographer, Jerome Robbins. It's not precisely that Balanchine sees himself as the self-pitying, morbid, overwrought Don Quixote, or the doddering, scrappy ragpicker of *Pulcinella*. But he seems to take an attitude, to create from a point of view only slightly exaggerated from his current situation.

The company is in a rather paradoxical condition right now. It's settled and successful. As long as Balanchine remains in command, I don't worry about its suffering from establishmentarian rot. His creative ability, the repertory that forms the backbone of the company, and the expressive range of his aesthetic are not going to go out of style or lose their interest for me. But it's just this preeminence that creates a problem for the artist — when you get your dream and can do exactly what you want indefinitely, how do you stay interested?

Lesser choreographers and companies adopt fads, find new stars, drop them, shuffle the repertory. Balanchine has invested in stability and uniform high-quality work; he has to keep giving us that. I think sometimes he's imposing his fantasies on the company, putting dancers with weird bodies or terrible technique into exacting parts, eliminating costumes from period ballets, rechoreographing new bits of old ballets, just to see what they'll look like. Whatever the reason, the company often looks kinky or uninterested or downright perverse. A kind of civil-service mentality seems to have affected much of this season; too many dancers looked as if they were doing time until they could collect the gold watch. The great performances came from people getting a crack at something for the first time.

I'm thinking particularly of Colleen Neary, who's been trying to get noticed for three years or so, and who grabbed every chance she could this winter. She reportedly learned the second lead in *Serenade* on the day of the last matinee, and was so good they kept her in it for a substituted evening performance. Susan Pilarre replaced someone too, as the third principal that evening, and brought a lovely quietness to the role. Pilarre is an unflustered, uncluttered dancer. Every joint of her arms doesn't break on every step; she takes time to be calm about what she's doing. Neary is not only big and technically secure, she's vivid, clear about the differences in the shapes of steps. She doesn't mug, but you can make out the evolving features of her face from the back of the theater. Together with a boneless, almost bodiless Allegra Kent and a fine corps, they pulled off a superb performance of this wonderful ballet.

Amid the seasons's dislocations, I also enjoyed Merrill Ashley, Bart Cook, Helgi Tomasson's inexhaustible excellence and good temper, and Edward Villclla's effectiveness in his acting roles. But the heroine of the season unquestionably was Gelsey Kirkland, who'd been injured herself and hadn't danced in New York for almost a year. With Melissa Hayden retired and McBride and Verdy out, the company was hurting for stars and was not anxious to pluck them out of the back row. So Kirkland really carried the big dancing assignments. And how she carried them!

This is one dancer who fills me with pleasure every time she steps on a stage. Technically she's a whiz, with fast, high-arched feet, long, straight legs, astonishingly accurate turns and secure balances, an unmannered musicality, and a sense of always knowing where she is and where she's going. She appears to have no idiosyncrasies, nothing extraneous she has to do to achieve the movement, yet she's not an expressive zero. The roles she took on this season gave her some interpretive latitude, and you could see her beginning to let the movement produce its own reaction.

In the Pas de Deux Mauresque of *Don Quixote* she emphasized the yielding, delicate, behind-the-eyes seductiveness to contrast with John Clifford's driving masculine role. In *Monumentum pro Gesualdo*, her softness became liquid, melting into the convolutions of the music. In the slow movement of *Symphony in C*, the one where Farrell used to be so sinuous and sexy, Kirkland gave away her energy into space and gathered it back, creating, with her partner, Nolan T'Sani, an absorbed but articulate private world. I felt I had never seen such a beautiful adagio. By being nothing but what she is, a very young, very good dancer, she gave credence to Robbins' fussy but superficial new pas de deux, *Four Bagatelles*, which she danced with Tomasson. And when she caught the bounce and playfulness of Jacques d'Amboise in his *Irish Symphony*, all I could think was what a fabulous *La Sylphide* she would do. Someday perhaps.

May 1974

Ravel Festival:
Mini but Memorable

AT THE New York City Ballet events have a gratifying way of not duplicating themselves. When the company is good, it's also apt to surprise us, so it doesn't matter a bit that the Ravel Festival failed to recap the fabulous excitement of the Stravinsky Festival three years ago.

The final Ravel program actually had eight new ballets on it, and like the two earlier programs, a lot of it was inconsequential. But some of it was breathtaking. For that we have Ravel to thank — and George Balanchine.

Le Tombeau de Couperin, musically, is itself a memorial — Ravel's tribute to eighteenth-century French composers, and following its cool, carefully meshed formalities Balanchine has set another of those gorgeously simple ballets that say so much.

The work is for eight couples, and it is altogether a group work all the way through. No stars, no pas de deux or individual variations. In the opening Prelude, they're arranged in two square sets. It's a dance of greeting — courtly bows and hands extending and entwining between partners, couples, women, men — and of promenading around the dancing-space. In the Forlane, dancers execute precise, elastic foot steps; the couples spread out around the stage and sometimes coalesce in two lines or circles. The Menuet is a little more active, a little more airborne; and the final Rigaudon is vigorous, a bit peasantlike, with a wonderful suggestion of a Virginia reel, only elaborate and complicated.

Sometimes there seems to be much less movement than there is in the music, but the dance never actually stops. The steps, like the preclassic dancing of the time, are close to the ground — terre à terre. At first there are no jumps, the women don't go up on their pointes, but as the dance grows more active, a fleeting but irresistible force seems to be drawing the dancers into the air, to rise, to jump, to lift.

Without being in the slightest mannered or "period" in his designs, Balanchine manages to give you the impression of an eighteenth-century ballroom. It's a social occasion, not a ceremonial one, but observing proprieties is essential to these participants' enjoyment. The dances are made of small, intricate figures, not long phrases. Each dancer or couple does certain of these figures and watches somebody else do others.

The sixteen dancers, who understand the style of it so well without trying to tell the audience they're doing a style, are absorbed in each other and in the complexity of their socializing. There's hardly a moment when the stage space looks random — they are always engaged in a pattern, they don't just dance around the way they would have in the nineteenth century.

I don't know what special gift Balanchine has that allows him to create a poetic image like this, but it goes beyond choreography. *Tombeau de Couperin* tells you what *The Goldberg Variations*, for all its straining and invention, cannot convey. Jerome Robbins is a good choreographer who makes successful ballets, but he is not a poet.

Perhaps this contrast is more evident now because Ravel is such a difficult composer to dance to. Balanchine certainly snared the danciest of Ravel for himself in *Tombeau*. Groping through the impressionistic spume and spray of *Une Barque sur l'Océan*, Robbins sends four men led by Victor Castelli wheeling and scudding across a stage before a rippling blue cyc. The piece shows you the spacious surface of the music. But when Balanchine deals with impressionism, in *Gaspard de la Nuit*, he refers to the specifics of the music only in a peripheral way, yet he connects with something deeper in it. He constructs a macabre world, glittering with dark light, where undersea women, dead murderers, elusive reflections tempt the viewer. I don't know if this music or the poems it was written to directly suggest the attractiveness of suicidal fantasies, the dangerous allure of the unknown, but Balanchine uncovers that for us.

Robbins' contribution to the final program was *Chansons Madécasses*. The songs are supposed to celebrate the mystery and eroticism of black Africa, but singer Gwendolyn Killebrew's French was unintelligible. A black couple, Debra Austin and Hermes Conde, and a white couple, Patricia McBride and Helgi Tomasson, schematically dressed in black and white practice clothes, seem to be alter egos. The dance had a lot of restrained passion on the part of the whites, but since the black couple did practically the same things, even in their own duet, it wasn't clear what was enviable about them, if anything. I liked watching the sensuous, rounded way Austin did McBride's movement, but it seems a bit de trop in 1975 to have this pointed out as a black-white difference.

I haven't mentioned some of the minor pleasures of this long evening — Balanchine's Isadora Duncan-esque solo for Patricia McBride, *Pavane pour une Enfante Défunte*; Peter Schaufuss actually smiling for the first time onstage, while doing things in the air like Baryshnikov, in *Rapsodie Espagnole*. Or some of the tacky things — the grindingly sexy movement that Spanish-flavored music like *Rapsodie Espagnole* and *Tzigane* brings out of Balanchine; the excesses committed by a new array of costume designers — deep maroons, electric blues, and slick fabric till I almost longed for Karinska pink.

June 5, 1975

Balanchine Waves a Flag

THE TECHNICOLOR HYPE that announced George Balanchine's new *Union Jack* was enough to sink the British navy. I had visions of another Bicentennial lead balloon, or at best an acid reply to Kenneth MacMillan's massacree of Scott Joplin, *Elite Syncopations*, which the Royal Ballet was committing across Lincoln Center Plaza.

Indeed, *Union Jack* has its conceits. A Hershy Kay score that turns perfectly good fife and drum music into something fancy and self-conscious. An excess of costume detail when there were so many people on the stage you needed every bit of clear space and line you could get. And a finale straight out of Busby Berkeley, where a battalion of dancers spell out "God Save the Queen" with semaphore flags as a series of flying drops turn the background into a British flag and the band plays "Rule Britannia."

But never mind. *Union Jack* could have been so much worse. And what it is, actually, all the pageantry and Anglophiliac justification aside, is pretty extraordinary. It's Balanchine once again launched on a seemingly undanceable idea, through which he succeeds in showing us new things about dance.

The hour-long ballet is in three sections: a series of variations on Highland dancing by seventy dancers dressed in full Scottish regalia; a series of dances based on the sailor's hornpipe, for forty-nine dancers; and, in between, a music hall turn with Patricia McBride and Jean-Pierre Bonnefous decked out in splendid rags decorated with zillions of buttons sewn in geometric patterns.

What with the masses of people onstage most of the time, the costume overload and so on, it wasn't the choreography that attracted me on first viewing so much as Balanchine's use of the dancers in both highly impersonal and highly personal ways.

The ballet begins with a trooping of the colors. Detachments of ten dancers appear, one by one, and go through almost identical formations, their ranks first set up in threes with a leader out front, then in two rows of five, and retire to the sidelines as another group enters. Each platoon wears a different color combination of jackets, kilts, and tartans draped over one shoulder. When the whole seventy of them are present, they do some more slow-march drilling, then clear the field so each group can do its own variation.

Even more than its predecessor, *Stars and Stripes*, this part of *Union Jack* indulges our love for parades. The dancers at first do nothing but a slow parade walk, their arms swinging in small, jaunty arcs. You admire the precision of their all-alike patterns, you marvel at their accumulating numbers filling up and reorganizing the space.

But also you explore their step, as more and more of them keep coming, that slow shift of weight, the knee raised, the standing foot firmly set down into the ground, the arms carefully placed and timed. Not a ballet walk at all, it's so much more assured and less rarefied. How fine to see a ballet dancer in touch with the pavement. And you begin to notice individual variations — Suzanne Farrell turning in her knees just enough to give her hips a wiggle, Jacques d'Amboise lifting his shoulders in a suggestion of strut.

The Highland variations are all foot dances — fast or slow, some on pointe, some with men and women in pairs, all with the arms placed importantly, either curving up to the sides or resting on the hips or just hanging down doing nothing. There's a reel in a running rhythm of three led by Peter Martins and Kay Mazzo, in which all of a sudden the feeling I'd had about seeing these dancers with their heels down crystallized, and they looked like honest-to-god men and women, rather than the sexually sublimated beings that ballet dancers usually are.

Throughout these variations Balanchine keeps his dancers strictly regimented, almost entirely in unison and facing the audience, with the leader in front of his or her group.

D'Amboise and Helgi Tomasson lead their groups in a sort of competition, Sara Leland's variation develops into fast, traveling pointe work, Karin von Aroldingen's has big kicky-marchy steps, and Farrell's is bouncy. Then all the groups return to concoct one of those magic Balanchine finales in which the dancers regroup and combine in various new ways but never lose the idiom. It keeps being a big Highland games and a big ballet over and over. *Why* couldn't they have had bagpipes and real music?

After that McBride and Bonnefous do their number, which is funny and cozy and also has some nice dancing in it, in a style of what I suppose is English vaudeville. They're like the king and queen of the hobos, she's very grand with the audience and he plays up to them, and you know they make tea after the show in the dressing room they share.

Then the scale builds back up again, with all the same principals as before coming back, and Bart Cook and Victor Castelli too. This time they're backed by five groups of eight, but the whole thing is less formal than before, with more anecdotal interactions among the dancers. The sailor's hornpipe is a near relation to the Highland flings and reels, being concentrated in the feet and not requiring anything elaborate in the body or the arms. It has more jumping though, and it sometimes goes rakishly off balance.

Again I enjoyed the way the dancers looked in their sailor outfits, so different from their ordinary garb, and the way they were able to do all their "character" bits — flirting, joking, and other hijinks — within the fast-paced structure of the music. But I have to admit I saw much less in this last section. Even with the McBride-Bonnefous interlude for visual relief, my eyes were working so hard to sort things out in the Scottish part, they just had to take it easy.

May 20, 1976

Recycling

IT COULD HAVE BEEN called *Vivaldi-Corelli*. If I hadn't known the New York City Ballet's new production to be a reincarnation of George Balanchine's old *Square Dance* (1957), I probably would never have recognized it. Not only that, I wouldn't have thought to connect it with Americana in any particular way.

The most obvious difference is the elimination of the square-dance caller and the removal of the chamber orchestra from the stage back to the pit. In the Joffrey Ballet revival of 1971, the fiddlers sat up on a special platform, stage right, with a wagon-wheel chandelier above them, and I seem to remember that the dancers wore something suggestive of the milieu in addition to their dance clothes, like kerchiefs tied around their necks.

After a few minutes the caller became annoying since he wasn't usually calling the steps, or distracting if he was, and the musicians took up altogether too much of the dancing-space. But the Joffrey production did have an authentic air of conviviality and a feeling that all the participants were in the same place together, contributing equally to the event.

With the space opened up and all the visual particulars out of the way, *Square Dance* is nothing but what it always was: a suite of dances for six couples and two principal dancers. Balanchine's movement idiom is really classical here, with no apparent regional quirks to broaden or give special nuance to the line. And yet, just by the way he deploys the troops, you can tell he has another kind of dancing in mind. For example, there's very little counterpoint in *Square Dance*, which is a compositional device Balanchine employs frequently elsewhere. Instead the ballet's ideas are often introduced responsively: first a soloist demonstrates, then a group follows. The floor patterns are clear and linear — fleetingly reminiscent of reels, squares, Texas stars — and the dancing is almost always in unison.

Yet the impression you get is not of regimentation, as in the Scottish games section of *Union Jack*, but of a continuous, highly organized, and demanding group activity. Maybe this is partly because there's so much traveling in the activity. In groups, the dancers bound or scoot across the stage, weave in and out of their own lines, seem as interested in getting from place to place as in the elaborate batterie of their steps.

Kay Mazzo leads the women in volleys of pas de chat, a jump to the side in which the legs pull apart with the knees bent, and then close, one at a time, on the way down; and in even more spectacular gargouillades, which are something like pas de chat except that the dancer stays up in the air long enough to circle each leg before landing. Toward the end of the dance, Mazzo demonstrates how fast her feet can work, springing up and changing position without getting far off the ground.

Mazzo and Bart Cook dance a pas de deux in which he first supports her as she raises herself on pointe and sinks into plié in one motion, in a variety of poses, another demonstration of the suppleness of the dancer's feet. Later she twirls fast from one side of him to the other, cutting the turns short at the end of the musical phrase, precisely when she's facing the audience. Most of the time, when he's supporting her, it's by lifting both their arms above their heads. This isn't a dance about intimacy, embracing, encircling, but about giving each other plenty of room to maneuver and show off.

Square Dance has always been known as a ballerina ballet — it was created for Patricia Wilde. This season Balanchine has added a new section for Bart Cook, a slow, solemn sarabande, in which he's alone on stage and does very little except take a few steps or a jump in one direction or another, with that splendid, long stretching and arching of his torso that he used so effectively earlier this year in the Melancholic section of *The Four Temperaments*.

I don't think it was only because it reminded me of Melancholic, but this solo contrasted strangely with the rest of the ballet. It's the only slow interlude, the only time all the other people are gone, and the only time you have the feeling a dancer is exploring his own inner distances. The ballet becomes more balanced with this chance to focus on the male soloist. But also, in this sudden moment of introspection, Balanchine has added a completely new dimension to the work.

This is proving to be a season of unexpected pleasures at the NYCB. Balanchine is slipping in new choreography everywhere — a new final section for *Baiser de la Fée* last winter, and just the other week the *Emeralds* section of *Jewels* acquired a new pas de deux and a new ending.

All these new choreographies, together with *Square Dance*, seem to show us Balanchine working from the inside out. It's as if he doesn't always have to show us a finished product. He can add to something we thought was finished and make us see it in a different way. I think this is amazing, as well as damned generous. And in the warm reception the audience gave him after *Square Dance*, I thought they may have realized how lucky New York is to have him for our own.

May 27, 1976

Madness at La Mancha

THE NEW YORK CITY BALLET isn't supposed to be good at storybook ballets. But George Balanchine's *Don Quixote* is almost as grand as the visions of its protagonist. The scale, the theatrical ambition of this work surpasses anything I've seen anywhere in the classical or the modern repertory. It doesn't quite work — the audience doesn't prefer it to the pallid *Cop-*

*pélia*s and *Swan Lake*s offered by other companies. But each time I look at *Don Q* again I'm amazed by what it's attempting.

Long ago Balanchine established the policy of doing one-act, plotless works and leaving the preservation of old-fashioned spectacle to other companies. But consistency is not one of his holies, and from time to time he's added a big traditional work when the repertory needed something popular. His *Nutcracker* (1954) sells out for five solid weeks every winter. Later, when the company moved into Lincoln Center and became more secure in its identity as a neoclassical ensemble with its own particular style, there was less uneasiness about going to ballet or literary classics for themes. Two-act versions of A *Midsummer Night's Dream* and *Harlequinade* came along, the latter based on an old Petipa ballet with characters from the commedia dell'arte. More recently Balanchine and Jerome Robbins collaborated on a new *Pulcinella*, which Stravinsky composed for Diaghilev's Ballets Russes in 1920. And this season the NYCB went into competition with virtually every major classical company by staging the old standby *Coppélia* as a showpiece for its summer home, the Saratoga Performing Arts Center.

Don Quixote was made during the first spring in the New York State Theater, 1965, when the company was luxuriating in its posh new environment. It must have been a time when Balanchine felt most confident of his powers, of his audience, and of his dancers, because not only is *Don Q* the biggest thing he's ever made, it's also the most expressive in a contemporary sense. In the mime and the dancing, the characters project feelings that might really belong to them or to the choreographer who speaks through them.

If *Don Quixote* isn't exactly autobiographical, it represents Balanchine's most sustained preoccupation with the mind of one character — the Don as outsider, idealist, crusader, who is comforted and inspired by his vision of perfect womanhood. Which would not be a bad way to describe Balanchine. The Dulcinea role of Madonna and Magdalene, servant and sovereign, was choreographed for Balanchine's then-favorite, Suzanne Farrell. It's no use pretending these facts don't influence our response to the ballet, especially since Balanchine has completed the identification by occasionally performing the mimed role of the Don.

I've been more disturbed by the personal associations in *Don Quixote* than by Balanchine's changes in the production from season to season. I didn't get to see the ballet until 1969, by which time the tinkering had already begun, and my feelings about it have come in the opposite direction from those of my colleagues. Most critics complain now that the continuity has been lost, the dancing mutilated — although Edwin Denby seems to be the only one who gave a good account of its initial assets at the time when they were supposedly strongest.

At my first encounter with it I felt like a voyeur; it seemed to me Balanchine was not only revealing himself more openly than I wanted to see him revealed, but he was covering himself with self-pity as well. Those very scenes that bothered me for their cruelty, though, were intriguing too. I grew more and more fascinated by the psychological sweep and the bizarre effects of the ballet. This season Farrell returned to the company after five years of doing yoga and other activities with Maurice Béjart's Ballet of the XXth Century. Whether being with Béjart or leaving him has improved her, she looks very different from the pliant, vacantly beautiful dancer-creature she was before. Somehow this new firmly centered, risk-taking Farrell has shifted the ballet for me, just enough, away from its old too-close-for-comfort implications of master enslaved to his worshiping pupil, so that I could look carefully at its weird theatricality.

The scenario takes the Don from his protective household out into the callous world, where, with Balanchinian interpolations of dancing, he makes various gestures in the name of chivalry, continually brings society's contempt down on himself, and finally is brought home in a cage to die. I've never read Cervantes' novel, nor do I think Balanchine would expect that in order for us to comprehend his ballet. To me the story line isn't always clear, but neither is the mind of the story-maker. The ballet's main device — and perhaps its main flaw — is that it's told from the point of view of the hero, an old man who is either senile or freaked-out on religious apparitions. The protagonist and his companion Sancho Panza don't dance, so there is no lyrical thread holding events together. The whole idea is more operatic — or cinematic — than balletic.

The dramatic events have tremendous power, and they reverberate long after they're over, but when pure dance sequences start, in the first and last acts, they're as if from nowhere — dissociated from the foreboding and nastiness that constitute the main tenor of the ballet. The dance numbers contain the only fast-moving action in the ballet, which creates a strange tension — a reversal of ballet's usual apportioning of what is ephemeral and whizzing past all the time and what we stop to think about. Consider the relative impact of *Coppélia's* big action scene in the toy workshop, and the expansive, almost meditative pure-dance last act. One kind of activity facilitates the plot, the other comments on it. In *Don Quixote*, it's the other way round. Something feels out of whack, like the ocean being to your west in California.

The Pas Classique Espagnol that opens the village scene in the first act is perfectly pleasant choreography, and it looked especially lively this season with Merrill Ashley in the lead, supported by Tracy Bennett at one performance I saw, Robert Weiss at the other, and the strong young dancers in the present NYCB corps. But the people in the dance seem to be there for the purpose of doing that dance and nothing else. They're set in position when the curtain goes up and they go away when they're finished. Nobody watches them except a few supers dressed as soldiers.

Devotees of Balanchine love the third act pas d'action best of anything in the ballet. Farrell's solo seems to be unique in all of Balanchine's choreographic output. Nowhere else is he so directly expressive in dance steps of a character's feelings. From a quiet beginning she grows more and more agitated, twisting her body, changing directions violently, balancing in distorted shapes that lead to other distorted shapes instead of to repose.

But there's a lot of other stuff happening here that has no discernible reason. A lot of beautiful Maidens do a ballet, and they have partners called Cavaliers, and Farrell has a partner called the Knight of the Silver Moon, and near the end two other characters come flying in dressed in black, Colleen Neary (Night Spirit) and Robert Maiorano (Merlin). Other people have told me what this allegory means, but the dance doesn't tell me, so I can't connect it properly to Don Quixote, who, by the way, was caught in a big net before it began and carried offstage.

To me, the core of *Don Quixote* is the second act, where the character of the Don and his society are most consistently worked out in one dance image — the court masque. At the end of the first act Don Quixote had become involved in a village brawl just as the Duke and his entourage were passing through. He's allowed to make an appearance at court, by some means that I think was made clear in an earlier version but is obscure now. Perhaps the jaded aristocrats think he would be amusing to play with for a while.

The court is an oppressively hard-edged, formal place, all gold and onyx, with no place to sit except a throne. A foppish major domo announces the guests, who enter in a sweeping, supercilious procession down the center of the room. Esteban Frances has created costumes for this scene that are brilliantly suggestive of the period — in heavy fabrics as burdensome as they are showy. The women wear tall helmets, high neck ruffs, dresses that sheathe the upper body and stand out stiffly from the lower, and precarious spike-heeled shoes. They hold themselves as if their role in life is to be magnificent breakable objects. Their partners, in tights and pantaloons and rakish mustaches, look incapable of handling anything of any utility at all. They all have smooth, discontented faces and a taste for intricate pleasures.

For a while they treat the Don as their honored guest. They dance a remarkable sarabande in which the movement is minimal and all the potency of their regimented existence is compressed into the almost sinister eroticism with which they eye each other. Various entertainments are shown them — dancers from the harems and slave markets of the Moslem world.

Then, at a signal from the Duchess, they put on masks and begin baiting the Don. This too turns into an elaborate ritual. As he's dancing with the hostess they poke him, trip him from behind. He's confused, tries to maintain his courtly attentiveness to his hostess. A man mounts his back. He doesn't understand. They taunt him more openly with capes, swords, red feathers. The imagery becomes more grotesque. The women promenade in a big circle around the Don, leading the men, who squat like monkeys. They dress him in a red cape and a crown of golden leaves, strike him with the flat of their swords, seat him on a wooden horse, and set off firecrackers that are tied to its tail. Women circle around him in white wispy beards. Finally a woman smashes a handful of white foam into his face.

This is all done slowly and deliberately — the aristocrats are savoring every minute, but so is Don Quixote in some way. It's as if he loves to suffer — the more passively he endures their cruelty, the more saintly he can imagine himself. After the torture, a vision of Dulcinea appears to revive him. But even her dance is taunting as she pulls him this way and that, never establishing a clear direction to safety, and then fades away too quickly for him to follow.

One of the extraordinary things about this scene is the way it lapses from reality into delusion. Sometimes we are a spectator to events in which the Don and Sancho participate, later we're put inside the Don's view of the frightful events. The first glimpse provokes our indignation at the people who can behave that way; the second image is disjointed and irrational, and doesn't make any judgments, it just *feels* awful. Nor can we tell the exact moment when we've slipped over the line of reason.

In fact, the entire ballet slides back and forth between these two theatricalities. The third act consists almost entirely of fantasies: he dreams of Dulcinea as a symbol of beauty and goodness who is kept powerless by the evil magician Merlin; he charges to the rescue but she's carried off. He's suddenly fighting a giant puppet version of himself that turns into a whirling windmill whose blades lift him in the air and hurl him to the ground again. Horribly, he's stampeded by a herd of pigs, becomes an animal himself, crawls docilely into the cage brought by faceless men in black capes. Then after he's brought home and put to bed by his servants, the last, overwhelming series of hallucinations: an Inquisitorial procession, the burning of his books, and his Dulcinea-Madonna statue miraculously beckon-

ing him to reach once more for divine mercy. He rises toward
her, arms pleading to be united with her, but she vanishes and
he falls back dying. The servant Dulcinea absolves his madness by placing two sticks in the form of a cross on his lifeless
body.

The composure with which Farrell now performs this act —
and all her other tasks as the "real" servant girl — makes her
seem almost unnaturally plain in contrast to the violent and
chaotic images fermenting in the Don's mind. You can't find
in his home and friends anything that would excite such gross
imaginings, and that makes his efforts all the more pathetic. I
think this contrast has to do with what Edwin Denby calls the
changes of scale in the ballet. The thing keeps going from
ordinariness — Dulcinea washing the Don's feet, Sancho
Panza shaving him, a bunch of Spanish girls dancing in the
village square, the Don and Sancho clomping in on a sleepy
old horse and a donkey — to extreme, distorted fantasy.

Though the transitions between these two states are so gradual that we don't always realize when they are happening, Balanchine has been very clear about the symbolic connections
underlying the changes. Almost everything "real" in the ballet
has its analogue in some later fantasy, almost every monstrosity
is an echo of a religious icon. Whatever is sound or innocent
in the Don's life gets tainted by injustice or burned by cant. In
the opening scene his books of knowledge release phantom
knights and Inquisitors like insects from a nest. The faithful
Sancho's shaving soap gets pushed in his face later to mock
him. The peasants' good-natured hazing in the village fore-
shadows the ingenious cruelty at court. Sancho, who's gone
through all his trials with him, finally becomes his keeper, leading him into the cage, which looks like the iron bars of the
palace gate.

In almost all these fantasies, the Don sees the world as altered from its proper size. The books that come to life are
themselves oversize, but the figures representing knights on
horseback are played by children. So is the first little princess
that he tries to extricate from that battle. Later he watches a
traveling puppet show where the actors are children, and takes
it into his head to intervene and save the Christian heroine

from the Turks who are trying to abduct her — and he wrecks the puppet booth in the process.

If the objects of his misguided benevolence are all miniatures, his enemies are giants. Even the Duke and Duchess and their court seem inflated in their high-heeled shoes, voluminous dresses, capes, tall hats. They're hidden from him too, these enemies, behind masks or armor or clerical garb. His derangement takes the form of a profound alienation — and also a vast arrogance. No one in the world is his equal. Those characters who match him in size are inferior in station — his servants, the peasants and village characters, the exotics who dance at court.

Only Dulcinea of all his fabrications is human scale — and his confusions about her are the most enigmatic part of the story. Dulcinea is not just a simple girl who works in his house, she's the princess he would save from dragons, the dead poet's mistress whom he rescues from her accusers, the good fairy who tries to save him from his tormentors, and finally the Virgin statue that remains a distant ideal. Though she's a religious symbol to him, he wants her to be human and humble too.

I find it impossible to avoid seeing sexual implications in Dulcinea despite the chivalric premise of the ballet. Her Magdalene gesture of drying his feet with her hair in the first act isn't accidental. I can't believe that she holds no earthly attractions for the Don, who's overstimulated by everything else around him. His final attempt at union with her Madonna-self is the only really clumsy stage business in the ballet; he stands on a narrow elevator platform that's covered by his carefully arranged fifteen-foot long nightclothes. As it slowly rises I see a phallic image, not a spiritual one. But even if she's supposed to be pure and his love for her isn't sexual, she's a temptress. Whether he's looking for consummation or consolation, his own mind thinks she's promising what she can't really give.

Despite all that he undergoes, I find it hard to feel sorry for Don Quixote. I keep wondering why his servants are so loyal, why Dulcinea loves him, why he's allowed out to commit his moralistic mayhem on other people's lives. He has no idea of the consequences of his heroic gestures or even the reasons for them. His code is as blind and absolute as the one he seeks to combat. He thinks he's too good for his world, but he doesn't even recognize the good that's around him.

Perhaps the dancers who take this role can't find its sympathetic core either. I've seen Richard Rapp, Jean-Pierre Bonnefous, and Jacques d'Amboise do it over the years, and they all maintained a tone of passivity throughout, except when seized by some zealous notion of charity. They were like sleepwalkers or psychotics who could rouse themselves only by giving vent to violent aggression. I always look for signs that the Don is losing his apparent contact with the events around him and drifting into hallucination, but I never see it. So I have to conclude that he's never really in contact. Perhaps Balanchine is telling us that the saintly man in society *is* mad, or that society will always see him as mad, or that the acts of society aren't any more rational than the ravings of a mystic.

Summer 1975

Rome Was Never Like This

WE'VE WAITED a long time to see the Bolshoi Ballet's most recent revision of *Spartacus*. The Bolshoi has been coming here and not coming here for several seasons. As the politicians played their inexhaustible games of cultural roulette, Moscow sent us stars, students, divertissements, but no repertory and no company. Now they're here though, even if you do have to get your briefcase inspected at the Metropolitan Opera House door.

I don't know what I thought *Spartacus* would be — I guess I was imagining some combination of "Intolerance" and "Les

Troyens," with a dancing Steve Reeves in the title role. Well, this wasn't it.

Spartacus is a story ballet that is nonstop dancing, like a lyrical ballet. It has three acts all right, and a plot. But the distinguishable characters number only four, unless you count a helmeted gladiator who expires at the end of his one scene. The characters are Spartacus, the Thracian prisoner who leads an uprising of slaves against their Roman masters; Phrygia, his wife; Crassus, the Roman general; and Aegina, Crassus' mistress, who softens up the slave-army for the final Roman attack by throwing them an orgy. There are no friends, servants, or any other persons of intermediate rank between the principals and the masses of their followers.

The story too is whittled down to its barest essentials — or rather to the incidents that afford the best dance possibilities. The connecting information and the sociological frame of reference is conveyed in a page of program notes. Choreographer Yuri Grigorovich's intention seems to have been to construct a series of danced episodes of extreme clarity and effectiveness, leaving out all the messy little realistic details, the digressions and elaborations that impede the momentum of ordinary story ballet. What resulted, though, is a work of such rigid formalism, such relentless impact that about halfway through I began to feel I was seeing the whole thing again backwards.

The ballet has no furniture or décor other than a small ramp across the back of the stage where various set pieces, backcloths, and arrangements of people are changed behind a scrim. Each scene ends with a tableau, the scrim drops like a cargo net to cover it, someone dances a soliloquy on the bare stage, then the lights come up on a new tableau, the scrim rises and the next scene begins. The only variation to this pattern is that at the end of each act a tableau is arranged downstage, and a backcloth comes in behind it. Double the impact.

Spartacus is a dance you see in increments. Six dancers come on from one side, then six from another. The basic module sometimes multiplies to twenty-four, with another squad in the wings or posing upstage. The more important stuff has more people, more unison movement, dancers working closer to the footlights. Nothing is ever *not* important or *not* strong though. The dancing always goes at high intensity and mostly at high speed. By eliminating the pauses, the mime, the stretches of lowered intensity that are found in conventional ballets, Grigorovich has produced a rhythmic monotony so thorough that it nullifies the mere volume of undeniably virtuosic achievement. The audience hardly knows what's astounding enough to applaud.

Except that Grigorovich's dance idiom is strictly classical, *Spartacus* reminds me of nothing so much as the spectacles of Maurice Béjart. Béjart has an amateur's enterprise in devising asymmetrical floor patterns, unpredictable — or illogical if you prefer — build-ups and encounters. But like Grigorovich his aim is propaganda and his method is mass movement.

Spartacus doesn't attempt to describe the battles, the escapes, the conversions, or the betrayals that carry forward its plot, except in the most schematic way. Spartacus' army divides into seven and five men; they leap back and forth across the stage for a while until the five depart; thus you know they've deserted him. But *why* they desert we have no idea. The Romans march in goose step; that makes them villains. Phrygia flings herself around a lot in her solos — she's free and warm, you see. Aegina's movement is narrow and sinuous. She's a betrayer. You don't have to care about them, you just identify with the ones on your side.

May 1, 1975

The Panov Myth Revisited

SAN FRANCISCO —Valery Panov's first ballet for an American company, *Heart of the Mountain*, does not clarify the celebrated Russian's artistic position as I'd hoped it would. If anything, it raises even more questions than before about who Panov is, why an international campaign had to be mounted to get him out of Russia, and what he aims to do with his talents in the West.

Valery and Galina Panov seem to travel in their very own smog of hype, evasions, rhetoric and — well, excuses. They gained our sympathy because they wanted to emigrate to Israel, but they found no suitable company to dance with in Israel. Since their debut in Philadelphia a year ago, we always see them at some kind of disadvantage — they're out of shape, their managers book them into the wrong spaces, they get injured. They've yet to dance in New York, where the main dance audience is. And somehow there's no American company in which they can settle down and dance the standard repertory; they only do their own special numbers as guest stars.

The Panovs have made a nice little sometime-niche for themselves with the San Francisco Ballet. The audience here likes their showy pas de deux, and the company likes their popularity. Now the company has granted Panov one of his dreams: a chance to choreograph. After the martyred years of longing for freedom and the threnodies to the creative spirit that would not be crushed, this ballet seems almost a dance of regret.

It's a look back to the past — not the Imperial Russian ballet past of Petipa, nor the glorious avant-garde past of Diaghilev, but the tacky, sentimental, sloganeering days of Soviet realism. *Heart of the Mountain* is a suite of dances based on the full-length *Goryanka*, choreographed in the 1930s and remade in 1968 by Oleg Vinogradov for the Kirov Ballet with Panov in the principal role. Excerpting Murad Kozlayev's movie-soundtrack score from the latter production, Panov has incorporated a lot of folk-dance material from the Caucasus region of Daghestan in his new version.

Heart of the Mountain is a sort of junior-grade *Spartacus*. I mean it appears to be that — one still has to hedge because I saw Attila Ficzere in the main part. He stepped in for Panov, who had been injured at the second performance, and some of the choreography was modified so he could learn it in time. The work is a series of group dances with expressive/virtuosic solos by the lead couple. Some kind of story is being told, but the ballet doesn't concern itself much with narrative; it just picks up the participants at points along the way and tells you about their frame of mind right then.

No program notes or other clues are provided to fill in those gaps, but I was able to piece together this much: a marriage is arranged, but the girl (played by Galina Panov) rejects her assigned husband, who thereupon stabs her and runs away. Panov has supplied a poem for the program which refers to the "cold and eternal" ways of the ancestors. He's also said the work is his tribute to Freedom, and to "the mountain people who . . . preserved their original character and remained loyal to their old traditions."

A curious brew. I don't know what in the ballet represents freedom and what oppression. The real tradition-breaker is the recalcitrant bride; she gets bumped off for defying the rules of the tribe. Does Panov sympathize with the rejected bridegroom, thereby sanctioning murder? Conformity is the constantly reiterated message of the unison group dances, the men and women of the community hovering around to make sure the prescribed ritual is carried out.

The rigid formalism of the work doesn't allow you much insight into the choreographer's attitudes. It's all done with the high-macho insistence that passes for modernism in present-day Russia. The men swagger around, showing off for the women with a stick-twirling dance. The women droop and sway in a line, their arms twined together. When the leading

man confronts his intended, he courts her with aggressive pirouettes and jumps, he lunges and grabs at her. When she
can't discourage him by gesturing her repulsion, she runs and
leaps violently away from him. He writhes in fury and frustration at her feet, and at last kills her. While three tribal elders
look on, she dies a prolonged and careful death.

Like its Soviet models, *Heart of the Mountain* does not attempt any psychological explanations. For Panov it seems to
be enough that there is a colorful conflict, that the maverick is
punished, and that the keepers of tradition live on, implacable.
I find these sentiments amazing in the man who became a
world symbol of the individual's resistance to social oppression.
The entire ballet confirms Panov's tradition rather than exploring those inspiring, stimulating influences he was supposedly
denied in Russia.

March 11, 1976

Ballet Théâtre Contemporain

POP DANCE is with us, so much so that I guess we are going to
have to start cataloguing its various types. The most attractive
representative I've seen of the European side of the family is
the French Ballet Théâtre Contemporain, which made its U.S.
debut in four performances at Brooklyn Academy.

This company specializes in movement. If the movement is
without style or subtlety, there's a lot of it, it's highly technical,
and it's given the utmost visibility by severely stylish sets, lighting, and costumes. I think people, especially dancers, like to
watch this kind of dance because it exploits all the possibilities

that dancers are built for. It's like finally being able to drive a car as fast as the speedometer will go.

The company's opener, *Danses Concertantes*, choreographed by Felix Blaska to Stravinsky's music, establishes a high-powered kinetic climate, with great hordes of dancers clad in red, green, blue, or black leotards, the solists in white, pitching movement at the audience in perfect unison. The individual dancer is unimportant compared to the mass effect. Even the soloists seem only slightly more noticeable versions of the others.

The audience's sense of motion comes from a lot of dancers doing a lot of things at high intensity. Groups move together into certain areas of the stage. They change direction or level en masse. What's important about these shifts is how they alter the total design of the stage, but there's almost no concern with the act of traveling itself, with *how* a dancer gets through space.

Requiem, choreographed by Françoise Adret to Gyorgy Ligeti's vocal score using fragments of the Catholic Mass in sustained, overlapping dissonances, works on the same premise. It seems to be darker in mood, mainly because a lot of it takes place on the floor and the dancers don't smile. There's one female soloist (Muriel Belmondo), who looks anguished but stoic. She wears all-yellow, while the others have leotards in dark primary colors with weblike designs.

A tubular aluminum sculpture forming a giant circle open at the bottom dominated the stage for the first part of the dance, flew out, returned at the end. I took it to be a symbol, perhaps of Woman, but only because it was too imposing to be mere decoration.

Ballet Théâtre Contemporain's director, Jean-Albert Cartier, is a former art critic and museum administrator, and the company prides itself on its spectacular décor and lighting. *Violostries*, a duet for Martine Parmain and James Urbain choreographed by Michel Descombey, is a rather standard predatory-female-luring-reluctant-male encounter, produced for maximum excitation. Glaring white light from the sides of the stage slams starkly into the areas of combat, like TV going after a riot. The woman's hideout is a glimmering showerbath of plastic streamers. The couple's tense stalkings and devouringly sexual meetings acquire superimportance in such a brilliant arena.

BTC doesn't seem very modern to me, however, because when you get beneath its scenic and dancing expertise the company is projecting twenty-year-old ideas. Its psychological themes, expressionistic movement, and symbolic designs are the sterile third-generation offspring of Martha Graham.

November 1972

Secret Places and Jackpot

ORDINARY BALLETS seem to come in flavors, like breakfast foods. There are costume ballets, erotic ballets, pop ballets, jazz ballets. Some companies try to keep one of each brand around for variety. The City Center Joffrey Ballet's chief choreographer, Gerald Arpino, specializes in these repertory fillers, and February 23 we got two portions back to back, a romantic ballet and a kooky ballet, both duets.

Secret Places, revived after a two-year absence, was choreographed in 1968 to the second movement of "Mozart's Piano Concerto No. 21," otherwise known as the Elvira Madigan Musik. The setting is an imaginary forest, suggested by Ming Cho Lee's tubular-steel sculptured birch grove and Tom Skelton's leaf-shade lighting.

In silence Donna Cowen walks through the place with that thrusting, expectant walk dancers have. A minute after she's gone Dennis Wayne appears. Then he's gone and she comes back. This cruising goes on for a long time, the dancers accelerating to running and then to big jumps. They keep missing each other somehow, even though they've got their eyes peeled and they're often onstage at the same time.

Finally, she jumps into his arms and the music begins. The rest is pretty predictable. They embrace dreamily, hold each other at arm's length as if they could see each other better that way, leap together in rapture. At one point he chases her offstage, and after a pause they come quietly back with their arms around each other. Whatever they did out there is primly withheld from us, but I suppose we're meant to imagine something intensely poetic so that the ballet will acquire a shape. Otherwise it's more of the same until the music's over.

Jackpot, the kooky one, is new. Glenn White and Erika Goodman appear to be some kind of intergalactic clowns imitating people. He's lit in a poison green spotlight all the time; she's in surprise pink. The music is a stream of electronic burbles and burps by Jacob Druckman. Over her leotard Goodman wears a tiny little skirt flaring out at the midriff in the new pregnant look — I guess she's an Earth Mother type. White has silver nailheads on the shoulders of his leotard, and at first he stands on a box wiggling his hips a great deal — perhaps he's lost his motorcycle.

She pops up from inside the box and leans out between his legs. He jumps off and wiggles in alarm while she beckons slinkily. He's kind of a throwback, you see, to the Moor in *Petrouchka*, who thought his coconut was sexier than any girl. But finally they bump hips a few times and after they've made contact, they vibrate together for quite a while.

When he's really juiced up he grabs her around the waist and runs around in a big circle shoving one of her legs out straight ahead like a plow while she reaches for the back of her head with the other. The second time around he comes up behind the box and crams both of them, with Goodman's leg first, right inside it. Whereupon there's an explosion, a puff of smoke, and some lights on the box blink on and off as the curtain comes down. JACKPOT! JACKPOT! JACKPOT!

March 1, 1973

The Concert

TRYING to think why there are so few comic ballets around like Jerome Robbins' *The Concert*, just revived by the New York City Ballet, I realized that we've become more sophisticated about movement since the mid-1950s, when it was made. So much of the humor in contemporary ballet depends on kinetic jokes. There's Gerald Arpino's *Valentine* from last season, for instance, where the take-off point was the ancient contest between men and women, but the fun came from the dancers' timing and changes of focus, from their pratfalls and surprises in 57 varieties, and from their subliminal struggles with an onstage musician.

While *The Concert* makes a lot of movement jokes too, it's basically about the silliness of people — situation comedy is what that sort of thing was called in the glorious young days of television. With swift unerring strokes, Robbins sketched a snooty pianist who plays Chopin as boringly as possible, and his audience: an effete music lover plagued by two ladies rattling their pocketbooks behind him; an imposing lady in pearls with her cigar-chomping, racing-form-reading husband in tow; a jittery young man; a debutante in a pink picture hat; and a muscular female who probably hates music and gives piano lessons to intimidated fourth graders.

As the music flows over their heads, the characters indulge in ever more grandiose fantasies. The debutante first bullies the shy young man in a pas de deux of stabbing pointe work and violent balances. In *his* dreams he beats her and carries her off in a swoon.

Later she fancies the more masterful approach of the philistine husband, who by this time has mentally murdered his wife and taken charge of an army of Cossacks. Just as the lovers are united in a fluttery duet, his avenging spouse shows up again as a sort of matronly Queen of the Wilis, and summons a troupe of incompetent butterflies, who bring down the curtain in a havoc of grand jetés.

The Concert stays within balletic ideas most of the time, and it's funny just as a ballet parody. Robbins gets great mileage out of the old joke about the girl who's on the wrong beat in the chorus, and the subservience of the male in classical ballet. But the piece remains human to the end. Robbins doesn't allow his characters to freeze into types or period puppets — his theater genius keeps them alive and changing.

I particularly enjoy seeing "serious" dancers do a work like this. It makes them tap resources they usually don't have to use, and gives their performance an edge of unpredictability. Sara Leland as the belle of the ball, Bettijane Sills as the wife, Francisco Moncion as the Babbitt, and Robert Weiss as the petrified partner were all splendid.

The young dancer who saw *The Concert* with me remembered soon after the curtain went up that she'd seen the ballet when she was ten years old. She was delighted all over again. She told me afterward: "The first time I saw it I wanted to dance with Jerome Robbins, and I still do!"

December 16, 1971

Siegfried's Revenge

BALLET IS a woman's art. Or was.

For 200 years the ballet stage has been inhabited by beautiful females with uncanny skills of speed, balance, accuracy, and elevation — women whose virtuosity gave tangible support to their stage roles as princesses or leaders, often endowed with

supernatural powers. Countless ballet heroes have fallen help-
lessly in love with these splendid creatures. Countless men
have unwittingly angered them and had to endure their punishment, or unwittingly pleased them and been rewarded. Even
when the plot is a love story — and most plots are — the ballerina is what you go to the ballet to see. A male dancer hoping
for stardom in this world learns to incline his head and step
backward with regal deference.

Siegfried, the prince in that most classic of all classical ballets, *Swan Lake*, is a vacillating playboy who can't find the right
girl. This annoys his mother no end, since he's just turned
twenty-one and isn't giving a thought to what is apparently to
be his only serious work in life, producing an heir to the
throne. Instead he has the bad judgment to fall for an enchanted Swan, who makes him swear eternal love. No sooner
does he get back to the palace than he's tricked into betraying
her by a magician's daughter. In despair, he rejoins his beloved and — depending on which version you see — follows
her over a cliff or sees her taken away forever by the powers of
Evil. Siegfried gets to dance only at those rare moments in the
ballet when he's having a good time, but usually he suffers. His
main job is to lift the ballerina and look noble.

Much of Western literature paints women as idealized figures, and the nineteenth-century ballerina embodied this ideal,
with her stage partners bowing and scraping in the background.
Villains, clowns, slaves, and other exotics often did stunning
solos in these ballets, but the sensational "character dancer"
somehow always stands lower in the ballet hierarchy than the
more elegant leading man who dances less.

Even the great Nijinsky achieved his fame primarily in a series of character parts; he was an ornament to the story rather
than the protagonist. His role in *Le Spectre de la Rose*, perhaps
the first ballet that totally belonged to its male lead, was an
extension of both the effete prince and the sensuous but not
quite real character part.

The Spectre, a vision conjured up by a girl who has just been
to a ball, is hardly what we would call a paragon of masculinity.
When American Ballet Theater revived the work two years ago,
with Paolo Bortoluzzi and Carla Fracci, I wondered how any-

one could have thought this petal-covered, limp-wristed, gently smiling creature had anything to do with a male image. A more romantic friend explained that the Spectre represented a virgin's ideal man in 1911. There must be people who accept these ultrachivalrous figures as models of masculinity. Woman certainly gets the best of it — this nonthreatening, nondemanding partner defers to her and allows her to assert herself without losing her femininity. Siegfried in another role is Leslie Howard as Ashley Wilkes.

Sergei Diaghilev's phenomenally successful Ballets Russes revised the world's concept of Western ballet, and the role of the male dancer with it. Over the company's two decades of existence (1909–1929) Diaghilev collected and presented a fabulous array of men and women dancers, choreographers and allied artists, Nijinsky among them. His last great male star, Serge Lifar, embodied the physical beauty and nobility of the romantic hero and excelled as a dancer. In addition to successes in the classical repertory, Lifar created roles in such precedent-shattering works as George Balanchine's *Apollon Musagète* and *The Prodigal Son*. These were true heroes at last, not just gilded playthings come to life.

In the new field of modern dance, where women were again the principal dancers and also created most of the choreography, Ted Shawn and José Limón made particular efforts to secure a decent position for men. When Shawn's company of men dancers made one of its early tours in 1935, a woman writer in Atlanta said that before she saw them "the very idea of male dancers disgusted me." She was converted by the company's forcefulness and muscularity, its avoidance of the sissy image. Shawn had concentrated on pure dance and ritual, incorporating folk, religious, sport, and work motifs appropriate to men. Limón made dramatic dances for an all-male cast — *Emperor Jones*, *The Traitor*; he based several scenarios on the conflict between two powerful men, played by himself and Lucas Hoving; and in general he tried to choreograph for the particular qualities of men as contrast or complement to those of women, rather than in subordination to women.

But equality of the sexes, in dance as well as life, hasn't worked out yet. I think the early modern dancers were searching for it. Doris Humphrey more than anyone could use men for their tenderness and women for their strength, without making them seem neurotic. But Humphrey was avowedly utopian, and the idealism of the early modern dance grew weaker while its message became more simplistic. Humphrey's community of powerful equals has evolved into a futuristic land of androgynes and look-alikes.

Today a lot of dance isn't concerned with discovering new forms and new roles at all, but with telling a story or exhibiting a technique. A great deal of it is popular dance, and as such it trades in popular stereotypes. The men are virile and the girls are feminine in the old familiar ways. We hardly notice how this reinforces sexism because it's so attractive and entertaining.

At the same time as this trend toward more accessible, naturalistic characterization, we've seen a sort of male backlash developing, whose concern is not to show the depths and confusions of sexuality, but to draw very clear, corrective models. Some years ago Erik Bruhn refused to dance *Swan Lake* anymore. Bruhn, probably the greatest danseur noble of our time, said as a contemporary man he could no longer believe the traditional *Swan Lake*. He choreographed his own version, with the Prince as the central character. In this version, danced by the National Ballet of Canada, Siegfried resents his bullying mother, and meets his downfall by choosing spiritual over sexual love. The villain has become a woman, called the Black Queen, alter ego of Siegfried's domineering mother.

This Siegfried isn't any more independent than the nineteenth-century original — he's still the victim of women. But he rebels against their power and bids for the audience's sympathy. Suddenly, as people have started reexamining other legendary plots, lady villains and traumatized heroes are flooding the stage in a great outpouring of Oedipal spite.

The Biblical brothers Cain and Abel showed up a couple of years ago, as symbols of the creative nonconformist versus the conventional drone, in a dance called *Sin Lieth at the Door*, choreographed by the Israeli Moshe Efrati. The famous fratricide was instigated by a female Demon. John Butler's *Accord-*

ing to Eve, for the Alvin Ailey company, showed the two brothers as pawns of their mother's favoritism. Ailey's star dancer, Judith Jamison, started the rivalry by loving up Abel and spurning Cain, then she stood around wringing her hands while the two men struggled spectacularly.

Eve, the great Mom of us all, is the originator of Sin if you want to look at it that way. Even the Serpent is often played by a woman, as in Maurice Béjart's *Nijinsky, Clown of God*, for example. Béjart's *Nijinsky* goes further, reinterpreting the life of the great dancer to show him as an innocent whose art, sanity, and finally his life are destroyed by a predatory woman. A childlike Nijinsky flourishes happily under the thumb of the impresario Diaghilev, his mastermind, father, and lover, until the advent of the classic temptress he eventually marries. The marriage costs Nijinsky his friends, work, and Big Daddy. His sexy wife thereupon turns into a symbol of spiritual love.

The renunciation of heterosexual love and/or the identification of woman as an eternal threat to man's existence are recurrent themes in today's dance. A whole series of ballets could be grouped under the title "The Making of a Homosexual." Antony Tudor's *Undertow* (1945) established the genre, with its disaster-prone plot and mandatory meanies: parents who show their rejection of their son by having violent sexual relations, the young girl who's too naive to give him real love, the pack of boys who initiate him into sado-masochistic manhood, the woman of the world who awakens castration fears. We're getting the same message, less literally, from ballets as vicious as Jerome Robbins' *The Cage* (1951), a charming little story of a tribe of female insects who kill their lovers after using them for impregnation, or as innocuous as Béjart's *Firebird* (1970), which does away with a story entirely to become an abstract representation of the revolutionary spirit.

Can there still be a mind romantic enough to see *The Cage* as a fantasy, to pretend those aren't real women doing that horrible number on real men? As for *Firebird*, the original ballet was about a Russian prince who catches a magic bird and sets her free; later the bird rescues him and his princess from a troupe of monsters. I agree with Béjart that this story "seems lame," but note that the good angel and principal dancer is a woman, the monster king is a man, and the rabble are up to no good. In Béjart's *Firebird*, the glorious mob is dressed in fatigues and smudgily made up so you can't tell the men from the women. The Firebird, who passes Idealism on to them with a kiss, is a man, and after his demise he is succeeded by another male, the Phoenix. There's no villain at all, so the revolution turns out to be a cult, inspired solely, as far as the audience can see, by the beauty and fervor of the hero, and of course by his male-ballerina dancing.

These ballets, despite their aura of homosexual propaganda and antifeminism, are part of a larger drive to redeem the status of men in dance. Alvin Ailey recently revived Ted Shawn's all-male *Kinetic Molpai* in his continuing effort to preserve the classics of American dance, and the Limón company has retained its strong male orientation even after its founder's death. Many smaller dance companies have rejected on principle the old habit of featuring women while keeping just enough decent male dancers around for a few special roles.

Even some of our big ballet companies are doing away with female superiority. The Joffrey Ballet seldom uses a traditional corps de ballet anymore, and this spring its company roster listed four more men than women. Striving to maintain its middle-American glamour image, the Joffrey has taken a path somewhere between the old-fashioned, women-centered ballet and the new antifeminism, and its chief choreographer, Gerald Arpino, has come up with a number of neoclassic ballets in which the men and women are surprisingly evenly matched. In these works Arpino demanded that both contingents work hard all the time; there are no long lines of girls in the background counting two to the left, two to the right; nor are the men relegated to carrying baskets of grapes or holding up the maypole. But in his hippest, most "modern" works, *Trinity* and *Sacred Grove on Mount Tamalpais*, men have the major dancing roles and establish the personality of the piece — the speed-soaked evangelists of *Trinity* and the blissed-out guru of *Sacred Grove* — while the women are reduced to ciphers.

While Arpino tries to preserve both male and female identities, more choreographers fall back on unisex. Several European companies — Béjart's Ballet of the XXth Century, the

French Ballet Théâtre Contemporain, the Netherlands Dance Theater among them — have scrapped the old repertory and tried to give men and women more equal dancing responsibilities. All dancers are costumed in streamlined leotards and tights. Girls never wear skirts, though they do wear toe shoes. By virtue of their physiques, men and women dancers are specialists — women can dance on pointe, can be lifted in the air; men can jump and turn and support. But the ballets are asexual. They're athletic, or spiritual, musical, moralistic, humorous, but they bypass or depersonalize any reference to sexual relationships. An increasing number of American modern dance companies have adopted the same approach.

Attempts to solve the problem of using men and women more equally while acknowledging their sexual differences have so far tended to look backward for a one-to-one reversal. Kenneth MacMillan successfully substituted a squad of Russian naval officers for the traditional corps de ballet in *Anastasia*. For the 1972 Stravinsky Festival at the New York City Ballet, Jerome Robbins choreographed *Scherzo Fantastique*, a pas de deux backed by an ensemble of three men. Gelsey Kirkland and Bart Cook did flashy Bolshoi-type lifts and chases, complemented by the fast and aerial corps.

But simply replacing men in the positions once held by women can, it seems to me, only lead to the same exploitative practices in reverse. Other than bigoted racial contexts, dance and the homosexual community are the two places I know of where grown-up male persons are commonly referred to as boys. Classic ballet has always carried an unspoken sexual come-on. Virtuously offering the notion of woman as gifted, gracious, and morally good, ballet literally presents her in the flesh. When the ballerina languidly unfolds her leg into a high extension or stretches her torso into an arabesque, she's calling attention to a shapely ankle, an arched instep, the long straight bones, and the rounded hip and ribcage. You can't mistake it if you're alive yourself.

Nor can you be unaware of the sexuality of modern ballet's strong, sleek, handsome men showing you thighs, buttocks, bulging baskets. The nineteenth-century ballet functioned quite openly as a showcase where dandies picked out their mistresses and little chorus girls found lifelong protectors. Perhaps inevitably, the featuring of men in ballet has created a new theatrical meat market. "I'm sure women's lib would agree it's about time that men got their turn at being regarded as sex objects for a while," wrote a "Dance Magazine" reviewer in justification of a recent boy-beautiful ballet. I'm not aware that women's lib has ever tried to reserve the status of sex object for women. In fact, I find the idea of any intelligent person wanting to grow up to be a sex object rather ludicrous, but it seems we have to take the suggestion seriously because so much dance these days is primarily a homosexual pitch.

Men as dancers and artists, and men as theatrical prototypes are being robbed of their full humanity as the roles reverse themselves, and so are women. The heroines of story ballets, after all, were remarkably bright girls. They were always thinking up ways to outwit the authorities. For every tinsel Sugar Plum in the old-time ballet there is a compassionate Giselle, a benevolent Lilac Fairy, a clever Swanilda. Even the lady villains usually had some reason to harbor their grudges.

Today's leading men seemingly don't need any dimension or character, nor do the women who oppress them. Take two contemporary trios, for instance, Louis Falco's *Huescape* and Kenneth MacMillan's *Triad*. (The latter also has a small male corps de ballet.) In both dances, the two men are interested in the woman and in each other. The woman represents a threat to their friendship/romance because she's a possible companion to each of them. The dance is played out on the level of movement tensions and balances — a cat's cradle of arrangements and entanglement and undoings — but the dancers as people are rootless, motiveless, existing only for the time between the rise and fall of the curtan. Take Béjart's *Symphonie pour un Homme Seul*. The hero, He, and ten pals are working hard at representing Mankind, when the heroine, She, comes around bothering them. Why are they disconcerted? Why does He look so tormented by her advances? Not for any reason we can see, except that She is female.

Why do the couples in Brian Macdonald's *Time Out of Mind* look as if they're trying to disembowel each other every time they embrace? Why is the woman in George Balanchine's *Var-*

iations pour une Porte et un Soupir, an obvious parody and put-down of the whole genre, shown as luring the man into a trap rather than offering him pleasure? We can no more imagine this man turning down the woman's provocation, though it's an obvious source of anguish to him, than we can see Kay Mazzo deciding to stay with her girlfriends in *Dances at a Gathering* instead of joining Peter Martins at the slightest tilt of his eyebrow.

This isn't simple warfare between men and women. The message goes beyond sexual partisanship. People in these ballets are passive, typecast, abstract. They are prisoners of their own biology. Their sex determines their role in society and their role in the dance. The man is always either a stud or a sensitive ambiguity. The woman is always a calculating bitch or a clinging vine. The ballet doesn't need to explain them or excuse them, or give them half a chance to rearrange their fate.

Summer 1974

Sprung in New York

IT'S ANYBODY'S GUESS what Rebekah Harkness' mural means to her. But the panorama of naked dancers so artfully yet unflatteringly deployed around the proscenium of the Harkness Theater became some kind of symbol to almost everyone who visited the new showplace of dance in its inaugural two-week season.

I'm sure a lot of the audience went just to see the mural. It was a sort of peep show; you had to get way down front in the orchestra to see all of it, and the ushers had trouble beating back the crowds in the aisles. The theater is closed now until the fall, and maybe, having exposed the infamous fresco to us, Mrs. Harkness will arrange for it to go away before anyone performs in the house again. Maybe it will just quietly disappear, as did a huge portrait of La Patronne herself, clad in toe shoes and a drape, that the press saw on a lobby wall a week before opening night.

I used to think of the Harkness Ballet as being a dance company — a rich woman's plaything or fantasy perhaps, but a dance company anyway. Now, with all this advertisement unavoidably splattered before my eyes, I'm getting the message that Mrs. Harkness needs dancers' bodies to glorify not dance but nakedness. The mural still haunts me, as the Harkness repertory does not. The exploitativeness of it, the excess, is a dance critic's nightmare. It should be called "Spring in New York."

The Harkness Ballet seems to be trying to bring to life and extend those images of physicality suggested by the mural. Yet where the mural manages to make overrefinement vulgar, the Harkness' dancing makes passion a bore. Choreographic ideas run to either vapid lyricism or gratuitous violence, but there's a curious denial of aggression in the dancing style, a washed-out look. There's no anxiety, no urgency in the transitions, no bite to the attack.

The same great brush of artifice that collected all those androgynous beings around the proscenium seems to have swept over the dancers, painting them in a climate of homosexual utopia. The women are less attractive physically than the men anyway, and they usually appear in passive, picturebook roles or as witches — Helen Heineman grimacing horribly as the victim of *The Lottery*, Manola Asensio playing the grotesque Vamp in *Souvenirs* as if she were a man in drag. Their slightest tendency to look glamorous is given sinister implications. Jeanette Vondersaar plays the Firebird like a femme fatale instead of a benefactress.

The men are shown sympathetically and prominently in almost all the ballets. In one number they wear low-cut crimson while the women fade away in underwear-peach. In others they seem to have all the biggest, most active movement. Bare-chested, dimpled, muscular, they court the audience, not their stage partners. I never saw a pas de deux catch fire. The men coldly held off or accepted their partners' advances, but never reciprocated. After the second performance or so, I noticed sly little dramas being enacted by the men — knowing looks, postures of annoyance or intimacy, secret understandings passing between them, which drew my attention from the pallid good form of the women. It was as if being with the boys was their real pleasure, while dancing with women was purely business.

The distorted and inflexible image of male and female roles that emerges from the Harkness repertory may be the result of an intentional gay-liberation message, or it may happen quite naturally because the choreography is vacuous and the men in the company are better performers than the women. It offends me to see women being put down so consistently, but even if the sexism didn't disturb me, the triviality would.

The most serious of the pseudoliberated Harkness ballets that I saw was Vicente Nebrada's *Gemini*, a duet for two men of different temperaments. Nebrada sometimes makes interesting use of sculptured space, and here he contrasted one man's thrusting, linear movements with the rounded and spiraling shapes of the other. But a popular astrology book will tell you more about Gemini's dual nature, and any relationship has to be more complicated than this pat juxtaposition of attitudes.

Gemini doesn't reveal anything about homosexuals. It isn't daring. The male duo idea provokes no choreographic breakthroughs, it's just another excuse for a ballet. At every performance there was a similarly mindless pas de deux, plus one or two larger but no less superficial ballets. Margo Sappington's new *Rodin, Mis en Vie* seems to be trying for a vision beyond the pictorial, but there's so much supplementary information that the audience has to attach to the stage action — the names of the statues, their moral, mythical, and historical meanings — that we settle for whatever passing excitement we can take in. The violent works are no less clearly differentiated as to character or feelings than the lyrical ones. There's always only one thing going on, anguish, mass rape, brutality. Ho hum.

I think one reason why I found the Harkness so deadening is that Martha Graham was in town at the same time. Graham is no slouch when it comes to exploring the intricacies of sex and violence. In a way I suppose she made the Harkness possible. Choreographers like Norman Walker and Brian Macdonald use the Graham vocabulary to beef up the emotional possibilities of ballet. What for Graham was a mode of expression became a set of expressive symbols. Using them, the choreographer no longer has to think what his characters feel or how they react; he has the ready-made tools for a standard construction job.

A piece like *Gemini* or Macdonald's *Time Out of Mind* is static. It merely illustrates a situation or a relationship. Graham never does this. Her less successful dances, like the recent *Chronique* and *Holy Jungle*, lack a commanding personal focus, and they get diffuse and complicated in the very diversity of the ideas she wants to portray. Too much that's too stimulating is going on, but never is *nothing* going on.

Of Graham's lighter works, *Diversion of Angels* perhaps most closely corresponds to the Harkness ballet-ballets. The genre is that of lyricism, the idealization of the male and female through pure dance. But where Nebrada's or Walker's dancers reflect music — turning when the music swirls, jumping when it pounds — or enact group rituals, Graham lets you see the music and the group *and* some specific people. Instead of simply giving the three leading women in *Diversion* more to do than the corps or standing them in the front of the line, she shows us individuals, personalities.

The girl in red is spectacular, roosts on one leg forever, cuts a swath across the stage with her enormous strides. The girl in yellow is coy, curled up, fast as a bird. The girl in white is slower, stately, more mature. The audience's interest in these women depends foremost on the movement Graham gives them to do, not on how much the dancers can make of their roles. *Diversion* is a whole dance that is about something. The Harkness ballets offer a tepid movement vocabulary to which a leading dancer's interpretation alone can possibly lend a semblance of life.

When it comes to dramatic dances, of course, Graham is unsurpassed at theatricality, expressive movement, emotional depth. What I found so wonderful, so endlessly inventive this season was the variety of ways she could see people behaving in relationship to others. Her women are not all the same, nor is any woman character the same all through a dance. Graham's women feel and act in a manner that goes far beyond our preconceived female character-types. They have consciences. They get angry. They exert their power over others. They hate, fear, love, exult, despair, hang back, doubt. In the end, they usually become transfigured.

Graham was less detailed in her examination of men's characters, and often her heroes are beautiful, slightly stupid jock-types, like Jason and Agamemnon. She doesn't waste much sympathy on these tin gods and doesn't care if the audience does either. But she is capable of showing men who change too. For instance, Adam in *Embattled Garden* is very ambivalent toward Eve and Lilith. He dominates them at times, but he also can yield. The Preacher in *Appalachian Spring*, one of Graham's most inspired creations, invokes hellfire one minute and laps up the admiration of his four feminine groupies the next.

It's true that all the blessings in *Appalachian Spring* are performed not by the Preacher but by the Pioneer Woman. It's true that most of Graham's compassionate figures are women, and most of her heroines, however villainous the plots they arrange, have been provoked unreasonably by their male betrayers. But it's also true that all her recent central characters have been men, and she draws them more flatteringly. Perhaps she's mellowed toward them, now that she's no longer competing with them onstage.

The Graham company was dancing with all the spirit that the Harkness lacked this season, that, in fact, they themselves have lacked in recent years. Graham's youthful dancers, the men particularly, are investing new energy in roles that we've seen grow stale, and the works seem deeper than ever now. Renewal, revival. I keep coming back to life images with Graham. The dancers make the work live, and the work makes the dancers live. There's more than sex in that.

Summer 1974

Nijinsky, Clown of God

I THOUGHT that nothing of Maurice Béjart's could disappoint me anymore, but *Nijinsky, Clown of God* did. I've seen Béjart's bag of tricks, and found his choreography stilted, his polemics tiresome, and his style overstressed. With *Nijinsky* he was bringing to New York a full-length creation. "Too big for any theater!" yelled the ads, and in the 5000-seat Felt Forum of Madison Square Garden, marvels might have been expected. But even as spectacle it wasn't much.

Nijinsky is a big production but a curiously mean-spirited one. Its ideas are routinely imagined, repetitious, sketchy. It's not much more than a pageant, an inappropriately grandiose essay on the brilliant but simple dancer who wanted only to love and to dance, and who finished his life in madness. Nijinsky, danced by Jorge Donn and spoken, in passages from the dancer's diaries, by his grandson, Vaslav Markevitch, stands at the center of a universe. Characters from his fantastic career and his even more fantastic delusions parade up and down ramps of memory, acting out symbolic roles, and eventually — as he becomes obsessed with religion, becomes God in fact — they preside over his crucifixion.

The whole thing is very heavy on symbols, but the more you delve into them, the less sense they make. Nijinsky is followed around by a sort of alter ego dressed in hobo-clown costume (Victor Ullate). The hobo has four confederates in sequin-covered, stylized Russian clown costumes. Dancers representing four of Nijinsky's stage identities (the Spectre de la Rose, Paul Mejia; the Slave from *Schéhérazade*, Daniel Lommel; the Faun, Jorg Lanner; and Petrouchka, Micha Van Hoecke), represent him in various encounters with Life.

Diaghilev, the famous impresario whose favorite Nijinsky was until he married, is played by a tail-coated Pierre Dobrievich and by an outsize tail-coated puppet, *his* alter ego. However, it's Nijinsky who is the puppet, literally jumping through Diaghilev's hoop, cowering beneath his parental commands. The woman Nijinsky married (Suzanne Farrell) — Béjart doesn't bother to personalize her with her name, Romola — is shown first as a flirt and a temptress, and later as a symbol of purity.

But aside from its poverty of invention and its muddled profundity, I think *Nijinsky, Clown of God* fails badly on two counts. This is the first of Béjart's ballets in which I've seen him choreograph traditional ballet. His own eccentric, rhetorical style won't do for those scenes of the Ballets Russes. And his ineptitude in the classic vocabulary stands out like a sore big toe.

Béjart shows you the costumes and the shapes of characters you can see in any book of photographs, but nothing more. He gives them a few trite steps with a semblance of their original style, and they run back and forth throughout the piece doing the same thing. A big number in which fauns, sylphides, and all manner of exotics cavorted together struck me as a supremely offensive put-down of all pre-Béjart ballet.

If this ballet doesn't honor dance, it doesn't honor Nijinsky either. It depicts him as a beautiful moron with no will or initiative but with a colossal ego. The complex innocence and instinctive artistry of his dancing career, and the intricate fantasies in which he enmeshed himself for more than thirty tragic years are barely suggested.

I imagine Béjart understands Nijinsky, in his shrewd/simplistic way, but he has no reverence for Nijinsky or Nijinsky's art. He reveres only the two-dimensional fiction he himself has substituted in Nijinsky's name. *Nijinsky, Clown of God* shouts Béjart with every step. Béjart the showman, the manipulator, the mastermind. As if Nijinsky, Diaghilev, the Ballets Russes existed solely to be exploited by Béjart.

November 1, 1972

Sacred Grove on Mount Tamalpais

Sacred Grove on Mount Tamalpais is Gerald Arpino's second worst ballet, unless I have succeeded in forgetting something even more terrible than a lurid version of Arthur Miller's "The Crucible" a few years ago in which everyone had hysterics in a multilevel set. Arpino is chief choreographer for the City Center Joffrey Ballet, and his job is to produce whatever number of new, preferably with-it ballets the company happens to need each season. At various times he has zeroed in on the public taste for plastic, rock music, prize fights, romanticism, doom, the Middle Ages, virtuosity.

Oddly enough, he is most effective when he concentrates on movement. When he gets involved with a plot or a message, as in *Sacred Grove*, everything comes apart. *Sacred Grove* is a fertility ritual, with all the references to love, ecology, mysticism, and long hair that can be extracted from locating it in Marin County, California. Arpino's hippies, however, are a lot cleaner than the types you encounter around San Francisco, and they don't ride motorcycles or sell hand-enameled roach clips. Perhaps those tribal customs will be investigated in a later Arpino ballet.

The love-in on Mount Tamalpais starts with processions, led by two nearly naked children, symbolizing innocence of course. Men and women cross the stage, meet, withdraw. The men walk Martha Graham style, with one hip swiveled inward, and sinking softly into the standing leg, holding their arms in a turned-in V.

The women don't do anything notable except pitter-patter around on their toes. Eventually a bride and groom are unveiled — there is a lot of cheescloth in this ballet — and they do a duet where the shapes are mostly balletic but the energy is ground out from the pelvis. The whole ballet is very wrist-y and hip-y, and what with everybody gazing ecstatically at everybody else, even the women look effeminate.

Scarcely do the bride and groom consummate their marriage than their Son is born. The meaning begins to get a little obscure from here on, and the audience becomes restless because there's no more sex. The Son, contrary to everyone else, is red-haired, practically naked, and seems to be awake. He dances with his father and the other angel-men. The mother has conveniently put on her veil again and disappeared.

After a long, meditative time, the Son does a balletic/acrobatic solo — perhaps he's Krishna. The former celebrants spread a great big piece of cheesecloth over the stage and wiggle it like waves. The Son advances through the billows leading a crowd of beatific children, all flashing mirrors from their upraised palms.

Eclectic as always, Arpino has borrowed from such spiritual texts as *Tommy* and Alvin Ailey's *Revelations*. He also relies on that grand guru of pop, Maurice Béjart, for plastique poses and tableaux and for mechanistic groups that pound their heels together or hurl their torsos about while lying down sideways in a diagonal line behind the soloist.

Visually the ballet is very fussy, almost gnomelike. Rows and rows of scrims with irregular holes cut in them hang down and sometimes fly up, and are lit in different colors. The girls have little organdy-flowered bodices over their tights, and the props include flower-wands with sleighbells inside them.

The score was especially written or possibly regrouped by the composer of Arpino's *Trinity*, Alan Raph, and it has a lot of nasal philosophizing accompanied by guitar playing and brass choirs and violins breathing sentimentally in the background. Starr Danias and Russell Chambers danced the love-dedication and Russell Sultzbach was the visionary cartwheel-turner.

November 9, 1972

Scherzo for Massah Jack

NOTHING GOOD can come of a ballet named *Scherzo for Massah Jack*. Lar Lubovitch dreamed up this catchy, radical-chic number for American Ballet Theater, and, as its title promised, it exploited everything within reach. It left me with a leaden feeling, possibly despair, in my stomach.

There is indeed a scherzo in the music (Charles Ives's "Trio for Violin, Cello, and Piano"), which Lubovitch has repositioned to suit himself at the end of the piece, rather than the middle, where the composer intended it. However, if you can imagine such an absurd thing as a scherzo being used as a dedication, and by the kind of character who would conceivably address anyone as "Massah," there is still the fact that no one in the ballet or connected with it is named Jack.

The ballet reeks with references to the Old South: a blond belle in a pink gown, a white-haired, white-suited, arthritic but feisty colonel, two young bloods with dueling pistols. But Lubovitch claims his dance is "a pure dance piece to illuminate the music." This is an odd way to illuminate music that the composer wrote as a reminiscence of his student days at Yale, circa 1890.

In bizarre juxtaposition to these reaction-triggering stereotypes, Lubovitch introduces completely nonspecific dancers in metallic body suits of fuschia, silver, and turquoise, which I took to be his pop-art version of red, white, and blue. They have various themes. Daniel Levins travels in fast turns, knees slightly bent, lower back contracted, arms flailing up and down like a demented stork. Bonnie Mathis and William Carter do a long duet ripped off from José Limón's *The Exiles*. Christine Sarry gets thrown around by Ian Horvath, and Zhandra Rodriguez is disputed over by John Sowinski and Warren Conover.

Eventually these people coalesce into some sort of group,

possibly a dance company or some other community. But scarcely do they achieve some kind of unison when they begin squabbling. The angrier they get at each other, the more artificial becomes the movement that holds them together, and the more it parodies the minstrel-show antics suggested by those other types in costume.

I lost track of coherent thought somewhere around here. The types do their thing: the duelers shoot each other; a woman runs in, falls over their bodies, and a baby bounces out of her arms and onto the floor; the colonel totters after the belle. Lubovitch's idea of profundity is to bring a big bundle or a bag onstage to symbolize something secret or subconscious. At some point the belle and the baby (now a very large bundle) are undressed and they emerge as dancers in fuschia, silver, and turquoise body suits. Keith Lee, the erstwhile baby *and* the erstwhile colonel, is black.

A lot later, the dancers cluster center stage and make big sobbing jerks with their torsos and big open-palmed, eye-rolling minstrel gestures of sorrow. They go out all bent over and creaky like the colonel, and William Carter and Ruth Mayer, the erstwhile belle, wave goodbye, and the music ends with a hiccup.

I didn't like seeing this ballet, and I haven't liked writing about it. It violates you and me and our country by turning our guilt into cliché, our horrors into cartoons, our prejudice into sensual amusement. I'm sure Lar Lubovitch would be flattered if I called him the American Béjart. Except it wouldn't be a compliment.

January 25, 1973

Weewis

CRYPTOLOGISTS and other word sleuths were advised by the City Center Joffrey Ballet management not to guess at the meaning of Margo Sappington's title for her first ballet, which had its première October 27. *Weewis* is not supposed to "mean" anything. I didn't understand the ballet any too well either, but even when something doesn't mean anything it means something.

Weewis consists of three separate duets taking place in overlapping segments, with all three couples remaining onstage throughout the piece. Each couple is entirely unaware of the others, and, with all the fadeouts and intercutting from one couple to another, there's very little thematic unity among them. Nor do any of the relationships progress or develop. Each couple is always doing essentially the same thing as when we first saw them.

Couple Number 1 interested me the most. Look-alikes Gary Chryst and James Dunne, dressed in mod-dyed T-shirts and bell-bottoms, could have been descended directly from the sailors in Jerome Robbins' *Fancy Free*. Their behavior was so uncannily similar to those competing, joking, horsing-around, showing-off pals that I couldn't help getting prepared for some kind of trenchant commentary on 1944 male good-guyism and other social institutions.

But Couple Number 2 turned out to be a black man and a white girl, Christian Holder and Rebecca Wright, wrapping themselves sinuously around each other in stereotyped sexy slow motion; and the third pair, Susan Magno and Tony Catanzaro, were classic 1950s love-hate soulmates, full of abrupt passion and tense refusals.

Magno and Catanzaro also seemed to be Robbins rip-offs, but Wright and Holder didn't. Maybe they were meant as an ideal resolution of the tensions of the other two pairs, but they weren't given special prominence as such, and Magno and Catanzaro had the last word, trading slaps as the curtain fell. The ballet doesn't really end, but announces the continuation of a cycle in all three relationships.

The commissioned score by Stanley Walden used the kind of brass and percussion anxiety music Leonard Bernstein wrote for some of Robbins' early ballets, with added touches of nervously rhythmic rock. *Weewis* looked to me more like a page from an artist's sketchbook than a finished composition.

At the same performance I saw that perennial masterpiece *The Green Table* (1932) for the first time in about a year. It looked splendid, with George Montalbano exploiting the role of Death more fully than anyone since the late Maximiliano Zomosa, who danced it so devastatingly when the Joffrey first mounted this revival. Christian Holder, who's done it a lot in the last couple of years, is a strong dancer but not a spatial one. Montalbano restores to the role that voracious expansiveness, grabbing out for space all around him, that makes Kurt Jooss's death figure so vicious. Some of the audience, after a trippy evening that began with Gerald Arpino's *Trinity*, had trouble figuring out that *The Green Table* is a serious ballet.

December 2, 1971

Interplay

PEOPLE USUALLY TALK about Jerome Robbins' early ballets as if they were minor works. All of his pre–1960 pieces that I've seen testify to the contrary, including *Interplay* (1945), just revived by the City Center Joffrey Ballet. Where his recent ballets are huge and full of portent, *Fancy Free*, *The Concert*, *Moves*, and *Interplay* were succinct and unpretentious. He told you volumes about style — about the people or the times — with the careless aplomb of someone young enough to know how right he was.

From a movement point of view, *Interplay* was a pop ballet — maybe the first. Without benefit of story it picked up the energies and gestures of jazz and applied them to the ballet vocabulary. This is very much what chief Joffrey choreographer Gerald Arpino does now with rock, so it's quite appropriate that the company should have inherited *Interplay*.

Set to Morton Gould's "American Concertette," *Interplay* is very formally structured, using four men and four women on an almost equal basis — except the men are the leaders. Christian Holder bounds across the stage, summoning the group into action. Gary Chryst shows off, then he too gets the group going. Rebecca Wright and Paul Sutherland dance a quiet duet, and the ballet ends with the dancers choosing up sides and having a contest of tricks, which no one wins except the audience.

There's hardly anything in *Interplay* that you would call jazz movement. The idiom is classical ballet — leaps and turns, balances, footwork and partnering. But there's a subtle change in weight and rhythm. Instead of stopping in between steps to adjust their placement, the dancers launch right into the next thing. Instead of skimming across the ground, they bounce and swing. Everything looks more connected than ballet usually does.

Once in a while their energy bursts out of its traditional design into a fast Lindy or a big hip-wiggle or a cartwheel. During the pas de deux, the other dancers stand around the edges of the stage snapping their fingers.

Very small bits of byplay between the dancers re-create the period. When a piano starts a slow blues, Wright turns to Chryst and asks him to dance. Naaaah, he gestures, I'm too tired. She saunters over to Sutherland but doesn't look at him until he takes her hand. The situation is so telling — could this exchange occur between youngsters today? And the casual way they do it, bold but disinterested enough to arm themselves against rejection, is immediately revealing of postwar American kids.

A special pleasure the night I saw *Interplay* was the stand-in appearance of Edward Verso as the fourth man. Verso hasn't danced in New York for over a year, and I miss him in every ballet he used to do, but particularly in this kind of ballet. I think Verso is the definitive dancer of Early Robbins. His body can absorb the choreography's shifts of speed and direction. He senses the contrasts between condensed, spiky drives and spread-out, floating spirals. He lets the changes keep renewing his vitality. Beside him Holder and Chryst look pushy and overtaxed.

October 24, 1972

Deuce Coupe

EVERY MILLENNIUM or so a ballet comes around that shatters all your notions of what ballet is or should be. Twyla Tharp's *Deuce Coupe* is one. I thought I was prepared for this. When they announced that Tharp was choreographing a work for the Joffrey Ballet with her own modern dance company, I knew it would be startling and I knew it would be good since Tharp has been knocking me out with her brilliance and her kinetic style for about four years.

Well, *Deuce Coupe* opened March 1 at the City Center, and I wasn't prepared a bit. Detailed discussion of this ballet will have to await cooler viewings, note-taking, and analysis. Right now, I'm still floating down from euphoria.

Deuce Coupe is based on the soft-core rock 'n' roll records of the Beach Boys, and it uses rock dance steps of the past decade. Its theme, or one of them, is the way popular culture influences ballet and the established arts. But the last thing you'd call it is a pop ballet, in a way. Instead of mouthing a popular style, slicking it up, throwing its banality back for the audience's smug self-recognition, Tharp uses the popular idiom as a tool to jimmy open the sealed vaults of convention. When you realize what she's doing, you wonder how you and everybody who came before could have missed so much.

Because Tharp makes these dancers move! All the other ballets you can remember suddenly seem like dull posturings and positionings, futile strainings after insipid effects. In *Deuce Coupe* the stage seems to vibrate all the time with dancers going. They run, they jitter, they hang, they flop, zoom and slide, they twitch, they spin. They stop. When all twenty-one of them are moving at the same time, you can't possibly keep track of everything, but the tempo and the drive are unmistakable. Anyway, it doesn't seem so necessary to have the dance all neatly lined up and chopped into precise portions the way ballets usually are.

This dance is about the flow and immediacy of crowds as much as it's about individuals doing their thing in crowds. If traditional ballet is a group of people moving together according to a plan, Deuce Coupe is a group starting from a common pulse and creating a momentum, irresistible and unpredictable as a wave.

To establish her dance idea, Tharp puts a serene Erika Goodman among the swirls of other dancers, methodically performing the steps in the ballet dictionary, in alphabetical order. Every once in a while you notice her get caught up in the gushing energy of the mobs. She wavers, hops inelegantly and rhythmically on pointe, or her shoulders start to wiggle. But she sticks to her principles, and you don't resent her for it. In fact, the other Joffrey dancers do a lot of her steps too, and Tharp's loose-jointed dancers borrow theirs. You'd think it would all look riotous and messy, and it does. But it looks inventive and funny and tremendously human as well.

For "scenery" Tharp has hit upon the perfect metaphor; the gorgeous graffiti that adorn New York's subway trains. Half a dozen of the actual artists come on during the ballet and with spray paint they create resplendent murals on slowly unrolling scrolls of paper. Near the end of the dance, they walk off abruptly, and their baroque signatures — like the moving trains where we usually see them, and uncannily like Tharp's dance itself — continue out of sight, leaving us with an empty but somehow livelier space.

March 8, 1973

Outa Sight Dancin'

CAN A BALLET be Art if you have a marvelous time looking at it? Twyla Tharp's *Deuce Coupe*, a triumph in an age of trash, spread a wave of exhilaration across the City Center Joffrey Ballet's spring season. The pop mongers and purists, who loved it as much as everybody else, smugly hailed it as high-grade trivia. It isn't. *Deuce Coupe*, fascinating and fun though it appears on the surface, is also that splendid rarity, an innovative ballet. It is perhaps the first work since Robert Joffrey's psychedelic film-ballet *Astarte* (1967) to demand that the audience overhaul its habitual way of looking at ballet.

Deuce Coupe challenges almost every convention we revere about the structure of ballet, yet it keeps its respect for ballet right to the end. People say it's formless and inexpressive because its form has never been seen before and its expression is so much more spontaneous than what we usually allow the ballet to show.

Deuce Coupe's trappings are modish: it has music by the Beach Boys, costumes that look like ordinary sports clothes, graffiti backdrops. But beyond that, it abandons the rarefied dynamics of ballet in favor of the casual energies of the street and the neighborhood hangout — that's what really makes it so recognizable to us.

Three things are going on here: rock dancing/the youth culture/disorder and cool alienation; ballet dancing/tradition/the single-minded removal of the artist; and some vast, varied province in between which is neither modern dance nor pop dance — a disciplined free-for-all of dancing that is reserved, competitive, exuberant, and stylistically unique.

The ballet opens with a slow, dreamy piano version of a love song, "Cuddle Up." We see Erika Goodman, who is going to perform the steps in the ballet dictionary pretty much nonstop.

Absorbed in their own world, Rebecca Wright and William Whitener do a balletic pas de deux with a strange look to it — steps that are continuous and slightly off-center — arms, shoulders, heads that pull out of alignment and drift back subtly.

When you think about it later, even this brief introduction is unusual. The stage looks bare with only the three dancers on it, Goodman moving contentedly along a slice of a diagonal and the couple almost stationary and withdrawn to an upstage corner. They do two entirely different movement themes simultaneously, finding two different rhythmic sources in the same music.

Suddenly the music swings into "Little Deuce Coupe," and the stage explodes with movement. One by one, twenty dancers come mincing or side-stepping across the footlights, shoulders hunched, heads rolling back on their necks, hands dangling in front of them. At this point you can't distinguish the Joffrey ballet dancers from the modern dancers of Tharp's company.

For about the first two thirds of the ballet they do what are essentially variations of the frug, boogaloo, monkey, and other rock dances. But Goodman stays among them, in her white ballet dress, doing all those refined things with the French names. And gradually you begin to perceive stylistic differences. Or rather, the dancers seem to embroider on the music and the pop steps according to their different kinetic dispositions. What started off looking like a party in the high school gym organizes itself into snaky, skittery lines, like a game of Crack the Whip at a roller rink. Tharp wages a very funny dance battle with Gary Chryst, each one speeding and whirling ahead of the other, and finally hurling their frustration into the ground with heavy, splayed-legged jumps. The Beach Boys sing about Alley Oop the caveman, and people begin looking beetle-browed and awkward, hunkering down and scratching. Big Rose Marie Wright gallops across the stage to "Long Tall Texan," with little Tharp in agitated, hopeless pursuit. "Catch a Wave" sends them whizzing clear across the stage balancing on the flats of their feet.

All alone in a flame-colored spotlight Sara Rudner, sexily aloof as a "Harper's Bazaar" model, does a solo based on the

shimmy-ing, pelvis-thrusting, fanny-shaking motions of burlesque. Before she's finished Erika Goodman returns to continue her ballet glossary with some sensuous, curving stretches
of neck, back, and arms. Two versions of Woman, though I
doubt if either one is precisely what the Beach Boys are describing in "Got To Know the Woman."

All during these sequences of social dancing and fantasizing
on the music, themes from Wright and Whitener's first pas de
deux have been slipping past our eyes, sometimes all but submerged in the torrential flow of events, sometimes showing up
more noticeably in the sections Tharp calls Matrix, which are
always accompanied by the "Cuddle Up" music. This theme
and its variations begin to dominate the ballet. The Beach
Boys sing a saccharine little sermon about pollution ("Don't Go
Near the Water"), and a line of girls makes swimming motions
that degenerate into spasms and disconnected shudders.

Donna Cowen emerges from this group trying to do the
smooth arm circlings of the Matrix phrase, but her movements
are jerky and out of control. She staggers frantically back and
forth on pointe, and is gradually caught and calmed down by
some men who are passing by. She goes off and her place is
taken by Eileen Brady, who does a long, bouncy solo around
five men dancing a Matrix variation in canon.

This leads to an even bigger canon variation and finally
Tharp's own version of the Matrix dance. The balletic line
that everyone else has been pulling slightly askew she now
nudges off even further; the smooth connections get weighted
into swinging, flinging accents. But they're the same steps, you
can still see that.

She starts alone on the stage, and the "Cuddle Up" music
now has words. People come back. Another procession across
the footlights: the Matrix theme, this time being passed from
one dancer to another, each one entering on a later segment of
the phrase. Once again the stage is filled with dancers; once
again it looks disorganized, but contains, in fact, a reprise of all
the movement ideas in the ballet, including Erika Goodman's.

The ending is strange — stranger than anything else in this
strange and wonderful work. Everyone gathers in a clump at

the side of the stage, the music comes to a climax, a girl is suddenly lifted in the air, and everyone freezes. The lights dim out, leaving the group in shadow and Goodman in a follow spot. Slowly one dancer after another wanders away. The girl who was lifted "dies" and is lowered to the ground. Goodman stretches toward something far away and four or five dancers stare at the girl on the ground.

It's impossible to convey in a few words the density of this ballet, its many moods and meanings, its wit and spontaneity, and the compositional brilliance that reveals itself as you go back to it again and again. Tharp's remarkable handling of the flow of energy in time and space seems to be its most original quality. *Deuce Coupe* never stops for a minute. The stage is never empty and never entirely still. The movement spins out in one piece, passing through those parts of the step that the dancer usually aims to hit, making transitions out of what is usually held for emphasis.

Tharp doesn't use conventional stage designs — lines, balanced groupings, symmetrically woven paths and patterns. She does care that the audience see the dance, but she counts on us to follow the movement phrase or the tensions and releases of energy as they flow or even overlap from one dancer to another.

After the first stunned and delighted viewing of *Deuce Coupe*, I've increasingly had the feeling that its movement structure is what is clearest, while its meaning is more ambiguous. At first you are merely caught up in the ballet's drive, its vigor and speed, its jokes and surprises. Later you examine your feelings: excitement was there certainly, and joy. But also some sadness, confusion, even — for some in the audience — anger that it isn't beautiful.

Are the dancers identifying with or commenting on the romantic, rather simple-headed Beach Boy credo? Twyla Tharp is from California, and though she's a little too old to have been a Beach Boy groupie, I think she harbors some nostalgia for the untroubled 1960s American youth they sing about. She knows it probably never existed, even in California, but that may only make her feeling for it more poignant.

It's even possible that for Tharp, classical dance and the

Beach Boys represent a similar kind of illusion: a kid's dream life composed of physically demanding play and not too much introspection, where the most serious problems are taking good care of your feet and wishing you were old enough to get married.

April 8, 1973

Tharpitis

THERE'S SOMETHING endearing about Twyla Tharp's dance that infects the audience. The sour grapes people think it's all being done by a ten-man claque, but I doubt if there's another choreographer who has been as radical and at the same time as appealing, as serious about dancing and yet as downright popular.

Ever since 1969, when she did *Medley* out on the grass at Connecticut College, all Tharp's premières have had the same exhilarating effect on me. For the first few minutes I'm stunned, disoriented, I don't know where to look or how to organize what I'm seeing. Gradually I get pulled into the energy of the piece. A line of gyrating figures careens across the space and magically resolves itself into a calm ensemble. Somebody starts falling over, and somebody you hadn't been counting on whirls into place for the catch. I get excited. I'm grinning. I'm gasping. I'm looking as hard as I can. All of a sudden it's over, and the minute I can pull myself together and think, I decide I haven't seen what's there at all. Then I start making plans to see the dance again.

Tharp takes away your security, all the things you've unconsciously learned through constant reinforcement about how to look at dance. Not only are the dancers using a different movement language, they don't guide you with carefully regulated designs, pauses, proportions, and sequences in their use of the stage and the music. Yet we can tune them in.

Tharp's dancers look like people; they look like us almost. Or anyway like our optimistic notions of ourselves. They're no icy symbols of beauty and perfection. She dresses them in real clothes, not idealized fluffs of tulle or scraps of jersey with a bodice or a collar sewn on. And, released from the confines of standard technique, they look as if they could move any way at all. They sometimes jerk, twitch, go off balance, shake their heads unaccountably. They twist, glide, slump into momentary repose. Most of all they flow.

Tharp's flow is one of the most remarkable things about her choreography, and one of the most consistent. She sees both the dancer's steps and the sequence of a whole dance as one continuous filament of movement. Her dance always has a surging propulsiveness. It skims over the ordinary positions and points of emphasis. The final gesture of a phrase is also the beginning of a new phrase. A departing group leaves behind one dancer to start the next section. The dancer's body is a collection of finely articulated parts ready to pick up and continue the impetus from each other.

I think it's the ongoingness of Tharp's movement that makes it seem "natural" to the audience, that allies it to social dancing and jazz more than to ballet's refined, controlled, parceled-out use of energy. This "natural" flow is also what leads many people to think Tharp is simple-minded: those "Oh, anybody could dance like that," and "It's just improvised" comments that hound every new Tharp effort.

Tharp's easygoing stream of movement conceals — or, remarkably, coexists with — a splendid choreographic mind. You can see her dances over and over again, and the new ideas you get from them each time don't just come from your own flights of fancy. The dances themselves are interesting; Tharp is interested in them. Each one is a new problem to her, and each, in a way, reinvents dance to solve itself.

The CBS-TV "Camera Three" production of *The Bix Pieces*, opened like a fashion parade — no preliminaries, just glamour shots of each dancer, with their names superimposed. These may be ordinary walking-around modern dancers who work in a grubby loft way downtown, but show-biz makes them stars, and they're as elegant and adorable as any other stars in this pink and silver video setting.

The Bix Pieces is about style, about our pre-Depression dreams of riches and fame: the understudy who goes on for the star, turns the town upside down, and finds handsome young men waiting at the stage door with flowers and limousines; the little girls taking dancing lessons in hick towns, who half believed they could tappy-toe their way to a new egalitarian, high-class success. Inside their heads some of them had made it already, and they moved with a concave, slinky hauteur because they knew they were being looked at by the unworthy.

But *Bix* is more than a dance about America's jazz age. It was devised as a lecture-demonstration for Tharp's trip to Paris in the fall of 1971. At last she was going to verbalize about her work, explain what was behind those disheveled, seemingly formless dances. And she did, marvelously, but she was too shrewd and too guarded about her feelings to let the words be read straight. So actress Marian Hailey delivers them in an affected, acting-school voice with exquisitely calculated timing, while Rose Marie Wright and Ken Rinker demonstrate, tossing off the steps perfunctorily. The style, the theatricality are stressed and the message is underplayed.

The message of *The Bix Pieces*, part of it, is that nothing is new in art. So ballet is part of show dancing, Haydn and Bix Beiderbecke live in the same ball park, and Tharp's dancing comprises all of them, rearranged. *Deuce Coupe* says the same thing about rock, subway graffiti, ballet, kids in love with cars, California in the sixties. It probably doesn't seem particularly odd to Tharp that she juxtaposes such oddly assorted ideas in a dance. One thing that sets her apart from other choreographers is that she doesn't try to make her imagery consistent. Pop ballets like *Trinity* or *Astarte* load you up with different versions of the same idea — the music, the dancing, the mime, the lights, costumes, décor — all express one energy, one sentiment. But with Tharp, after you make your way through all the information coming at you from off the wall, you see many possible meanings, many ballets, many connections.

Deuce Coupe in its second and possibly last season looked just as fresh, just as genuine as it did originally. The graffiti had become so elaborate you could hardly read them, and the dance looked a bit exaggerated in spots too. But that's where New York has gone in the last six months. I've about resigned myself to never seeing *Deuce Coupe* again. Future productions without Tharp's dancers wouldn't be the easiest thing for the Joffrey Ballet to cast, but maintaining the ballet's unsentimental drive and its precise disorderliness would be an even greater problem without the choreographer's gritty presence on the stage.

It's hard to imagine *Deuce Coupe* later on, when the subway cars have all been cleaned up. This is such a good ballet that it deserves to be kept in the repertory, or revived for historical reasons. But it's so contemporary that I suppose it'll be a period piece by the end of the Nixon era. Tharp thinks of *Deuce Coupe* as being about kids growing up any time, but there's something very much of this time to it — something to do with lost ideals, with passing into the age of expediency and realizing that nobody believes his own platitudes. The Beach Boys sing about how it's not nice to pollute the water and how we should all save the environment, while the stage is disappearing in a cloud of spray paint and the dancers are sucking lethal vapor into their lungs.

Most other pop ballets use the means and sensibilities of another time to comment on the present or reinterpret a popular theme. *Deuce Coupe* uses things nobody has thought of using, and says things we only half-suspected. It is a product of its time. What it *is* is its message.

Tharp's new ballet for the Joffrey, *As Time Goes By*, is short, clever, kinetic as hell. Also classical and quietly witty. After four viewings it looked very unassuming to me, just a dance-dance about music and movement, the sort of intricate little essay Tharp used to make for her own company before she started exploring popular music. She's returned to Haydn, who must be one of the world's most amusing and fluent composers, and has set the last two movements of his "Farewell Symphony." The piece is a babble of farewells and dance jokes when you first look at it. Then it becomes clearer, but not too clear. Like *Deuce Coupe*, there's always more going on than you can take in at once.

Beatriz Rodriguez' opening solo in silence is allegro ballet laced with those odd dislocations of body parts, those big transformations with smooth, almost lazy recoveries that we've come to think of as Tharpian. As Haydn's minuet begins, five other dancers join her and they slip through a long chain of decorous attitudes and preparations that melt or click into surprise partnerships. Haydn leaves the music dangling on an unfinished cadence, and the dancers redeploy themselves to begin The Four Finales, a glorious rout in which you can just pick out elements of various overworked dance endings, exits, and climaxes, all overlapped and out of joint and meticulously mistimed. Finally, to Haydn's famous adagio where the musicians leave one by one, Larry Grenier spins out an extraordinary solo in one long, sinuous, self-involved phrase of movement, while the stage fills with dancers and empties again. You can't remember where he came from and you can't imagine where he'll stop. The curtain goes down while he's still dancing.

I'm not inclined to take the title of *As Time Goes By* too seriously — it might have come about by accident. A harried person from the Joffrey publicity department runs into the studio a week before the première and pleads: "Twyla, time is going by. The papers are screaming. We've got to have a title for your ballet!" Without taking her eyes off the rehearsal, Tharp mutters, "Okay, call it *As Time Goes By*. Now don't bother me." However the title came about, the ballet seems more concerned with continuity than with time itself. It shows us the bridges between things, the awkward foldings that precede the beautiful unfoldings, the movements that connect rather than the poses that separate. The beginning is the end is the beginning. Amen.

December 1973

They Danced It at the Movies

I DISCOVERED Fred Astaire last summer. That sounds preposterous I know, but keeping up with the live dance in the world doesn't leave much time for movies or nostalgia. Anyway, it turned out neither one of those things was what hooked me on Astaire.

When I hiked over to the 80 St. Marks movie one cloud-bursting Saturday afternoon in August to see "Follow the Fleet" and "Carefree," I knew Astaire in his later role as sophisticate and old-pro song and dance man. The cane and the soft shoe, the tails and the patent leather and the glamorous girl. That part is only a residue, the last lingering glow from the prodigious gifts he had in his 1930s and '40s musicals.

Astaire was a dancer in every way and with every part of himself. Like the Africans or Asians, dancing for him was less an isolated talent than one expression of a drive that could take many forms. He could play the drums and piano, swing a golf club easily, move across a sidewalk or a room with the same bounce he had on a dance floor. Maybe because he was such a total mover, he could impress a theatrical credibility upon the most improbable dance situation.

In his movies Fred Astaire danced on dance floors and stages, but he also danced in hotel rooms, in offices, on the decks of ships, on a bar, in an amusement park, in the woods, in a gazebo, and in places fabricated by the Hollywood imagination, like the gleaming, Tinker Toy engine room of an ocean liner, or the tiered, polished concoction that represented the plaza at the Lido in Venice. Astaire made you think those were all real places, and places meant for dancing.

The movies have always had problems trying to mesh the naturalistic style of the plot with the mannered action of dancing or singing in musicals. They usually either found a pretext for an exhibition — Ann Miller plays a hoofer doing her act — or tried to make the number fit into the plot as a sort of theme and variations — first the couple say they love each other, then they sing and dance about being in love. Or they stressed the setting, a locale that inspired a particular kind of action — Gene Kelly's Paris, for example, or the work-dances in "Seven Brides for Seven Brothers." In the first two instances, the place doesn't affect the dancing at all — it could happen anyplace; in the last case, there'd be no dancing without the specific place. But with Fred Astaire you can't always spot the exact place where he starts dancing.

Still tracking down Astaire, I went to see "That's Entertainment" and found that this attitude toward place is one of the main things that separate Astaire and Kelly. It wasn't only that they were very different types of dancers, but that Kelly's dance became an expression of where he was. With Astaire, the place became an extension of his dancing.

Aside from the fragments of Astaire numbers, and a lot of trivia for future speculation or whatever you do with trivia, "That's Entertainment" is a rip-off at the four bucks they were charging here in the Big Apple. Hollywood-style, the movie flashes on moments, names, faces, great punch lines we all know and love, but doesn't show anything with any development or context. You wonder how they chose what to include. There's nothing of Ray Bolger dancing, for instance, but lots of Frank Sinatra dancing. No Marilyn Monroe but lots of Kathryn Grayson and Esther Williams. Hollywood at its most heavily self-congratulatory.

Every once in a while it peeks at its own scroungy side, but quickly draws back. I love backgrounds, and I would have been fascinated by more of those broken-down sets — can't somebody do a documentary before the rest of the Hollywood back lots burn down? — or more of the footage of movies actually being shot on those monster sound stages. But as I said, I'm not into nostalgia. I want to know what is present in things. The ample coverage of Judy Garland was a revelation, because I could see for the first time, looking at her over all those years, that she was frightened. Her smile wasn't real, and something behind the eyes was always saying Wait, I can't get all the way out there, I've gotta hold back. In some shots it almost looks like panic.

Liza Minnelli, who plays the Younger Generation in the movie, is given sincere, hard-hitting things to say. She hesitates and stumbles over words sometimes, like the actors who play real people in commercials. "Thank GOD for movies!" she exclaims at one point, and whether she's scripted or not, I couldn't agree with her more.

I would rather sit through most Astaire movies — ridiculous plots, jibbering comics, and all — than see Astaire's numbers strung together in a row. I love to see what people wore thirty years ago, and how the sets were made, and how everybody moved when he wasn't dancing. I'm interested in what character types are being perpetrated, and how types get broken. There were lots of rich people in those movies, for instance, and a disproportionate number of servants of the rich — valets, waiters, dress designers, stewards, and secretaries. The rich were either stuffy and talked with affected accents, or slightly demented, which nobody noticed, and talked with affected accents.

Women were often smart and self-reliant, but they knew they had to play dumb with some men. It was also taken for granted that no matter what she did for a living, the girl wouldn't do it anymore after she married. Astaire, on the other hand, always seemed to have some work or other that he never worked at, since he spent his afternoons at the country club or roller rink pursuing Ginger Rogers. He didn't live anywhere permanent either, was always a transient, or if he did have a home, he was never in it.

Movies keep things as they were: that's their big advantage over live theater. They tell us about our past, both as artifact and as reality. The choreography is there, and so is the performance. The first time I recognized dance as a distinct entity in the world — comparable to the movies or the newspaper business, say — was when I saw "The Red Shoes" half a dozen times as a teen-ager. Until I went to see it again last summer, I had preserved nothing of the dance image in the film, but the aura of the *world* of dance was so strongly created that I kept it for years.

Now I understand that the dancing was quite terrible, those snatches of it that you saw behind the story, but the atmosphere of dance still rings true — the feverish changes of fortune, the fanaticism, the luxury and the sweat that rubs off on everybody. The film's morality is repellent, of course. Once again the woman must give up her profession in order to marry, and the incredibly male-chauvinistic climax has the ballerina's husband and the impresario sadistically demanding that she choose one of them over the other — no compromises — both of them will have all of her or none. Of course she throws herself in front of the train. Interestingly enough, the Red Shoes ballet, which symbolizes the movie's plot, tells you that you'll get punished for dancing too. Not only do the shoes take possession of the girl, making her dance incessantly till she drops, but at the end she's denied the solace of both love and religion by her former lover, in the guise of a priest.

I was surprised,·though, at how ambitious the Red Shoes ballet was as cine-dance. It's full of ingenious camera tricks, and in fact, as choreographed it would be impossible to do on a stage. Film can send the bewitched girl running through the corridors of life, getting older and tattered, in the space of a few minutes. It can summon up her fantasies — a man materializing out of a dirty scrap of newspaper, a magic ballroom — as no stage machinery could do. It may be hoky to see the crimson slippers suddenly pop onto Moira Shearer's feet in a trick shot, but that's precisely the kind of transformation that film can make, and what better place to do it than a fairy tale.

I still think "The Red Shoes" is a visually beautiful and exciting film, but my perception of its values has changed drastically since the innocent days when I first saw it. The point is, the experience is still intact for checking. The film exists. No amount of memory-jogging can ascertain what we've lost or distorted of our past, or tell us how faithful what we've retained is to some finite reality. No amount of posthumous knowledge can really alter the event for us once it has taken root in our own image-factory. And no amount of insight from other people can create a fully imaged event for us that we haven't once experienced ourselves.

Or, as someone said to me last summer after I showed two hours of Martha Graham films to the writers at the West Coast Institute for Dance Criticism, "I've read all there is to read about Martha Graham and looked at photographs, but, never having seen a Graham dance, I really had no idea what her choreography was like. Now I do."

If you're shocked that someone reviewing dance for a major publication in a major city has never seen Martha Graham, you just don't know much about dance criticism in America. Newspapers routinely send people to cover dance who are essentially illiterate about dance, though they would scarcely send a reviewer to the Boston Symphony Orchestra who didn't know what Beethoven sounded like. Up to now, though, they've had little choice; the dance literature is simply not available for study.

This summer I decided to see if I could include in our critics' training a survey of dance literature — not literature about dance but literature *of* dance, choreography — on film. Petipa to Monk. You could not have seen all forty of the dances we showed in those three weeks, not in the last season or any other season of live New York dance. Many are not in any current repertory. Many will never be done again, for all the reasons that even highly significant dances disappear from the scene. Many *will* be seen again, though, and those nine critics at Mills College will now have looked at and analyzed those works, learned what period of the past they came from and how at least one company once danced them.

The Mills film series was laboriously put together over all of last spring, and you can't look up the titles in any catalogue, because they came from many commercial and private sources. The series had gaps, big ones. No Jerome Robbins, for instance; Robbins won't allow the films of his ballets to be used for this purpose. The quality of the films varied enormously, and some were stupidly ginked up by arty cameramen. But enough were really valuable to convince me we ought to do it again.

For years I've been saying, like everyone else, that film is no substitute for live dancing. That's true, but it's not the end of the subject. There are some things film can do for dance, things that live dance cannot do for itself. Dancers have a superstitious distrust of film. I think they fear anything that is retrievable about their art — they think memory and verbal distortion can serve them better than accurate records. So they make film and store it away somewhere like the program from a past performance.

The thing is, film is being made, every day. Cassettes, video discs, cable TV, prestige-run movies are here. Despite the often irrational or arbitrary controls that are placed on existing film, a lot of it will eventually be seen. Until dancers, managements, unions, distributors, technicians, and archivists get together to reevaluate the uses of existing and future films, and insist on better filming conditions and techniques, a priceless potential is trickling off into cloud cuckooland.

November 1974

Real Decoy

THE BEST OF Eliot Feld's recent ballets have been like mementos — little reminders of other times, other styles, with hardly anything of their own to say. What's admirable in them is the economy and assurance with which Feld can suggest these bygone precedents. His new work, *The Real McCoy*, is that kind of souvenir.

There is a certain approach to ballet repertory that decrees novelty without profundity. You dude up an old style in a new arrangement, in preference to repeating the old ballets year after year. This doesn't seem an altogether bad idea, except that with each new gloss, the original motivation fades. Soon we're seeing a comment on a style rather than any indication of what provoked the style in the first place.

Feld's *The Gods Amused* is in some ways more palatable than Balanchine's *Apollo* — there's nothing old-fashioned or tacky about it, it has none of the awkward gestures of invention, and no extended discourse is needed to make the point. Just a few quick strokes, poses, flights, and we get the idea. It's a sort of rush-hour version of history.

So is *The Real McCoy*. Set to George Gershwin piano music, the ballet wants to recall — I'm not sure what, but the dance images of famous Hollywood musicals anyway. Fred Astaire is in it surely, and maybe Cohan and Gene Kelly and some others too. But the ballet is no literal rerun of Great Screen Moments.

Feld, as an ordinary walking-around joe, conjures up a top hat, a cane, closely followed by a great-looking girl on a blue satin couch. Before long they're backed up by a dancing chorus of men with bowlers and walking sticks. Eventually, of course, the fantasies are all swept away on a cloud of syncopation and Feld is left gazing up at the rainbow-studded backdrop.

This ballet is about effects, machinery, more than it is about dancing. Everything slides into the next thing with remarkable ease and clarity, and each change suggests a whole catalogue of half-forgotten plots. The bellboy who delivers the girl on the couch comes out of a dozen posh hotels — a hundred. Feld pushes the couch around — it's on casters that roll smoothly — and he and his dream girl, by the simplest adjustments of posture, are flirting on a hotel lobby divan, sitting on a park bench, rowing on the lake.

The girl, Michaela Hughes, is sort of a Gertie Lawrence type, very suave and carefully made up and languorous in a long, pale gown, and she lifts her shoulders and smiles with a fascinating combination of innocence and complicity. No wonder Noël falls for her.

Feld has a nice dance near the beginning, to "Three Quarter Blues," in which he kind of tries out the cane and the hat, as if to prove the inevitability of Fred Astaire, given those props.

With Hughes he does a ballroom number with a funny, stamping-dance middle section. They also do a drooping-yearning "what-if-we-have-to-part" bit to the Second Prelude that moves us up twenty years to Gene Kelly — Astaire never danced about what *might* happen, he was too engrossed in the joy of the instant.

The dancing in *The Real McCoy* is tight, cramped, striving for the right shape. But the thing about the Hollywood musicals that made you feel so marvelous was the way the characters abandoned themselves to the dance, no matter how corny or contrived it seemed. Astaire's most endearing quality, I think, is that.

Feld has said this ballet is a kind of homage or dedication, to movie romanticism I suppose. Yet, unlike Twyla Tharp, who has also paid her tributes to the silver screen, Feld doesn't explore the dancing energy of the past. Nor does he tell us what that past means to a man — or a choreographer — of the 1970s. He just wants to parade the symbols for us to admire.

December 19, 1974

Time Collapsule

TOO BAD we think all ballets have to be big ballets. Kurt Jooss's *The Big City* (1932), once you get over the shock of its brevity and its abrupt ending, is a marvel of succinctness. After seeing the Joffrey Ballet's thoughtful revival of the work twice, I realize it's another one of those times when you have to change your normal orientation drastically, and your visual equipment is not quite the same afterward.

The mode in dance these days is toward expansiveness. Ballets are supposed to be explicit, to linger over the artfulness of their design, the poignancy of their sentiment. We feel cheated when the ideas aren't given enough time to be thoroughly worked out and explored. In addition, anyone who's been looking at experimental dance has been seeing a lot of slow, deliberate movement, repetition, and the continuation of the image over very long intervals. We associate this stretched-out sense of time with cinema techniques.

But Jooss was working at the other end of the movies' development. *The Big City* is not just cinematic, it virtually *is* a film — but a film of the silent and the primal talkies era, when the visual impact had to be strong and immediate and the pacing had to move right along so as not to lose the spectator's presumably tenuous interest. I think it's the condensation of ideas that makes *The Big City* seem over before it starts. In fact, it's fourteen minutes long, only one minute less than that endlessly unfurling ribbon of a dance, Twyla Tharp's *As Time Goes By*.

In the first of three scenes, Jooss suggests a city street, not literally but by presenting a variety of characters traveling through the stage space in very formal patterns. There's a lot of contrasting motion in this design, out of which we can identify the hero, a workingman type, and his girl, maybe a secretary; some top-hatted, fur-swathed society men and women; a newsboy, an old woman, others. But they move in straight lines, usually facing the audience, with bodies held in doll-like poses. It seems so queer and unnatural, until you think how regimented city scenes really are, and how inexpressive the people in crowds appear, pushing antlike on their errands along sidewalks, stairs, corridors.

The workman does a very short duet with the girl, who likes him, until one of the playboys woos her away. In the next scene we see four children playing in the slum street where the girl lives. Their dance is like a faked action sequence in a silent movie — a tip-toe Ring-Around-the-Rosy that melts into a shadowy fight. The shopgirl enters with her rich paramour, who gives her a silver-wrapped box — ritzy clothes in it — and she goes off to change while the playboy adjusts his gloves, ogled by the children and their straight-backed mothers.

The girl and the rich lover go to a night club, where men in tuxedos and girls in poison green flapper dresses and red stockings dance the Charleston. Almost immediately the scene fades into a workmen's dance hall, where drably clad people do a sedate waltz and the hero longs for his girl. He grabs another girl and starts dancing with her. William Whitener, gaunt and slouching, makes you feel the stolid bewilderment and resignation of what used to be called the lower classes.

The scene fades back to the night club; the dancers look even more kinky than before, jerking their torsos around in a frenzy of dissipation. The playboy has found another girl by this time, and after one more dissolve, where both groups of dancers dance to their own music simultaneously, the heroine runs desperately across the stage and out, and the hero glumly looks for her — in the other direction.

The overlapping of the dancing scenes is wonderfully and simply done, by having one group gradually move upstage and disappear behind some black drapes, while the other group is coming forward. What makes it look like a movie fadeout is this use of the *depth* of the stage to make the change, instead of the normal practice of having groups enter and leave at the sides.

It's amazing what Jooss tells us and doesn't tell us in *The Big City*. He doesn't, for instance, show the girl being seduced — the rich man's self-assurance and his aristocratic clothes are enough to turn her head. He doesn't show the betrayal either, it's inevitable. Nor does he have to do anything more to establish the upright character of the working people than to show us their plain way of moving and their gentleness with each other. It may be morally simplistic, but it's technically ingenious.

This ballet will probably be called a period piece. That's a critic-word to okay something you're supposed to respect but don't really like. I don't think it needs that kind of apology. *The Big City* obviously means something to the dancers right now. It's very alive right now to me too, whatever period it came from.

March 13, 1975

For a Minute, the Smoke Clears

EVEN THE BEST-MADE ballets throw a lot of hyperbolic dust in your eyes. It's so hard to see what the ballet is, behind the miasmas of technique, the repetitiveness, the role-playing, the unreality of something so obviously made of flesh and blood. Kurt Jooss's ballets don't indulge in any of that stuff. They are clear and deep and essential. The Joffrey Ballet's all-Jooss performance, celebrating the choreographer's seventy-fifth birthday, was a wonderful breathing space for me.

Jooss has been badmouthed by the virtuosity mavens as someone who didn't know how to exploit the body. He's been dismissed as a "period" artist and greeted with snide ho hums by the sophisticates. What they lack in Jooss I can do without. Jooss makes it possible for us to see the full dimensions of carefully structured movement — there isn't any fuss in the way. He seems to conceive nothing that doesn't resound in experience, but he's not trying to expose the "personalities" of dancers.

His characters are types, his situations familiar. He isn't telling stories, he's describing the feelings that life evokes in us, the complexities of the person behind the label. So in *The Big City*, he doesn't have to stage some violent confrontation to show us the difference between the idle rich and the poor-but-honest workmen of his metropolis. He has them dance at the same time, one group in rhythms of three and one in four. The people don't clash, their rhythms do. They might be able to make some superficial accommodation to each other, but they'll never blend.

In *The Green Table*, all of the characters who fight — the soldiers, the guerrilla woman — do some of the motions of the Death character. They are both the strongest adversaries of Death and his accomplices. The Profiteer does some of the same things as the ineffectual diplomats — they avoid fighting but none of them could exist without war.

I think one reason Jooss didn't use more of the academic ballet vocabulary is that by itself it isn't specific enough. If any character can do an arabesque, it has no meaning. Jooss's movement looks so simple because it is appropriate. It wears fantastically well because it's so true all the way down. You perceive the Profiteer's oiliness, his slippery character at once. Later you may notice his movements are sinuous or the shapes he makes are usually circles rather than straight lines. At another performance, you see that he's not just aimlessly sidestepping the issue, but after considering it from all angles, he zeros in with the deadly speed and accuracy of a hunting bird.

Whatever you may have imagined about *A Ball in Old Vienna* (1932) — if you're thinking of other ballets that nostalgically re-create café life among the demimonde, or the bourgeoisie in its days of wine and roses — forget that. This work, newly revived by the Joffrey along with the only other Jooss ballet anyone can remember, *Pavane on the Death of an Infanta* (1929), is formal and succinct. Its subject, I think, is the attractiveness of a society that works in harmoniously organized patterns.

Five couples are attending the debut of one of the girls. Her two maiden aunts have a husband picked out for her but she prefers someone else. When she dances with the intended, they trip all over each other, but she's perfectly matched to the other boy, and so is the erstwhile suitor to the girl he likes. So everyone gets the right partner and the aunts approve after token opposition.

None of this is acted out naturalistically. It's danced, within the bigger framework of ballroom dances, mostly waltzes, arranged in lovely traveling lines and circles. Dressed in a particularly pleasing color scheme of white, dark blues, and tans, these amiable people are very much alike, but they're neither automatons nor saints. Secure in their community's well-understood design, they're also free to be individuals.

In the *Pavane*, the communal patterns become constricting, even terrifying. This remarkable dance is only a few minutes long, set to the Ravel piano piece of the same name. The

Infanta (Francesca Corkle) stands between a line of men and a line of women courtiers. While they turn their heads and rotate their arms in tiny ceremonies of presentation and respect, she runs and twirls up and down the narrow corridor that's permitted her. She never gets outside the rigid barrier of protocol that hems her in, and of course never can know the safety of the courtiers' regimentation either.

The courtiers, dressed in red and black high-necked, long-sleeved costumes with severe flat discs around their arms in place of ruffles or flounces, take only a few steps in line, always facing front except when they turn and bow to the princess. The Infanta seems pressed flat, her angled-up arms often echoing the wide panniers of her skirt and the tassles of curls at the sides of her head. She wants to move from side to side; the aristocrats are locked into a rut of forward and back.

The princess is vulnerable, overwhelmed by the formidable and cold process of royal behavior. Jooss is saying that the monarch is as victimized as her subjects. Finally she just lies down on her back and dies. Whether she wastes away or commits suicide or what, Jooss doesn't show us. He merely proves that there's no way out.

There isn't any present-day counterpart of Jooss's humanism. Robert Joffrey is to be congratulated for retrieving these ballets, and the Joffrey dancers for giving them to us with such quiet dedication. Happy birthday, dear Kurt Jooss. And thank you.

March 25, 1976

Modern Dance Now

DURING THE 1972–1973 season José Limón died. Martha Graham surfaced after a two-year descent into a personal purgatory, vowing never to dance again but to lead the efforts to preserve her past choreography. During the season more than fifty modern dance companies were eligible to tour with financial assistance from the National Endowment for the Arts, and ten or twelve modern dance companies bombed on Broadway. Merce Cunningham was trashed at Brooklyn Academy, and Twyla Tharp choreographed the smash hit of the year for the Joffrey Ballet.

Where is modern dance now?

We have to redefine our terms a bit. Modern dance, when it was being invented, was any concert dance form — predominantly American — that wasn't classical ballet. You could tell it because it was done in bare feet; people moved in ways that hadn't been thought of before, working more on the ground than in the air, more in the torso than the limbs; their attitudes toward music, subject matter, the body were unconventional; and modern dance was always created and performed outside the established temples of culture.

It wasn't hard to separate modern dancers from ballet dancers — they did it themselves. What they wanted more than anything else was to make each dance a unique statement on its own terms. If a way of moving didn't already exist to say what the dance wanted to say, they found new ways. Each dance presented a new challenge that demanded new forms. The modern dancers were supreme individualists, and they sometimes came to be thought of as cultists because, unlike the graphic artist, who invents and executes in one stroke, they had to train other dancers to do their movement before they could create anything. So the modern dance became synonymous not with a single style, but with the names of the people who were developing styles, and with the dancers whose physical presence made those styles real.

Today the modern dance has long since acknowledged the usefulness of ballet technique for training the body to move in highly specialized ways. The power and flexibility of modern dance have infiltrated classical ballet too. This intermingling has resulted in a synthesis, really a separate style: the modern ballet idiom practiced by a number of important choreographers here and in Europe. On an anonymous stage somewhere, without a program or dancers identifiable from any particular company, you'd have to get down to the fine points to distinguish Glen Tetley from John Butler from Gerald Arpino from Hans van Manen from Norman Walker from Lar Lubovitch — from Alvin Ailey and John Cranko!

In modern dance's early days — which I would define as ending by about 1960 — the choreographer was paramount. But the choreographer was thought to engage in an almost unconscious, even mystical act: he or she made dances out of an urge for self-expression. In 1973 Martha Graham told me: "I didn't know what the word choreography meant. I wanted something to dance." Everything in modern dance was directed toward the realization of this creative urge — techniques, dancers, companies, the giving of concerts and the establishing of schools, all served the moment when the choreographer was ready to work out a new idea. And each new idea, even if it didn't survive in the company's repertory, was presumed to advance the choreographer's knowledge or add something to the dance art. A new dance was a major event that had nothing to do with press agents.

If this was a highly romantic view of creativity, the times favored it. Modern dance in the 1930s and '40s had abundant talents and a need to explore. Economically it was possible to get something done on a modest scale, and to consider yourself an important figure if only a few hundred people ever came in contact with your work. The idea that every modern dancer had within him or her a potential choreographic talent was fostered long after enough alternative styles had been devised to satisfy the most rebellious student, long after the search for new dance ideas became an academic exercise.

After that first explosion of creativity, the modern dance began to weaken. Graham and Doris Humphrey and Charles Weidman and Hanya Holm produced a second generation, Limón, Anna Sokolow, Erick Hawkins, Merce Cunningham, still discovering but also using past discoveries, seeing what styles could do, perfecting forms, getting in touch with their audiences. No one thought they were doing anything but modern dance. But in 1966 a single work brought together so many postmodern dance concerns that I now see it as a turning point, a symbol of a new era. The work was Paul Taylor's *Orbs*.

Orbs shocked and dismayed me at the time. It was, as far as I could see, a ballet, despite its nonclassical movement and bare feet. I couldn't accept the idea that a modern dance choreographer would deliberately make a dance easy for the audience to understand, that he would relinquish the obligation to search for new movement or new forms, or that he would use "classical" music (Beethoven's late string quartets) to create a programmatic, illustrative dance. I couldn't explain the calculated, almost businesslike way *Orbs* looked. Taylor either had to be regressing or going commercial.

Orbs wasn't the first modern dance to do any of these things, but it was probably the first to acknowledge all of them as not merely byproducts or shortcomings of the creative process. Everything that the modern dance had been trying so desperately to avoid, Paul Taylor allowed to happen in *Orbs*. And the act was all the more telling because Paul Taylor was not some failed genius grasping at expedients. If he betrayed the insiders, he opened up modern dance to an entirely new audience which had found the art esoteric and difficult before.

Orbs came at a time of growing curiosity about dance, and it was endorsed repeatedly in the nation's most influential dance pages by Clive Barnes, who had lately arrived at the *New York Times* from England and was having trouble with the more rigorous manifestations of modern dance. Barnes admitted that he thought modern dance was best when it looked most like ballet, and he predicted hyped-up theatrical forms that ideally would borrow from both modern and balletic sensibilities.

Perhaps this was the only answer to the decline of modern dance's potent founding generation at the same time that truckloads of excellent young dancers were coming out of school and looking for action. The *Times*'s endorsement of eclectic theatricality may have only legitimized what was going on anyway. The modern dance companies that originated in the 1950s and '60s survived, if they survived at all, by figuring out how to look more acceptable to their audiences, their critics, and their backers.

In one sense, modern dance now is just going through what happened to most of the other arts long ago. It is establishing a popular version of itself. For those of us who have always taken dance seriously, it's hard to realize that what a lot of people are doing isn't serious in an art sense at all. They aren't trying to be creative; they're trying to be popular. Corresponding roughly to the jazz-folk-rock area in music, pop dance is entertaining, very well produced, and doesn't tax the audience's mind unduly. Pop dance is in its infancy, and trying to distinguish it from art dance is a murky, often emotional process. Pop uses the techniques and staging of serious dance — of the ballet idiom for brilliance and clarity, the modern for expressiveness and currency. Dance critics still review this new form rather than pop critics, and our pervasive dislike or our contorted efforts to get with it aren't helpful. I can see many reasons for the success of pop dance, and I think it's capable of making great progress. If we stopped thinking of it as commercialized modern dance, or pretentious show dance, maybe we'd stop being disappointed in it.

Although dance is ipso facto supposed to lose money — and the entire dance field is geared to nonprofit operation and substantial public funding — pop dance does very well at the box office. Producers like City Center and Brooklyn Academy often use big ticket sellers like Alvin Ailey and Maurice Béjart to offset the losses of less popular companies. But invariably it's the producers who get the advantage. I don't think the companies themselves are making money yet, not on the scale that pop musicians are making it. Nor, under the hand-to-mouth financing of the nonprofit system, can they experiment with their own resources, find ways to reach more people, and make better spectacles.

Very few modern dancers actually admit they're doing pop, but almost all companies, lacking the clear choreographic identity that was the original reason for having so many companies, are adopting whatever else will bring them an audience. Sometimes it's a very individual company style. Louis Falco, one of José Limón's heirs, has allowed his mentor's strong, successive movement to become more lush and round. Falco's dancers have a sexy, indulgent way of moving that turns people on, especially other dancers. He also has incorporated some of the techniques of improvisation and group encounter, including verbalizing. Some of his dances are so naturalistic, in the old Nichols and May style, that you begin to think the dancers are revealing their real personalities.

Falco's modifications of modern dance are polished versions of what in other cases looks like degeneration. Modern dance technique, whether X's or Y's, was especially demanding because it required the student to replicate someone else's movement patterns in his own body. Dancers went around from studio to studio in the early days, to find a technique that fit them. Now most of the techniques are borrowed, hand-me-down, a little of this and a little of that, all aimed, more or less healthily, at producing a mobile, adaptable dancer rather than a more focused, more limited X Dancer or Y Dancer.

What young dancers are doing looks to me more and more technical, and less and less pulled together. They seem able to do anything that is asked of them, except create that edge of assertiveness by which we recognize an artist. They're good at groups, and often develop a warm, easy ensemble style, though what they have to say with it may be muddled or trite.

For the first time in modern dance history, we are seeing a considerable amount of "repertory" — that is, new and old works by many choreographers being performed by one company. No longer does the modern dance company act as the exclusive interpretive instrument of its own director-choreographer and no one else. This is a big shift for modern dance, reflecting again the decline of the overriding artist-ego. So far it seems to work best on a very small scale, when you can concentrate on how one or two dancers reinterpret the work of another choreographer.

Some startling ideas have come out of this in the past season. Ze'eva Cohen danced Rudy Perez' *Countdown* and Wendy Perron did William Dunas' *Gap*, providing new meaning for dances originally done by and for men. Carolyn Brown developed a "score" for a dance called *Bunkered for a Bogey*, in which she provides choreographic instructions in words and pictures, and the dancers collaborate in the creation of the work by making certain decisions that she leaves open to them. A young dancer named Marjorie Gamso has sent several friends fifteen Polaroid pictures of herself dancing, and has encouraged them to choreograph new dances based on the pictures.

All this is very positive, I think. Modern dancers as well trained as the current generation should have the chance to work with different choreographers and think about each other's ideas, and it's high time choreographers stopped hoarding their own works, refusing to let anyone else do them. But as the repertory idea has worked out in practice so far, the big works haven't been too successful stylistically. Not enough attention has been paid to the qualities and performing attitudes that made Limón's work look the way it did, or Graham's or Sokolow's. Companies that do a lot of repertory, like the Ailey or Utah's Repertory Dance Theater, have acquired an all-purpose, technically stunning, and stylistically bland way of doing everything. Their reconstructions overdramatize the drama and leave the movement unfulfilled. The creators did it the other way around. Converting the classic modern dance repertory into staple, contemporary dance is not only unacceptable, it's a rip-off.

The other great breakthrough, and problem, of the modern dance's present era has been public financing. Dance, the least organized and institutionalized of all the arts, was the most vulnerable to bureaucratic pressures. Modern dance was the most vulnerable of all. As an art form it had no traditions, academic structures, or supplementary sources of support to shield it from the appetites of the "public interest." In less than ten years, the modern dance field has transformed itself administratively from a disorderly, unpredictable mob to a set of convenient categories into which the appropriate applications could be sorted and processed, and the corresponding audience numbers applied. Dance is particularly difficult to fund on artistic grounds because there's so much of it, the variety is unimaginable, and the ways of evaluating it are so nebulous. You can hardly get two critics to agree on what a new choreographer is doing, let alone whether he or she is any good. So, government funding relies partly on extra-artistic formulas to arrive at the relative merits of art.

Much of the government subsidy to dance has been wisely apportioned. The granting agencies have been particularly foresighted, I think, in feeding the flow of new ideas by giving small amounts of money to young, experimental dancers. But there seems to be something inherent in the funding process that pulls it away from individuals and toward bigger corporate units. Dance has acquired, for the first time in this country, a class of professional middlemen.

Again, this has hit modern dance hardest. The big ballet companies for the most part have been privately founded and sustained, and have created such unassailably important images that their recent campaigns for public money have commandeered large chunks of the annual state and federal appropriations, placing a great strain on the amount that works its way down to the many small companies. In the places where panels deliberate these things, a big proposal always gets more attention than a small one, a legislator with a thousand irate voters on the phone is a lot surer about which artist he'd better help or not help. So the impresarios of modern dance have played an increasing role as intermediaries in the funding apparatus, by developing markets for touring and by building multi-company "festivals" of high visibility and broad audience appeal. The typical modern dance package is so diverse that no one can complain of his interests being left out, and it's impossible to monitor the quality of any one component alone.

Modern dance has dreamed of being on Broadway for years, and it's always been understood that, apart from Martha Graham and one or two others, no single company would be strong enough to carry a whole season; they would have to join together. Somehow this got translated into the idea that *everybody* had to be on Broadway, and no one company could carry a whole evening's program. Was it the restless, parochial minds of the producers or the mythical, often invoked but never satisfied "public interest" that made this presumption? For many years the free dance concerts in New York's Central Park have offered a profusion of attractions on every program — in 1972 never less than three, sometimes six or more — thus insuring completely superficial exposure to everyone. But al fresco in the park and dance on Broadway are two different things.

In 1972 the City Center American Dance Marathon at the ANTA Theater, produced by Charles Reinhart, boasted "18 dance companies in six weeks — at least two companies on every program!" And the 1973 Jacob's Pillow festival was taking a "gang's all here" approach as it announced twenty-four names for its nine-week season. The Pillow, directed by critic Walter Terry for the first season after the death of its founder, Ted Shawn, also created for me the perfect image of how utilitarian and undifferentiated dance has become in the minds of its entrepreneurs, by announcing that Margot Fonteyn would appear on its microscopic, summer-camp–rec-hall stage.

The sampler approach may indeed attract new audiences, but what it's selling is entertainment, not quality. In fact, some of the ANTA participants were of distinctly inferior quality, and the season was planned so that every night there would be a strong company to draw for a weaker one sharing the program. This not only shortchanges the companies, it shortchanges the audience. Though the ANTA Marathon spanned an extensive range of modern dance, the audience was given almost no help in locating what it was about to see in the thirty- or forty-year period spanned, so every dance had to be looked at by itself. Historically important works and artists had to make it on the same terms as Alvin Ailey. Audiences tended to be partisan — well-known companies drew their own fans, black companies brought bused-in groups — and for every piece you wanted to see, you had to sit through at least one you didn't want to see. Some evenings the factions broke into open hostilities, and other times people just watched everything pas-

sively while munching on snacks and chatting with their neighbors. The Marathon was an artistic and a financial disaster.

I think this sudden jump into prominence has hurt modern
dance. The producers have chosen to underplay the form's
strongest assets — its individuality and seriousness — and have
encouraged audiences to view it superficially. The trashing of
Merce Cunningham was the result.

The Brooklyn Academy of Music, to which we all looked
only a few years ago as a real haven for modern dance, has
discarded most of its idealistic plans about resident companies,
decent length seasons, a really loyal audience, and has become
mostly a booking house. Cunningham's was the last of several
"resident" companies still connected with the Academy, and
his 1972–1973 "season" amounted to a big four performances.

It was Cunningham's choice to do all four programs
as Events, hour-and-a-half-long sequences of dance, whole
dances, parts of dances, in no particular order, with no intermission. This is hard on any kind of audience, but the crowds
that filled the Academy were completely bewildered and turned
off. When they saw they weren't going to get the entertainment bargain they had paid for, via subscription coupons (any
ten events for a discount price), cheap student seats, or theater
club blocks, they staged every kind of nonviolent disturbance
it's possible to make in a theater. One ex-Cunningham dancer,
typically, remarked to me that at least it was a reaction to the
dance.

I think this gives those audiences too much credit. They
didn't understand enough about the dancing to be angry with
it. Their reaction was contempt; just as everywhere else these
days, they'd been sold a bill of goods, and by god they were
going to retaliate. To me it was shocking to see one of the
great artists of our time treated this way. Merce Cunningham,
Joe Athlete, TV Susie, it's all the same — or so the promoters
would have us believe.

Mass taste is not something that modern dance can satisfy.
Now that the opportunity is beginning to present itself, some
modern dancers are going to settle in the pop field, and some
will be very effective there. But we must find ways to allow for
exploration to go on, and in fact to be subsidized as fully as

entertainment is. Public assistance to the arts has failed if it extorts compromises or imposes penalties on the creative artist.

The best modern dance has always been personal, even peculiar. In the history of Western dance, I think, it's the only scene where a whole approach to dancing can be built up from scratch by a single individual, and can, by the force of its language, make inroads on the great classical system. Martha Graham and Anna Sokolow would be remarkable for their contributions to ballet alone, though neither one of them ever tried to make modern ballets.

At the maniacal rate we are consuming everything, a choreographer has to be stubborn, even arrogant, to keep himself or herself outside of the jaws of culturedom. Sokolow has, and, at fifty-eight, she continues to grow. Her *Three Poems*, choreographed in 1973 for the students at the Juilliard School, had the familiar Sokolow look of intense drama rising up out of basic movement, but she's become more sparing than ever with her materials. Time, space, and gesture are condensed and crystallized — like some complex, beautiful stone you fish out of a California stream, the dance seems capable of enduring for thousands of years.

Cunningham has always stayed out. Now, having dispersed his own repertory into some seventy unrepeatable Events, he's dared to deactivate his company entirely until 1974, probably to gain time to rethink its direction. The enormous experimental dance field, which I haven't mentioned at all here, is Cunningham's progeny, though very little of it is engaged in pure dancing at the moment. Cunningham's own dancing and choreography are slightly but unmistakably becoming deeper and more personal.

The spirit of the old modern dance survives, through a blend of Cunningham and the most exacting classicism, in Twyla Tharp. Tharp is everything the old modern dancers were — individual, tough, far out, charismatic. Instead of allowing her work to merge and fade into some facile eclecticism, she has turned the ballet vocabulary to her own account. Tharp's steps and the virtuosity of her dancers may be balletic, but the compositional mind, the use of space and flow are hers alone. Amazingly — or perhaps not so amazingly, since she herself says that art isn't new, merely different — her work is inspired by familiar jazz music and dance styles, contemporary energies, and humor. *Deuce Coupe*'s sensational success can't have depended on its obvious aura of pop, since the Joffrey doles out pop almost every time it takes the curtain up. The success of *Deuce Coupe* was a popular success, but a modern dance victory. I hope the dance brokers were watching.

Fall 1973

José Limón 1908–1972

THE LAST TIME I saw José Limón he was striding across the lawns at Connecticut College, just as I'd seen him do so often before. He was busy rehearsing his own company, and putting the finishing touches on a revival — *Emperor Jones*, for the American Dance Festival's ad hoc repertory company — just the way he'd spent so many summers. But this was 1972, and José was dying. His face had the slack doughy look of catastrophic illness, but his body clung to its lifelong habits; it looked almost strong enough to beat off the thing that was trying to devour him. I didn't speak to him then. I hadn't been close to him, and I knew that trying to remember me and be gracious would cost him some of the dwindling reserve of energy that was left. He had better places to spend it.

José affected you like that. You felt the plain earthiness of the man even as you saw him reaching for some higher sphere, pushing his body beyond its reasonable limits. Everything he did seemed to be on a scale larger than life — and you noticed it especially because he never played the privileged, isolated Great Man. He lived among students and dancers, he didn't ask for special deference. Sometimes you'd see his wife, Pauline, arranging food, rest, trying to get him to spare himself, and it always came as a surprise.

José worked hard, and he made work seem heroic. It was the extra drive in his dancing — the more than ordinary intensity and earnestness — that made him a star. He didn't have much subtlety — at least not when I saw him in the last ten years — but I don't think he was concerned with that. He involved himself with supermessages, superpassions. His stage gesture was characteristically large and open, he focused past the mote in his eye.

People often thought Limón's dance was terrifically pompous, and it's true that he tended to bear down hard on his argument. His characters appeared in all their grandness or villainy right at the beginning; instead of building them up gradually, or allowing them to be uncertain, he wove them intact like motifs through a carpet of events and other dancers. This technique was most effective in *The Moor's Pavane*, where the four roles were almost equally balanced and pitted against one another. The characterizations didn't change, but the tensions of the dance kept rearranging themselves as different members of the quartet took charge.

The drama of equal adversaries was the formula for Limón's long and successful partnership with Lucas Hoving. It didn't matter whether Limón was good and Hoving evil (*La Malinche, Moor's Pavane*), or the other way around (*The Traitor*). Their two personalities were mutually provocative and complementary. Looking through my files, I find that I saw them dance together for only two seasons, plus the original cast revival of *Moor's Pavane* in 1967, yet their image is still with me. Theirs was a performing relationship one seldom finds in dance; so much more often we remember man-woman duos, or even trios, like that of Limón's own protégé, Louis Falco, with Jennifer Muller and Juan Antonio. But Limón never became as closely associated with a woman partner as he did with Hoving. Pauline Koner, of course, was another powerful ingredient in trios and more extended dramas, but if José Limón wasn't dancing solo, he seems to have needed the strength and size of another man to match his own.

He took a fairly conventional view of women's roles. Unlike Doris Humphrey, who often pictured women as leaders or equals with men, Limón saw women as evil and bitchy (Emilia), or as madonnas (Betty Jones in *Missa Brevis*). His heroines, La Malinche and Carlota, operated behind the scenes in a world where men held the power. Women could be soft and soothing, insidiously manipulative, inspiring and supportive, but it was Limón's men who accomplished things. The single exception I know of was his 1971 composition, *Dances for Isadora*, a suite of impressions of Isadora Duncan. Although he marred the piece with a conclusion that cruelly caricatured Duncan's last years, the dance indicates that he might have been moving toward a new perception of the possibilities for the female dancer.

But the male dance always challenged his imagination. Beginning with *The Traitor* (1954), Limón made a series of men's dances that continued developing as late as *The Unsung* (1970). Most of them followed a narrative line drawn from history or literature, but *The Unsung* was more impressionistic. Though the eight dancers were named after American Indian chiefs, the dance was a series of solo variations suggesting different qualities for each character, and it ended with the poignant image of them all rolling across the stage into oblivion, like tumbleweeds across the plains.

Throughout his career Limón worked consciously to restore the male dancer to his former grandeur. He wrote admiringly about the dancing warriors and priests of ancient times, and he despised what he considered the decorative and effete position of men in Western ballet and ballroom dance. When I began looking at dance in the early 1960s, Limón's company was at one of its peaks, and I still remember the strong male image it projected. I thought of his dance as not only masculine but grown up, as compared to most everything else I saw at that time.

In trying to account for this impression, I can easily see that the themes were impressive, the characters real, the struggles believable. But there was more to it. Limón's movement style actually looked more masculine. He liked to have men in the company who were physically big and strong, but he used more than this brute element in his men. Drawing perhaps on work movements, he gave his men a lot of large, vigorous detail in the arms and upper torso, and demanded great agility from the legs and feet. This reversed the balletic prototype where the man does all the heavy work in his legs and makes his arms into elegant, effortless curves.

I am struck too by Limón's egalitarian use of the group. Like Humphrey, Weidman, and others, he showed men and women working together, as well as in separate groups. Limón usually used the company as a mixed chorus unless there was a dramatic reason not to. And what strength emanated from those communal circles in *There Is a Time* and *Missa Brevis*. This was no artificial society, its sexes rigidly and forever differentiated by their highly specialized professional skills. Limón wanted us to see these choruses as men and women, too, not merely as sexless, abstract instruments.

A *Choreographic Offering* and *The Winged* were exceptions to this, but in a sense those were both wholly exceptional dances for Limón, since *Choreographic* was an abstract tribute to Doris Humphrey which intentionally used her own dance themes, and *The Winged* was not only an abstraction but possibly the single Limón dance that had neither a dramatic theme nor a musical inspiration.

These two works, with *Missa Brevis*, were the most impressive results of Limón's many experiments for large groups. He had access to sizable numbers of dancers, through his classes at Juilliard and Connecticut College School of Dance, and he mounted many productions with them. Some didn't succeed, but even when they misfired, these works gave tangible expression to the very special visions of Limón. That anyone could even imagine modern dances of such scope was astounding.

Limón didn't have a light hand with humor, and I think this might have saved some of his more grandiose projects. In 1962 he was choreographing "The Odyssey" — all of it, some people thought — as a long story told in flashback to the faithful Penelope upon the hero's return from his twenty years of incredible adventures. The dance had some genuine comic moments: pianist Simon Sadoff, onstage in the role of Zeus, engineered the whole plot, cigarette dangling from his mouth, like a tough rehearsal director of a schlock musical; Ruth Currier as Circe draped herself sexily on top of the piano at one point, in one of Tom Skelton's reddest downlights; Louis Falco, a very young Hermes, sped in and out like the office boy. Friends who were watching the piece take shape thought this nuttiness could be more than incidental, and wanted Limón to call the dance *Believe Me, Penelope* but he couldn't bring himself to do it. *I, Odysseus* didn't survive the summer.

Like all the great romantics, José Limón took his art seriously. His heroes were always tragic — stricken by their own flaws, doomed, betrayed, or enslaved by others. It's fascinating to me that, until the very end of his mature career, he consistently turned to European, Judeo-Christian literature for his characters and music. Even when his work reflected his own Hispanic and Indian background, he looked for the foreign adventurers whose personal greed he placed in conflict with the peasant symbols of ancient empire: Cortez and La Malinche; Maximilian, Carlota, and Juarez. When he tried to express the simpler side of his heritage, the land and its moods, the folk festivals and legends, he lost his focus, he overchoreographed, got maudlin. Curiously, it was Doris Humphrey who more successfully explored the Latin spirit without reference to particular personalities, though she must have been inspired by Limón as a dancer for some of the color and vitality in such works as *Ritmo Jondo* and *Lament for Ignacio Sanchez Mejias*.

The long, many-sided personal and professional relationship of José Limón and Doris Humphrey is one of the most intriguing in all of dance. Each was a distinct, individual artist, and yet each imparted something essential to the other. It's clear that he was her heir choreographically. He danced and taught his version of her technique. He shared her musicality and her sense that dance ought to be about the progress of man. During the years when she was artistic director of his company, she certainly influenced his works as well as choreographing her own, but to what extent she shaped and edited for him I don't know. I feel, though I didn't know Doris Humphrey, that it was she who gave the company the sense of amplitude, of range and stature that it still carried five years after her death.

I think Humphrey dreamed the dreams — Limón celebrated the dreamer.

I think Humphrey was the greater choreographer. Her movement concepts were inventive and rich, far beyond the way they're commonly understood today. What Limón contributed was a kind of specificity. Where Humphrey's characters were nearly always abstractions or prototypes, Limón's were real or literary personages. She fashioned whole communities, conflicts, loves, ideas, injustices into dance forms. For her the movement was a life-metaphor, and how ingeniously she could pack a phrase or a group pattern with meaning upon meaning! Her dances almost never told stories, they presented ideas, illustrated conditions, built up universal traits of a people or a period.

Limón humanized the things he wanted to say about life. His dance was much more fallible, less crafted than Humphrey's. You could poke holes in his dance argument, see where he'd gone haywire in telling his story, but you could always grasp it. People related to Limón's heroes because they could recognize them. And, I think, people responded to the splendor of his ideals. Humphrey pictured utopian harmony, the infinite versatility of disciplined forms. Limón thought man could transcend forms. Man's unruly will, his limitless desires, interested Limón more than man's ultimate perfectibility. He not only approved of our gaudiest ambitions, he exceeded them.

May 1973

They've Got a New System

ALTHOUGH DANIEL LEWIS no longer dances with the José Limón company, he has to be considered one of Limón's legitimate heirs, since he knows the late-Limón repertory and has reconstructed many of these dances for other companies. Lewis' own company, Contemporary Dance System, doesn't do any Limón works but it does do Anna Sokolow and Doris Humphrey, and I think it's a good example of how the old modern dance crosses over into our times.

One or two of the CDS dancers seem to be trying to dance in the old modern dance style, giving you a sense of the gravity of what they're doing. Most of the others come out of Limón and Juilliard in the sixties, and they look much less rigorous in the body, in their technique, and also in the head. Then, a few of the company are ballet trained, and they place their weight precisely but don't engage it in either a firm, sturdy way or a soft, indulgent way; they don't look like one thing or the other.

The last of four CDS programs at Pace University, which included Sokolow's *Steps of Silence* (1967) and *Lyric Suite* (1953), Humphrey's *Day on Earth* (1947), and a new work by Lewis, *Rasoumovsky*, showed just what this new crop of modern dancers can and can't do.

Lewis' piece, set to the second movement of one of Beethovan's Rasoumovsky Quartets, was like a vaguely abstracted *Tommy* or *Sacred Grove on Mount Tamalpais*. I know there's Christian symbolism in it because people frequently fall upon other people's backs with their arms spread out in cruciform shape, and one man seems to bless his companions, sadly. But the events in the dance aren't at all dramatic. Rather, they're a series of academic-looking leans, falls and rises, slow and lucid and sort of declamatory. No repetition of a phrase gets any different nuance from another. The dance seems to want to create a neutral texture out of which a few specific references can take shape.

Rasoumovsky seemed pointless to me. It lacked even a minimal sense of conflict or asceticism to put its bland sensuality into focus, and the sense of empty if pretty formalism came as much from the dancers as from the choreography. *Steps of Silence* depends less on strict dance execution than on creating a general air of passion and desolation, and here the dancers' sense of each other as a group was a great asset, as well as their timing and their development of dynamic crescendos and letdowns independent of music.

Steps is not one of Sokolow's deepest works, maybe because what she's saying about the lonely crowd has been said before, by herself and others. But her imagery is stunning. The force of her contrasts can turn the simplest action into tragedy. A girl runs in compulsive circles — then jumps into a man's arms, her momentum suddenly cut off. Another girl runs among other people, holding out her hands, pleading with them for something; they never look at her, never move.

As these driven souls run in and out, their clothes begin to look tattered, and finally they're stripped down to their underwear. While a storm of crumpled newspapers blows across the stage, they lie huddled on the floor, inert for long, long moments; then suddenly pull together in one shuddering mass, then lie quiet again. It reminded me of the convulsions of a sea bird I once saw dying of oil pollution.

When they had to harness this intensity to the more technical, musical *Lyric Suite*, the CDS dancers lost most of it. *Lyric Suite* comes from the last great period of modern dance — so does *Day on Earth* — when composition, thematic ideas, and emotional expressiveness through movement were more important than they are today, and more closely integrated in each dance. When you see "acted" versions — like Nureyev's *Moor's Pavane* — you're getting about 25 percent of the dance's original power.

Besides that, I think dancers of that era had conviction, as if doing that choreography made them instruments of a higher intelligence or sensibility. Carol-rae Kraus has this sense of herself, and her performance as Woman in *Day on Earth* was profound and beautiful. Matthew Diamond was serious in the role of Man, created by Limón, but Peter Sparling, who has appeared in other recent revivals, is more masculine, realizes the inherent patience and enduring commitment in Humphrey's movement.

This parable of life, love, work, death, and regeneration is a masterpiece of condensation. Some people consider Doris Humphrey a cold, intellectual choreographer, which may only mean that most of the dancers who perform her work now don't ever get to its emotional depths.

January 30, 1975

Respectable Anarchy

CONTEMPORARY DANCE SYSTEM looked, at first, as if it was going to carry on the dynasty of José Limón. Its founder-director, Daniel Lewis, was a principal Limón dancer and régisseur in Limón's last years. He and Laura Glenn and some of the other dancers had been trained by Limón at Juilliard; they were his heirs if anyone was.

But CDS seems to have become a Juilliard outlet instead. A small distinction perhaps, but a crucial one. The difference between stasis and growth. CDS now is a company of correct, unadventurous dancers who do correct revivals of classic modern dances and produce new choreography of stunning irrelevance. At the beginning, a dance company needs a sense of mission, of breaking ground, of doing some unique thing. To start out punching the academic time card is worse than ending up that way.

What's missing from CDS's performing is dynamism, even

the spurious kind that high-powered professionals can turn on when the choreography gets dim. They opened their week of performances at the American Place Theater last Tuesday with a tribute to one of modern dance's great dynamos, Anna Sokolow. The whole program and most of the season were devoted to her dances, and it was announced that Sokolow will become their resident choreographer.

I'm glad Sokolow will have a permanent group with which to work, but there's something strange about the way CDS copes with her demands. Sokolow's particular dance style emerged in the 1950s, when we were living in a pretty repressed country. The dancers who created for her belonged to the generation that stuffed its neuroses under the mattress and let them fester. Sokolow choreographed about that, insisted that her dancers feel that frustration, that anger or fear or despair or helplessness. Today's dancers, children of the sixties, don't look as if they've ever suffered psychic deprivation in their lives, nor are they going to start doing it there on the stage. And the idea of an academic Sokolow — pallid, dispassionate — is just a contradiction in terms to me.

The appearance of Jeff Duncan as a guest artist in the Panic section of *Rooms* drew this contrast clearly. Duncan was with Sokolow's company in the fifties and his dancing is highly charged, musical. So he's gray-haired and over forty, so you see him working hard to keep up with the pace, to make his stops as well as his starts explosive, to last the punishing thing out to the end — so what. He does the dance as far as I'm concerned.

Rooms — misdated on the program, it was actually composed in 1955 — is Sokolow's masterful portrait of lonely people, people who long to communicate with others but can't. It's about the kinds of crutches, fantasies, and delusions that they construct to keep themselves from taking that frightening step out of their own doors. Hannah Kahn as a woman who entertains a pretend lover, and Laura Glenn as a creature tormented by some kind of demon that keeps coming back and buzzing around her head no matter how desperately she tries to shake it off, were the most convincing of all the CDS dancers, but even their emotional tone was sad, not obsessed.

Sokolow's *Ballade* (1965) is an important work though small and unrecognized. The dance is set to Scriabin piano pieces, and after the costumed romanticism of Balanchine's *Liebeslieder Walzer* it cleared the slate again, getting back to the simple expressive power of that kind of music, unencumbered by costumes, props, or period manners. *Ballade* paved the way for *Dances at a Gathering* and another cycle of romanticism to begin.

Ballade is all running, sweeping flights across space — two couples who seem to be totally absorbed in their partners — and a disturbing something that comes out of the air or the music, pricking at their serenity, interrupting their oneness. At the end they've lost whatever attachments they held so tenuously, and each dancer jumps in circles, alone. The quartet of dancers I saw looked as if they couldn't breathe, even when the dance was most expansive.

Sokolow's new work for the company, *Moods*, was a brief sort of lexicon of Sokolow attitudes. People stand close together, they lift an arm, a leg, a face, but not to each other. People stare at the audience while stepping over other people's fallen bodies. A couple sways with arms about each other and heads straining apart. In the end the seven members of the group are spread out over the stage, isolated as they were when they stood right next to each other. Gyorgy Ligeti's music is fragmentary, but so are Sokolow's ideas. Nothing in the piece is developed into a sustained image.

December 11, 1975

When Is a Mime not a Metaphor?

IN ANNA SOKOLOW'S 1961 *Dreams*, revived last weekend by the Mary Anthony Dance Theatre, a man and woman embrace. The tighter they hold each other, the less they seem to feel, until they are frantically clutching at the flesh next to theirs, as if trying to make sure it's there. A man runs in place, bent over, his arms hanging down. He looks over his shoulder from time to time, expecting to see someone watching *him*. Atonal music of brasses and percussion drives him more and more frenetically until he falls, one hand to his face, as if he had pushed himself down. In Mary Anthony's *Cain and Abel* (1970) Cain watches his parents caress his brother. When he tries to join the family circle, they push him out, and he stands apart, cringing in a spasm of rejection.

Sokolow's encounters are less literal, but somehow much more meaningful. Anthony can only mean what she says: parental favoritism can have unpleasant results. But Sokolow can mean many things because her dance image isn't anything real — it has to resonate in us, in our personal savageries or desolation, before it can make sense. I think a lot of people aren't willing to invest that much of themselves in dance these days, and that's why Sokolow is sometimes dismissed as being about 1950 and the passé Lonely Crowd.

Modern dance seems to be evolving into ever more narrative and theatrical forms, from abstraction and suggestion to representation. I think Mary Anthony's company is caught somewhere between the two. Anthony herself is a member of the older modern dance generation but her audience seems to be younger and more into the surface pleasures of movement. I saw two of the four concerts the company gave at Marymount Manhattan Theatre, and they were a convincing argument for the old days. *Dreams* was one of the rarities of this season, and four of Charles Weidman's *Fables for Our Time* (1948) were the other. For some reason the two revivals were only shown twice each. The remainder of the programs consisted of new dances and repertory by Anthony and company members Daniel Maloney and Ross Parkes.

Mary Anthony seems to be basically two choreographers. In the Humphrey-Weidman-Limón line of succession she makes pieces like the new *Seascape* and Poulenc's *Gloria* (1967). These are very design-conscious dances. The dancers' bodies are angled or curved into very particular shapes, but the shapes don't travel, they don't expand or evolve.

The *Gloria* seemed particularly static to me, possibly because Anthony's phrasing didn't respond to the changing rhythms of the score. Oh, they counted out to the same numbers I guess, but you didn't see the off-balance, uneven quality of fives and sevens contrasting with the regularity of sixes. I'm sure the composer wanted to get at the feeling of these eccentric meters, not just to create an unusual sound. *Seascape* had a nice, soaring bird feeling — it reminded me of Limón's *The Winged*, with a few arabesques and things borrowed from *Swan Lake*.

The other Mary Anthony does story ballets like *Cain and Abel*, portraits like *In the Beginning — Adam*, where the movement is more sensual and psychologically significant. Grahamish, I'd have to say. Somebody ought to do a study of why so much of the post-Graham choreography, including Sokolow's, wound up in catastrophic neurosis or sexual deviation. After all, we're all a little unhinged once in a while, but one anxiety attack doesn't make a suicide. It's as if, once they got those twisted body shapes and conflicting energies to work with, dancers couldn't figure out how to undo them.

The Graham movement idiom, with its constant rubber-band stretching and spreading of tensions, does lend itself very well to dance with a homoerotic appeal, and Mary Anthony's men seemed to spend at least half their time wearing loincloths and Johnson's Baby Oil, and industriously flexing and rippling their thigh muscles.

Daniel Maloney's new *Night Bloom* was a graphic and Freudian version of Genet's "Our Lady of the Flowers."

Parkes, the tormented hero, grappled and groped with what seemed to be his male and female alter egos while a Primordial Figure who acted like his mother kept stalking in and throwing an umbilical cord at him in disapproval. Parkes's 1,2,3,4,5 had, inexplicably, only three sections. First a quartet of women with another woman in the center, doing stereotyped sexpot movements: the insistent hip thrust, the flexed wrist held to frame an elongated neck line; you know the catalogue. Then a loincloth trio. Then the quartet came back, this time with a man replacing the woman in the center and doing the same female come-on.

I don't know how Charles Weidman came to get mixed up with all this body glamour and pessimistic introspection, but what luck that last year before he died he set four of his Thurber Fables for the company, *The Unicorn in the Garden*, *The Moth and the Star*, *The Shrike and the Chipmunks*, and *The Courtship of Arthur and Al*. These small gems of dance and literature reflect the sweet and kooky nature of both Weidman and Thurber. In the world of the Fables the women are all nagging wives who get punished or cute featherbrains who get chased by henpecked men, and the men are all shy, unappreciated poets, and I don't know why the role clichés don't infuriate me. But the style is disarming, the fantasy pleases instead of offending. Whimsy isn't something we see much these days, it so easily slops over into camp. I thought the Mary Anthony dancers were just a shade too broad to catch the slightly reticent, slightly wavering style of the Fables, but they were very good anyhow.

October 16, 1975

Ballet Anonymous

THE LAST TIME the Netherlands Dance Theater came here was in 1968, and my memories of that event are almost entirely tinted gray. Now they've come back, with a whole new repertory, new costumes, sets, scores, dancers, but I find the things I've just seen at Brooklyn Academy are equally forgettable.

This is curious because the company is attractive and modish. The dancers are very good and the productions as slick as a spread in "Vogue." But the choreography to my eye is a vast, inconsequential chain of movements that takes forever to arrive nowhere. There's not a thing the dancers can do to make it interesting. Or perhaps I should say the whole philosophy of this company doesn't allow for the very things that might relieve its dullness.

The Netherlands is the first company I've seen that is completely committed to the idea of modern ballet, a hybrid form that uses the technical prowess of the classical and the expressive amplitude of modern dance. Nearly all dance companies today do a certain number of modern ballets — fashion demands it, and the killing pace at which we're consuming dance — but most companies can still be recognized as either ballet- or modern-trained, or as interpreters of one principal choreographer.

The Netherlands, since its founding in 1959 by the American Benjamin Harkarvy, has relied on the eclectic, balletic/modern sensibility. Though it is a multichoreographer company, its artistic personalities are practically indistinguishable. The company specializes in modern ballet style rather than in choreographic identities or points of view.

In this important way it differs from Maurice Béjart's Ballet of the XXth Century, which also purveys a modern ballet style, with chic décors and dazzling dancers. No matter how annoying or tiresome Béjart is, you're always aware that a person is behind the ballet, urging his ideas on you. You may not agree with the ideas, but there's no doubt that a living, insistent spirit conceived them.

Netherlands Dance Theater choreographers seem to work at effacing themselves as well as the dancers who execute their ballets. They demand the strength and accuracy of classical ballet, the flexibility of modern dance. Yet the dancers don't show off with great displays of virtuosity. Solos seldom bring anything out of the dancer that any of the others couldn't do. Duets tend to be multiplied or repeated with different partners, so that you don't start setting off one couple from the rest.

The dancers have a friendly performing style but they're impersonal. After three performances I couldn't identify a single one without looking at the program. The exact, neutral way they have of doing movement creates a strange contrast with what they dance about. For a great deal of the Netherlands repertory is about sexual conflict and liberation, the kind of thing Martha Graham started looking at through dance forty-five years ago. Graham turned these passions into a symbolic language, heroic, nonliteral, like the fugue or the Ionic column. The modern ballet choreographers, who all derive from Graham to some extent, have preserved her themes and some of the shapes and energies that she unearthed. But the weighty concentration of Graham has been modified by a lightness and a balletic, outgoing delivery, together with a more sensuous inner approach to the movement.

So the effect of a piece like *Mutations*, Glen Tetley's well-publicized nude ballet, is highly exhibitionistic. It doesn't tell you anything much except that dancers like showing off their bodies, without costumes or with them. They use the same intensities and designs as in all their other ballets; their contact with each other doesn't contain anything new.

This may be partly the fault of the choreography, which seems to be groping for meanings beyond its power to show. Or is it that the meanings are far simpler than Tetley's prolix movement vocabulary? *Mutations*, with its heavy message about the confining effect clothes have on the emotions, its ritual smearings of red paint, its homemade-looking films, is symbolic without conviction. It brings the dancers closer to the audience but we both remain as invulnerable as ever.

The most interesting work of the season turned out to be Louis Falco's *Journal*, a theater piece continuing Falco's exploration into the lovable, twisted psyche of you and me, ordinary neurotics all. As a girl's voice begins telling childhood memories to us, the curtain rises on a very dim space where you can just make out some surrealistic shapes — voluminous chairs, buckets with smoke pouring out of them hanging from twelve-foot-high brackets — as if you were six and woke up scared at night in your bedroom.

People come in and play together — follow-the-leader games of laughing, screaming, shoving. Later they get into more personal confrontations and competitions, finally pairing off into perpetually squabbling couples. Like Falco's earlier *The Sleepers*, *Journal* has the dancers verbalizing all the time, often hilariously, about what awful things their relationships are doing to them. The dancers' timing and good-humored physicality served this piece well, although they lacked the spontaneity and floppy familiarity with their own weight that endears Falco's company to me.

The rest of the repertory ranged through Hans van Manen's bloodless, academic *Squares*, set to a measure-for-measure imitation of Satie's three "Gymnopédies"; his low-key, unison TV-jazz dance, *Twice*; a predictable set of variations on a theme of aggression — women's duets, men's duets, heterosexual duets — set to sound effects that are actually named in the program, and titled *Situation*; an inadvertently well-named *Grosse Fuge*, set to Beethoven, with the women in body suits and the men in those long skirt-trouser combinations that Martha Graham invented for her women's costumes.

Tetley contributed a long, flamboyant piece called *Small Parades*, to early Varèse; company artistic director Jaap Flier choreographed a neo-Graham duet called *Hi-Kyo*, in which a man and a woman slithered around in a forest of ropes; and I also saw a desperately cute, pseudo–Paul Taylor piece to Handel by Charles Czarny, called *Concerto Grosso*.

I suppose the Netherlands Dance Theater in all its remote perfection and abstract concern for now topics is a reasonable development to come out of European dance. Where the ballet has worn thin, but the tradition of strong, personal choreography was never especially prized, dance companies have turned to this kind of compromise. It's highly professional entertainment, aesthetically above reproach, and, I imagine, satisfying to its audiences in precisely the ways I find it disappointing.

May 7, 1972

Blight of Spring

ONE COULD DISMISS *Le Sacre du Printemps* as just another locker room ballet. It wouldn't be Glen Tetley's first. At this point in the year I might enjoy making literary sport of a trashy ballet that nobody will ever see again, but I'm afraid Ballet Theater is going to be dragging this one out for some time to come. *Le Sacre* also raises a lot of disturbing questions, and maybe the end of a long, decadent season is a good time to consider some of them.

What is choreography anyhow? Is it an aesthetic version of a basketball game — a series of stratagems for keeping many moving bodies on display? A lot of the audience probably thinks so, and there are certainly enough people who are successful at making dance that way. I think Glen Tetley's success is based partly on his aptitude for these stratagems. He appears to have an acute sense of the borderlines between art and gymnastics, art and vulgarity, and he stays unerringly on the safe side of them, but as near them as possible.

Tetley also has a knack for making something look impressive. His ballets often come with a gloss of seriousness — a philosophical argument, a portentous theme or dedication, a provocative title. In this case, he's chosen the most loaded piece of music of the twentieth century. Stravinsky's monumental work is still shocking, still wonderful after sixty-three years, and even an audience that knows nothing of the various controversial ballets it spawned must be dazzled by its range and power.

Is the choreography supposed to duplicate the music or is that just a form of slavishness that's lost on the audience? Tetley reflects the general moods of the music, nothing else. He seems unable to set a dance phrase of any complexity or depth — or he doesn't think it necessary. His staging looks complex because a lot is going on; it looks as if it's about feeling because the dancers are straining so hard to execute their tasks.

It's this element of physical stress that so many modern choreographers use to incite the audience's passion. Tetley's *Sacre* is violent; his bodies lash out and thrust in distorted shapes, knot together in agonized copulations, or stiffen in a rigor of ecstasy. His dance has no line, only mass. It has no rhythm, only the pounding of the blood.

Yet it's also meant to "mean" something, I take it — something more than just a celebration of rutting time down at the gym. It has "figures," characters who do special things, symbolize other values, distract you from seeing how impersonal the proceeding really is.

Mikhail Baryshnikov begins it. Dressed in briefs, with blue body paint outlining his musculature, he dances a long, desperate solo in which he could be searching, growing, yearning, dying, pleading, almost anything. After a lot of orgiastic dancing by twelve couples in briefs and unitards, he sees Martine van Hamel standing downstage and he looks at her, transfixed, while the others clasp their partners and bundle on the floor.

Just when he starts to advance on her, he's picked up by a group of men and shoved lengthwise at her. The men throw him around, unresisting, and I conclude he has died of mysterious causes. He's dragged out. Van Hamel dances the closest thing in the ballet to a love duet, with Clark Tippet. Baryshnikov is carried back on. He's manipulated into several bizarre positions by the men, all of which I take to be phallic. Finally the whole ensemble forms a line down to the footlights, the women on the floor, the men in a wavelike chorus of Graham handstand-falls, through which Baryshnikov somehow makes his way.

At the front of the line he pushes himself out through Tippet's legs, or between Tippet and van Hamel, and is — well, reincarnated? Alone again, he dances faster, more brilliantly and more desperately. The group comes back and while it dances an orgiastic circle dance, he fastens himself into a trapeze-harness upstage. On Stravinsky's final ascending glissando, Baryshnikov zooms up and straight at the audience, prevented from rocketing through the dress circle and clear out to Columbus Avenue only by the fall of the curtain.

I guess he's supposed to be the Spirit of the Eternal Screw or something, if you consider screwing to be the ultimate legal act of aggression, and if you are male. The women in the ballet are forgettable, passive, except for van Hamel, and her apparent importance to Baryshnikov is never explained. She and Tippet convey something beyond pure biological attachment to each other, but like everyone else their dominant emotion is pain, not joy.

Or maybe Baryshnikov is some sort of sacrificial figure — he does, after all, dance in the ensemble, partnering Rebecca Wright, before turning into a phallic object. Maybe this ballet is a sort of pessimistic Après-Sacre, a sequel to the original in which a Chosen Maiden comes from the ranks to die in order to renew the procreative urges of the tribe. Or maybe he's a sort of modern-day Christ figure, or am I thinking about three other ballets?

Baryshnikov is a truly marvelous dancer. A prodigy. I almost weep at the sincerity he devotes to a role, even so punishing a role as this. Or as thankless a role as being the only living body propping up the most inexorably lifeless performance of *Petrouchka* I've ever seen, the same night *Sacre* premièred. This man is giving us, and ABT, more than we deserve. The artistic decay of the system that offers him to us only makes his dedicated genius more poignant.

July 1, 1976

Myth

ALVIN AILEY'S new ballet, *Myth*, takes place behind a scrim, but that's not the only reason it looks like a blurred old reproduction. There's just enough resemblance to Martha Graham about it to make one see how uninspired it is. Consuelo Atlas is the fresh young girl. Clive Thompson, Kenneth Pearl, and Freddy Romero are the three men she loves, or perhaps three facets of her ideal love. After she's danced with them all, she has reached fulfillment as a woman.

You can tell this because of the gorgeous lighting, by Nicola Cernovitch, featuring projections of bare tree branches that get warmed by an orange solar orb, and finally sprayed with a bloom of white dots as the three men hover protectively over Atlas in a final tableau.

Even in her more sentimental recent works, Graham was never so simplistic. There's always been a hint of mystery or anguish just below the surface that lets you know Graham has penetrated into a darkness before showing you the light.

Ailey has used a movement vocabulary of barefoot ballet — Romero's attitude turns and circling jetés, for instance; modern-expressive stretches and earthward lunges; and Graham gestures. These last Atlas performs with vapid sexuality — raising her hands to the back of her head with a mild contraction of the torso, lazily touching one ankle to the other calf, swaying her hips and arms in something like a fast hula. All of it looks round and spongy-soft and robbed of its Graham power, or any other kind of power. Which may be the point, since many people nowadays love undemanding dances; the flabbier the romanticism the better.

On the same program at City Center I saw Ailey's revival of *Suspension*, a work by the early modern dancer and teacher of almost everybody, May O'Donnell. Ailey's program note places this work in the "early 1940s," which would make it very advanced indeed for its time. However, "Dance Encyclopedia" gives its première date as April 6, 1952, and in the intervening decade Merce Cunningham began choreographing, a crucial reference point for all modern dance. Nobody was quite so far out after Cunningham came along.

Suspension is a very handsome dance, though almost completely without dramatic implications. It designs the bright blue stage with rising and falling motion, weights and balances, masses and lines of people. Consuelo Atlas begins the piece, reaching and pivoting, folding and rolling on top of two upstage boxes. After a long time, six other dancers enter and do stretches and turns, jumps and falls all over the stage, while Atlas revolves on her perch.

Dynamically, the piece is quite smooth. The group accelerates, slows down, but doesn't get more excited. What interested me was the shifting spatial patterns, and the fact that Atlas, fastened to her small spot, seemed to embrace great expanses of space, while the group, with endless room to move, seemed hemmed in by their own bodies.

Suspension, if it's a precursor of anything, sets the stage for Ailey's own recent abstract ballets, *Streams* and *Archipelago*. As always, I respect Ailey for caring about the past and for bringing fine old dances back to life.

December 22, 1971

Alvin Ailey Company

ALVIN AILEY'S fall season is his company's first as an official component of City Center. In the two performances I saw, the company looked more commercial than ever, yet, through excellent dancing and occasionally distinguished choreography, it manages to stay just this side of schlock.

It's a fascinating and dismaying business, watching the company get a tiny bit more showy with each successive season. In Donald McKayle's chain gang dance *Rainbow 'Round My Shoulder*, for instance, singer Leon Bibb now takes some of the folk song accompaniment with a lot of dramatic tempo changes. At one point I noticed the phrase "I'll call your name" had expanded to "I'll call, call, CALL your name!" Of course, the dancers stepped up the emphasis accordingly.

Several new works and revivals were announced for the season, but two of these turned out to be vehicles for the company's stars — *Nubian Lady*, choreographed by John Parks for Judith Jamison, and Ailey's *Love Songs* for Dudley Williams. Ailey may be the first to bring us modern dances that have utterly no choreographic aspirations except to provide flattering steps for popular dancers. Not that Jamison's strutting, sweeping possession of the stage, or Williams' beautifully shaped spins and contractions aren't special. They are. But isolating these qualities from any choreographic context, plunking them in front of us in all their crude, meaningless magnificence downgrades both audience and performers. This kind of excess is what killed old-time ballet.

The one really new dance of the season, John Butler's *According to Eve*, turned out to be another vehicle for Jamison, as was made clear by the spotlight that followed her around, and an initial solo that resembled parts of *Nubian Lady*. Jamison played an alluring Eve in a body stocking and long eyelashes.

Michihiko Oka and Masazumi Chaya were Cain and Abel, wearing dance belts in fetching chartreuse and pink. The dance is a distinctly strange version of the primal murder story. It's pretty clear though that sex has a lot to do with it, and that Mom gets the blame.

But no matter how show-biz Alvin Ailey is, he retains a certain rare integrity concerning his own heritage as a dancer. In a new series called Roots of the American Dance, he is reviving examples of early modern dance choreography. I missed Ted Shawn's famous men's dance, *Kinetic Molpai* (1935), which was taken out of the repertory when a dancer was injured, but I did see Katherine Dunham's *Choros* (1943). Dunham is known today as a precursor of modern black dance, since she incorporated many South American and Caribbean rhythms and forms into her choreography. She also anticipated Ailey as a concert dancer who ran a very high-class but very commercial company.

Dunham's was the first dancing I ever saw, when she was doing Broadway seasons in the 1940s, and I remember almost nothing about it except the color and gaiety. *Choros* lived up to that all right, but in other respects it surprised me. Although based on an early nineteenth-century Brazilian quadrille, with very formal floor patterns, its main character is balletic. Occasionally you see the side-to-side quickstep and the shimmying torsos of the samba, but there are more brisés, arabesques, classical arms, and nice stretched-out bodies. Ailey's dancers are all ballet-trained nowadays and they may be tilting the balance of the dance a bit by merely doing what they do well. Dancing the lead in some performances was Sara Yarborough, formerly of the Harkness Ballet, whose mother, Lavinia Williams, danced with Katherine Dunham.

December 2, 1972

Inner City Company

THERE ARE MANY nice things about the Inner City Repertory Dance Company, but I think the nicest is that it originates in Los Angeles. I wish we could see more of it here, but its continuing presence on the LA scene is a very healthy sign for dance in that part of the country. The two-year-old company, based at the Inner City Cultural Center and headed by Donald McKayle, made its New York debut with twelve performances during the ANTA American Dance Marathon.

Donald McKayle, one of the senior generation of black choreographers, is someone I've always admired for his integrity. He was choreographing black themes early and effectively, but he never pandered to prevailing fashions in black art. During the 1960s he had a series of companies that stayed together for a few weeks or a season, and he divided his energies between show choreography and the concert stage. By moving to the West Coast, where much movie and TV work is, McKayle seems to have gotten his two careers more into balance than ever before. Both the Inner City company and the new choreography he's made for it seem more settled, more fully thought out than a lot of his earlier work.

The company is young, integrated, and beautifully trained. Their style of performing is less showy than some of the hipper modern dance companies. They don't push and cajole every ounce of effectiveness out of every single possibility, the way Alvin Ailey's company does, for instance. This makes for a less high-powered experience, but a more sensitive one. With Michele Simmons as the woman envisioned by the men in a chain gang, McKayle's 1959 classic *Rainbow 'Round My Shoulder* regained the poignancy it lost in a slicker revival done by Ailey last season.

In his early dances, *Rainbow, Games,* and *District Storyville,* all included in the Inner City repertory, McKayle went through the literal, narrative explorations of the black experience that many younger choreographers are repeating today. His newer works are less concerned with character and message, more involved with movement.

In *Barrio* and *Songs of the Disinherited* he doesn't try to show a barrio or its inhabitants going about their funky life-styles. Instead, he tries for a blend of modern dance and jazz or Latin styles. Popular entertainment has already mined these sources pretty heavily though, and I found McKayle more interesting when he was concentrating on the various vocabularies of modern dance, in *Sojourn* and *Migrations*.

I thought of *Sojourn* as an academic modern dance, a resolution of the off-balance shapes and tortured dynamics, with the psychological burden removed. Much as Alvin Ailey has objectified the lyrical, idealized side of modern dance, McKayle here abstracts its tensions. Ailey celebrates the dancer in harmony. In *Sojourn* McKayle's dancers become the vehicle for discord. Led by Leslie Watanabe, the five dancers group and regroup, crouch, spin, flash across the stage as if in a flight from nowhere or a conspiracy that has no goal.

Equally plotless, *Migrations* uses seven women to suggest some elements that might be connected with bird flight — Wind, Calm, Precipitation, Weeds. The final section, Flight, gives them each a short, very virtuosic solo that you might expect to be done by men. These women leaping and turning in seemingly inexhaustible succession demonstrated what great reserves this company has, not only of strength but of imagination.

November 4, 1972

Some Other Stuff That Black Is

FIRST I'LL TELL YOU what Dianne McIntyre's dance doesn't do. It doesn't make sexy, flowing shapes. It doesn't sell you with line-ups or supersonic pirouettes. It doesn't patronize you with arguments you already support. Some people don't even think it's "black," meaning it doesn't match the stereotypical black dance that's an amalgam of all of the above plus ballet, Graham, and rhythm.

McIntyre's dance is black in a particular way that hasn't previously been explored by black choreographers, and that perhaps even McIntyre hasn't fully crystallized yet. Her approach is straightforward, pragmatic. I'd say gutsy if I didn't think you'd start picturing Judith Jamison. She deals with what she finds, develops what she has, rather than striving for the images that have previously worked. I think her being a woman is part of it — not only because virtually the entire contemporary black dance idiom has been shaped by men, but because McIntyre is the kind of woman she is.

There's a moment in *Memories*, her dance of an old woman's dreams. Bernadine Jennings, the woman as a young hopeful starting out to look for work, knocks on imaginary doors, finally gets an offer — to scrub floors. A look comes over her face of disbelief and then infinite sadness. Who me? Scrub floors? You see at once the pride she has in herself, in her intelligence and ability to do better. Then she drops to her knees. She's no slave, and she doesn't have to dance about how grand she'd be if she weren't scrubbing floors. I'm sure she'd react the same way at the chance to be a stripper.

Black women in dance are eminently exploitable; McIntyre doesn't trade on either their beauty or their submissiveness. She's made a remarkable series of solos for herself that keep showing you this indomitable, slightly wild, frail creature who survives, who is not a character but a force. The latest, *Piano Peace*, was shown at her recent La Mama performances. To some blues by Mary Lou Williams, she launches herself into space like an unfledged bird that knows instinctively how to fly but can't make its wings do the right thing.

Her movement is large, almost unnaturally large. It seems to be all reaching, not enough compacting for balance, not enough rounding for prettiness. She seems always in danger of tipping over or coming apart. It's her intensity that keeps her together, and the way she can let the space absorb her lanky energy by sending herself into spirals with parts of her body twisting in counterdirections. Sometimes she seems embarked on an idea that's perfectly reckless, but then she'll fall and hug the ground, soaking up its security in order to venture out again.

With McIntyre, energy is about 90 percent of the job. The dancer has to generate that energy, because the usual aids to catching the audience's eye are absent. The dancers in her Sounds in Motion company have to be unusually sensitive to each other's energy changes; often they don't even work to musical counts. *Etude for Moving Sounds* was a big improvisation with about fifteen company members and students, percussion and piano accompaniment by Babafumi Akunyun and Hank Johnson. The other improv work I've seen this year seemed pale and indulgent in comparison.

Instead of getting into one intensity and digging it, McIntyre's dancers allow themselves dynamic change. For instance, one sequence started with individual twisty-violent jumps. A woman got lifted, then another, then many. The lifters and the lifted drew together into one big mass of people that kept in continuous motion, with one or two women always in the process of being raised overhead or scrambling down again. Another group came out from the side with slow, pressing-sliding steps and made a circuit around the boiling pack. Gradually they raked up all the wriggly people with them, until everyone was sliding and spreading out in a circle. The circle accelerated into fast walking in all directions, individuals falling and getting up again, but more of them falling, until they were all motionless on the ground.

Even if the dancers had a predetermined order in which this sequence was to be done, they couldn't have kept it alive without being acutely aware of the whole group's dynamics and the effect their own actions were having on the group all the time.

This stress on dynamics works for good and bad in McIntyre's more formal choreography. It keeps the group work very immediate and real. Her work in progress, *The Voyage,* is a chain-gang-with-escape-fantasies piece, but the chain gang looks much less like a chorus line than its precursor in Donald McKayle's *Rainbow 'Round My Shoulder,* because the dancers establish their own tempos, build and spend their own crescendos of desperation. The movement isn't designed either. It isn't laid out with the idea of placing parts of the body in certain places, certain shapes. The dancers seem rather to be concerned with doing something — punching, grabbing, leaning — in a certain general direction.

What's bad about it — what I've been saying all along, I guess — is that it lends itself less readily to form. The ideas tend to be diffuse, the dance patterns don't cohere quickly enough for the audience to perceive what they are. As almost her only alternative to these energy-cyclones, McIntyre will lock into an idea with freeze-poses or facial expressions that, coming after so much spontaneity, look more like caricature than decisiveness. So far she shows ideas in their primal and finished stages of development, but not in the process of getting clearer.

April 8, 1976

Riches and Rags

TWYLA THARP'S DANCE is about dancing. It doesn't stun
you with heroes or intimidate you with metaphysics. It's not
decorative in the body-beautiful sense, or "designed" in the abstract sense. There are no pompous program notes or obscure
signals. What Tharp is doing is so plain to see. Yet its very
simplicity draws you deeper and deeper into the work; what
seemed almost too easy is revealed to be wonderfully rich in
invention.

Her new work, *The Raggedy Dances*, was given on the
ANTA American dance series, and I was lucky enough to see
three of its four performances. It's so new, even for Tharp,
that it drove from my mind her last work, *The Bix Pieces*,
which I saw once, in September. Perhaps that in itself indicates how she regards dance.

The Raggedy Dances is a suite, to piano rags, by Scott Joplin
and others and Mozart. There are eight rags, in which the
dancers in various combinations explore the energy and good
humor of the music. The dance idiom is early jazz — understated and meant for listening to almost as much as looking at.

Perhaps one reason for the current popularity of Scott Joplin's music is its lack of insistence. It goes gliding smoothly
on, not bashing at the beat or piling on volume. It makes odd
harmonic excursions and rhythmic hesitations that keep our
attention without battering our senses. Tharp has transposed
this feeling to her choreography. What you notice first of all
about *the Raggedy Dances* is the way the dancers' energy flows
continuously. What they do is more like folk or ballroom
dance than concert dance because they're always moving,
never stopping to emphasize a design they've carved out of
space.

Also unlike conventional stage dancing, their movement

doesn't consist of going from one big body change to another, one stage focus to another. Effortlessly they can shift their energy from wide-swinging arms to jiggling hips or shoulders to rebounding foot-stamps. Often two dancers or two groups are working at the same time with contrasting energy ideas — very fast, skittery steps against cool, sweeping strides; floppy non-chalance against poking, jabbing vehemence.

In the opening section, as Tharp and Isabel Garcia-Lorca swirl in the background, Sara Rudner and Rose Marie Wright travel across the front of the stage several times, first at an easy stroll, then gradually changing speed, pushing and pulling one another. Then, when they've gotten going really fast, they play a game: stop! go! stop! — flipping on and off the faucets of each other's motion. They giggle at the surprise and excitement of it, and so does the audience.

But *The Raggedy Dances* is more than the comedy of disparate energies. There are solos and duets, where you get to see how personally Tharp's choreography fits each member of her elegant company:

— petite, mop-headed Sara Rudner grinning and shaking something at the audience, sexy as all getout;

— Rose Marie Wright, with long, loose bones and half-closed eyes and a slow generosity in her smile;

— Isabel Garcia-Lorca, draping and redraping herself over thin air, as indolent and slightly awkward as a fashion model;

— Nina Wiener, almost balletic except for her short, curly haircut and the smooth transitions she makes between difficult steps;

— Kenneth Rinker, the lone man of the group, neither the dominator of all these females nor their patsy;

— and Tharp herself, a compact bundle of determination and unexpected changes.

There are a couple of larger numbers where the group swings from casual unison to semicanon and back to unison again, or works out multiple thematic ideas with one propulsion, something like a flock of birds in transit.

Near the end of the dance, Tharp appears in a spotlight, dressed in a minuscule purple bikini, and does a deadly serious parody of a stripper's routine. It's a very weird dance — ugly and fascinating and somehow sad. She moves very little, least of all through that expanse of torso, but of course this forces us to notice every tiny undulation even more. I don't know if Tharp was angry when she made this solo, but to me it was a bitter comment on fake eroticism and the overexploited female body.

Finally, when the possibilities seem all but exhausted, Rudner and Wright do a whole new set of dances to the Mozart "Variations in C Major" (the tune we know as "Twinkle Twinkle Little Star"). Far from being a gimmick, this astonishing coda shows the natural connection between ragtime and the classics. They have exactly the same spun-out rhythm, the same infinite capacity for decoration, the same negligence about virtuosity.

Twyla Tharp is a choreographer who thinks. On top of everything else, this is a miraculous gift.

November 12, 1972

Elegant as Old Shoes

THE COSTUMES for Twyla Tharp's new dance, *Sue's Leg*, are beautifully cut replicas of the dancers' own practice clothes, made in coffee and café au lait colors of luscious fabrics like satin. The dance too has an air of elegance overlaid on what is naturally unkempt, and it all comes from Fats Waller's piano playing, to which the dance is set.

Sue's Leg was premièred two weeks ago in St. Paul and given again last weekend at Wesleyan University in Connecticut. I saw it twice there, because the work was repeated at the end of the program, following another new Tharp work, *The Double Cross*. If there's anything better than a whole new set of Tharp dances, I guess, it's being allowed to see one of them all over again right on the spot.

This newest addition to Tharp's anthology of dances about American jazz and popular music doesn't convey anything specific about 1920s or '30s dance styles, but it tells a lot about the kind of class that comes from nitty-gritty roots. The movement is Tharpian — bodies relaxed, mobile, highly articulate in both the large and small parts — but, as in *Eight Jelly Rolls*, *The Bix Pieces*, and *The Raggedy Dances*, it's adjusted slightly to take on the characteristics of the music. Here, it seems more casual than ever, more expansive, like old shoes.

Sue's Leg isn't lighthearted precisely, and it isn't cool either. It just flows along on its own energy, finding ingenious things as much fun to do as lazy ones — sprawling flops look as good as soaring arabesques that swivel around on one foot. While Fats plays a noodling introduction to "Tea for Two," Rose Marie Wright and Tom Rawe banter back and forth, trying out shuffling steps and turns, just getting ready, vamping. Later, when the song gets going, Wright solos while Rawe and Ken Rinker jog around her, one man always arriving downstage center to throw in a little ornament, just at the same instant when the piano is making an embellishment too.

There's a lot of sham insecurity in *Sue's Leg*. People balance waveringly on one foot, but instead of falling over, they recover perfectly — they've been in control of their uncontrol all along. Rinker settles into a crooked-legged split, timing it to suit himself, curving his legs as precisely as a ballerina would keep hers straight. Rawe does a silent tap dance to a song with tap dancing on the sound track. Rawe taps with the accompaniment sometimes, against it sometimes, as if he could take the musical crutch or leave it.

The dancing is very smooth — imperturbable. Wright has an easygoing competition with the two men, seemingly taking one step for every two of theirs, and still staying pals. Tharp's solo to "Ain't Misbehavin' " is all mincing, fanny-wiggling, itsy-bitsy cutie-pie girl gestures, but she isn't really showing off, the way she did that self-absorbed slow shimmy in *The Raggedy Dances*. This girl is a dancer, she just happens also to belong to an era when girls wiggled.

To end the piece, the quartet gets all twisted up, with people sloping to the ground and being hoisted up again very fast, but almost before you can see how intricate it is, it untangles itself and the dancers are lined up hand in hand, bowing. Then they take off for one last chorus that somehow works its way around to the exact same dénouement again.

Sue's Leg, by the way, isn't about anybody's leg. Tharp is developing repertory for her company, having consigned all the old dances to videotape, and this piece is the first leg of a new series of works. It's dedicated to Suzanne Weil of the Walker Art Center, who brought Tharp and company to Minneapolis–St. Paul.

Tharp's other new dance, *The Double Cross*, was made during the company's one-month Minnesota residency. It's a fast montage of contradictory musics — like a drill sergeant barking orders while the dancers make tracks, a pointe solo for Rose Marie Wright to the Parade of the Wooden Soldiers, Rinker and Rawe doing slowed-down calisthenics to Schumann's "Träumerei." There's a big knotted rope hanging above the stage, and at one point two speakers recite a very knotty, theater of the absurd-ish text that may be about the appearances and the realities of things. This is one I need to see again too, but after all, how many gift horses can you get in one evening?

March 6, 1975

There's Always More

NO MATTER HOW much shallow virtuosity or turned-off non-dancing you may see in a given season, someone's always busy somewhere figuring it all out again. Sara Rudner's hour-long solo, *Some "Yes" and More*, made me feel wonderful — made me believe for a whole afternoon that the possibilities of dance aren't used up, never will be used up, and that it was only a failure of confidence that ever made me suspect otherwise.

Some "Yes" and More is thirty-two short dances performed without breaks except those intervals Rudner gives herself for rest. Or the rests may be dances in themselves. I lost count early in the proceedings although for a while Rudner held up fingers to tell the audience what number she was on. The whole thing seemed like one dance to me anyhow. A dance about all the raw materials and all the ways Rudner thought of using them.

She entered the big white room of Lucinda Childs's loft wearing a black silk Chinese jacket, white cotton pants with red pants peeping out the bottoms, and sneakers. She stood quietly for a moment in a corner and suddenly smashed into motion, with a few turns initiated by one flinging arm. It was like blowing off the steam of preperformance nerves — a safety valve. Then she could settle down.

Each section of the dance seemed to start with some particular thing Rudner had an impulse to do, and then it would continue with elaborations on the theme. Some of her train of thought was quite basic — accelerations or decelerations were a favorite way of varying a movement — sometimes she got intricate or even weird. But it never looked academic or compartmentalized. She seemed to be gathering up ideas from herself, incorporating what she'd used already if it suited a new turn of events. Because of this, the dance seemed to get more complicated as it went on.

Rudner first traveled the room, scanning it, circling it, making circles within her circles. She stepped briskly around — I can never think of her as just walking — making each transfer of weight a new starting point from which she could produce turns or little spatterings of foot-slaps. She sprinted across the length of the room, with giant steps that became turns in the air or broadjumps. Along the same path, she did a series of sliding-to-the-side steps and hops, sometimes clicking her feet together in the air.

She did collapsing falls to the side, pushed herself partway up, and fell again. Then, slowly drawing up one leg, she began twisting and rolling over. First you noticed the languid sensuosity of it; then she speeded up, slowed down, speeded up even faster until she was thrashing violently, her limbs like trees in a storm. She began crossing the space again, making big leg gestures that took her into circles and jumps, and sometimes threw her into sliding falls. Then her arms propelled her, like windmills, in circles, and down to sitting on the floor and back up again in one scooping motion.

Standing facing the audience she made an inscription of eccentric wavy designs with her arms. That seemed to suggest a ballet port de bras, which became derailed and turned into corkscrew gestures. In a later variation, she did a similar succession of shapes but held her arms so tense that they vibrated. Then that led her into a lot of kicks and thrusting leg gestures without the use of the arms, and some huge, wild thrashing-around jumps in which, just when you thought she was going out of control entirely, she sank to the floor, one leg beautifully stretched in front of her, and folded her body and arms forward like a dying swan.

She worked herself up to a series of falls, then dissected the fall by slowing it down, then slowing it down more and lowering her body piece by piece, slowing it down even further and interrupting herself, holding back, more, more, and finally spiraling cautiously onto her back as if every inch of the floor's surface was suspect. Up again, she swung herself around in arabesque, with one hand held to the side of her head. She fell to the side, keeping the hand there, so it propped her up when she got to the ground. She lay on the floor and twitched, one portion of the body at a time.

Getting to her feet, eyes closed, face searching the ceiling, she alternated folding her body double in different ways, some of them almost handstands, and lifting her upper body and face toward the ceiling, arms in the air. There was a long catalogue of things that began from hip rotations. There was a manic, stamping tap dance that became a bouncy, easy tap dance. There was an odd period of introspective relevés and pliés that turned into slow pivoting steps with her pelvis tilting too far out and her chest sunken in, and then a molasses walk with one shoulder pulled slightly out of plumb or her head skewed to the side.

Suddenly she seemed to see someone she knew just outside the window and began a talking pantomime sequence of hyperactive gestures, dancing, names she wanted to remember, cheerleader routines. As unpredictably as she'd begun, she stopped and said thank you.

We know what a terrific dancer Rudner is, from her years with Twyla Tharp. In this dance I saw her distinct from Tharp although not denying what is Tharpian in her background — the fine articulation of body parts, the masterful control and subtle gauging of tempos, the ingrained sense of the phrase, and the command of a broad range of dance modalities. Rudner is more space-conscious than Tharp or Rose Marie Wright, the other longtime Tharp exponent. I think this is why her gestural references are so clear — in one flash of motion out of all that welter of motion she could bring to my mind a piece of Tharp's she'd danced in — *The Bix Pieces, The Fugue* — or some other dancing she'd been associated with. I'd also never perceived the force of her performing personality so intensely before. She wasn't dancing merely for herself or for some vague audience-blob out there, but for us, that day in that immediate place. It was almost as overwhelming as the time Merce Cunningham danced solo at the Whitney.

Some "Yes" and More is the kind of thing a choreographer can do early in her career. Later on she begins choosing and winnowing out and refining — she gets clearer perhaps, and more effective with what she needs to say. But for us it's fine to share her vistas right at the beginning.

February 26, 1976

The Harsh and Splendid Heroines
of Martha Graham

MARTHA GRAHAM'S MIND is a transforming mind. She converts literary, historical, and social images into danced reality. Although it's impossible to identify the process of creating a dance with complete accuracy, we know that some choreographers begin with a personal statement or observation and then have to find a theme and a style by which to make it. Some choreographers say they work purely from a movement or a musical impulse — people as diverse as Merce Cunningham and Anna Sokolow, George Balanchine and Twyla Tharp. There are ballets that bring celebrated sculptures to life, and ballets that put stories into motion, and ballets that attempt to suggest a bygone period or a way of living.

Graham seems to start with the world's messages, then she states them in personal terms. I don't know of another choreographer as literary as Graham and at the same time as theatrical, as universal in the themes that inspire her and as personal in the method of translating those themes.

Like Stravinsky's, Martha Graham's range is as important as her endurance. Graham may be the first American dance artist to survive into her own posterity. Other choreographers have lived a long time, but only Graham has created a continuously strong body of work that keeps regenerating itself on new dancers, finding new partisans. The New York spring season at the Mark Hellinger Theater spanned almost thirty-five years of protean work and attracted large, appreciative audiences. Opening night Graham remembered that she'd once told a disapproving friend after an early concert: "I'll keep it up as long as I have an audience." The force of her personality probably won her adherents in those first years when her work was so radical. But behind that presence was and is a marvelously comprehensive intelligence that is evident now in the scope of the repertory.

A Graham dance looks nothing like a ballet or any other Western theater dancing I can think of. It's basically a soloistic form. The action centers on one person at a time, or at the most two. When any more people than that are active on a Graham scene, they usually assume choral patterns, losing their individuality in order to merge with the group. There aren't any real group interactions in Graham, as there are in Antony Tudor, for instance, where you often see several movement ideas or expressions contributing to the progress of a scene.

For a body of work the stature of Graham's, the dances are unexpectedly small. In several of the fourteen works given last spring, the principal dancers outnumber or equal the members of the chorus; some dances have only two, three, or four principal dancers and no chorus; and almost none of them has more than ten dancers in all. This must have come about in part because Graham's company was limited in size — even now she has only twenty-six dancers, about one third of what a major ballet company can get away with. And, of course, until the past decade or so, Graham herself was the central figure in her own work. Even when not choreographing for herself, she made movement that was essentially self-generated and self-directed. The dancer moves to call attention to herself, to define her immediate state or attitude. Graham's choruses, like traditional ballet choruses, are multiples of one, or sometimes multiples of male-female duets. She didn't think of a group as a collection of individuals or interwoven musical motifs as Doris Humphrey did.

Whether the dance is about a Martha-figure and her subordinate characters, or about a small group of related individuals with a unison chorus commenting on their actions, it proceeds in episodic fashion, one self-contained scene after another. The intensity of each episode is kept concentrated. So few characters have to carry the whole import of the dance that each one becomes crucial.

Graham often leaves the dancers onstage when they aren't

dancing. There they become frozen observers or efface themselves entirely. The main action gains even more potency because of this constant presence of the other figures in the story. The characters can't escape their past or their community or their fate, whatever those temporarily suspended, brooding presences represent. The typical Graham dance doesn't have the kind of continuity and flow that is created when dancers enter and exit in a freer, more overlapping kind of timing and grouping. It doesn't give you a sense of belonging to any other place, or having any other existence, than the one you see at that moment, in that space.

Within this rather severe and particularized framework, Graham's dances speak of the American temperament; of religion, rite, and atavism; of the anguish of artists and the obligations of kings; and of woman's struggle for dominance without guilt. Graham's dance is above all personal, and because it reflects a far-reaching mind and sensibility most of it traverses the nebulous line between work that is merely insular or eccentric and work of genius.

I think before anything else about Graham's dance crystalized, her movement language did. Within five years after she left Denishawn and began choreographing on her own, she was moving in a way that was unique. The earliest of her dances that could still be seen in recent years — on film or in short-lived revivals — showed her using the body much as she does now, although the style has gradually moderated, softened. Where ballet dancers and "expressive dancers" up to the 1920s had looked for harmony in the body, Graham exposed its discord. Her shapes and pathways were twisted, angular. Instead of concealing the dancer's exertion and trying to make her look serene, Graham made dancers use their tensions, show their power. She kept movement close to the center of the body; the dancer had to do more than move to another spot to change her relationship to others.

As her company grew, as her thematic focus broadened from the concerns of one individual to the transactions of groups and societies, this same way of moving served to define character and situation. Through movement, Graham externalized her own emotional states into something that could stand for much more.

Jason (*Cave of the Heart*) and Agamemnon (*Clytemnestra*) don't walk, they strut. They spread their elbows and clench their fists and their bodies bend only from the tops of the legs. When Graham mocks them, she mocks the arrogance of all kings and the rigidity of kingly succession. Medea's Princess-rival is quick, rounded, playful, but also vain and credulous, while Medea is contorted with jealousy, and shrewd as her obsession can make her. The center of the body, especially in Graham's women, tells you what is going on. They shrink back in fear, narrow themselves in repressed fury, wriggle seductively, flatten out, and expand in their rare moments of calm.

Graham may start out with very specific plots or legends, but there's always more in what the characters do than mere reenactment. *El Penitente* (1940) is a little passion play for three peasants in a flagellant sect in the Southwest. One man plays the role of man the sinner, a woman is Eve and the Marys, and another man a black-robed Christ-figure in a sad mask crowned with thorns. The Christ-figure is very straight up and down, even dancing a lot of the time on the balls of his feet. He towers over the Penitent, chastizes him with a gentle slap, walks spread out like a cruciform, tilting from side to side, as if he were a bit vulnerable or could be swayed. This is not at all the way Christ is pictured in traditional art, but it's one way a naive Indian might imagine a benevolent, paternal deity.

Deaths and Entrances (1943) started out to be a dance about the Brontë sisters — I'm not sure Graham ever considered the black sheep Brontë brother, who also secretly wrote stories all his life. As the dance evolved, though, it lost whatever specific references it ever had to the events at Haworth parsonage; Graham has said the Brontës were only a springboard. What the dance does tell you about is three women trapped by their own indecisiveness and gentility. The women fondle objects that seem to suggest action, but they're unable to act. Characters not definitely real or fictional run in and out, little encounters take place and are broken off, rivalries are intimated but quickly contained.

In one terrible moment at the end, one of the sisters, alone onstage and temporarily free of all the other lives that have been constantly encroaching on her own, gives way to her frustration. She ought to stomp around or smash something, but no, she keeps her rage all inside her body. Shuddering and wrenching, as if she would tear herself to bits from the inside, she hovers over the chess board where the endless familial game is played. She makes little stabbing gestures and steps, pulls back, not daring to breach the boundaries that her mind has constructed. Then it's over, the sisters return, the game begins again. The pattern continues.

It must have been the appalling proprieties of being a minister's daughter in the nineteenth century that drew Graham to the Brontës in the first place. The artist struggling to get liberated from the Puritan's body *is* Graham. Though she no longer practices any religion, she still reveres much that religion represents. She seems, on a more or less visible level in her dances, always to be grappling with the confinement versus the security imposed by tradition, the disastrous results of trying to conceal one's nonconformity, and the bliss of being able to give in to a higher authority.

When I visited her a few weeks after the spring season, she looked anything but a Puritan, wearing a spectacular emerald green caftan with the kind of confidence in her own glamour that some women possess even if they're not beautiful or young. Graham was in a mood for reminiscing, and she spoke without rancor of her Presbyterian forebears. She told me the Ancestress in her Emily Dickinson dance, *Letter to the World* (1940), had been modeled after her grandmother, a "severe but just" woman who always wore black. "It's a death image, a fear of death," she said. "Children are afraid of people in black. I never touch a child when I'm in my black practice clothes." And she recalled the stern dicta of New England preachers like Jonathan Edwards and Cotton Mather, who promised that man was nothing but "a spider in the hand of God. He's holding you over a flame and he can drop you in if he wants to." Their terrorizing sermons led to the creation of the Revivalist in *Appalachian Spring* (1944). "Fortunately I didn't know many preachers," Graham told me dispassionately.

Graham remembers, as a child, kneeling for morning prayers at home and peeking at her grandmother through the rungs of a chair. She also remembers that "very remote and dignified" lady, in her high-buttoned black dress, sitting right down on the ground in Needles, Arizona, on a very hot day, when the train that was carrying the family across the country broke down. The mixture of intimidating authority and ridiculousness in these images found its way into her dance.

But the dread and the revulsion came out too — in the huge, lurching, monster-strides of the Ancestress, a creature without any resilience in her movement at all, who stifles all chances of escape, breaks apart lovers, presides over funeral processions as if they were orgies. And in the demonic, hellfire frenzy that takes possession of the Revivalist when he's supposed to be preaching a wedding sermon. Yet even in these grisly portraits there is comfort. The Ancestress cradles a momentarily frightened Emily between her knees, and the Revivalist in his stiff, comical way, flirts with four adoring little choir girls.

I was delighted and a little amazed to hear these stories, for I'd always thought Graham's message was so lofty, so cerebral. There does seem to be a breaking point in her total output, when her sources became less personal and more literary. Up to the mid-1940s her dances were drawn from her American heritage, from her political and emotional sympathies, and from real or theatrical characters with whom Graham identified. The scenarios must have developed from her imagination, like *Appalachian Spring*, or been suggested very freely by assorted written texts, like *Letter to the World* and *American Document*.

It would take a critical biographer to investigate thoroughly all the reasons why Graham's approach changed in the forties. But after the small transitional works, *Hérodiade*, *Dark Meadow*, and *Errand Into the Maze*, she stopped doing dances about herself in reference to Mankind, and did dances about Mankind as represented by herself and her company. All her famous Greek pieces were made after 1944, all her dances about Judeo-Christian protagonists — Judith, Saint Joan, Samson Agonistes, and others — and all her big, abstract lyric dances for the group. In these latter works, one feels her intellect at work making connections. The psyche she probes is universal, interpreted by Freud, Jung, and the explicators of myth. The journeys back into her own memory and experience seem fewer and more generalized. Graham was deliberately making her characters larger than life; they didn't merely act out our passions, they symbolized our moral and emotional conflicts.

In *Errand Into the Maze* (1947) we can almost see this extrapolation taking place. *Errand* is a duet, a very strange duet. The man doesn't court the woman in any conventional sense, although what she interprets as hostile advances could be his attempts to seduce her. A huge bone or a branch or yoke spans the man's shoulders, and he must keep his arms wrapped around it, but robbed of his arms and hands he's still a formidable attacker. The woman is alone at the beginning of the dance, and survives alone at the end, having wrestled the man to the ground after a decisive third encounter. Narrow and tentative in her body at first, nervously poking and slithering through space, at the end she swings open her lower body, pelvis and leg, in wide, slow figure eights, as she gazes out of the entrance to the maze.

I've tried to be very factual in my description, to tell nothing but what you see on the stage, but Graham's imagery is so forceful that it can't always be separated from the actuality. There is no real maze; the woman steps along a serpentine path made by a tape laid on the floor. Later she pulls the tape up and slings it back and forth between two branches of a tree-like structure, barring herself inside, or keeping the man out. After vanquishing the man, she undoes the tape and frees herself.

A program note for *Errand Into the Maze* tells us that in this dance "the heart" does battle with "the Creature of Fear," without naming or attaching this heart or this Creature to any known persons. But we do know, perhaps from the dance's title, that it's a reference to the Greek legend of Theseus and the Minotaur. In a brilliant stroke, Graham shifted the whole focus of the myth by making the Creature's antagonist a woman. Gone is the standard tale of a hero who saves his people by seeking out an oppressor in its lair. Now it is an investigation of the hero's — heroine's — mind; her inner state of fear and tension, her positive action in going to confront the thing she fears.

Ariadne's thread, which in the myth provided an escape route for the hero, has become a path the woman embarks on to get in touch with danger, a path she no longer needs to retrace after she has arrived at the heart of her fear. We don't know if the dance is "about" making yourself do something you're afraid of doing, or "about" traveling back through your subconscious to encounter the source of your hang-ups. It could be about all these things, or many others.

Above all, what *Errand Into the Maze* shows us — apart from what it suggests and symbolizes — is a woman who thinks, acts, makes more room for herself to operate in. If Martha Graham has one message, that has to be it. She was an early if undeclared feminist, so early that she couldn't entirely shake off society's expectations for her, or the armor of guilt, conflict, repressed violence that society decrees for its female mavericks. Graham's heroines are all nonconformists — artists, doers, women with power beyond their sexuality. And they all suffer for their unorthodoxy.

While I was thinking about this article, I came across the following in Virginia Woolf's diary (August 19, 1918): "The heroic woman is much the same in Greece and England. She is of the type of Emily Brontë. Clytaemnestra and Electra are clearly mother and daughter, and therefore should have some sympathy, though perhaps sympathy gone wrong breeds the fiercest hate . . . Electra lived a far more hedged in life than the women of the mid-Victorian age, but this has no effect upon her, except in making her harsh and splendid." Graham's women are hedged-in, neurotic because they cannot submit to men and tradition, driven to acts of hate and acts of courage, and sometimes, when they give in to their need for masculine domination, reduced to simpering dolls.

Graham not only recognizes her occasional need to be dependent on a man, but apparently feels this need diminishes her. Her two self-satires, *Acrobats of God* and *Every Soul Is a Circus*, both show the heroine as star, but a star who turns all

Don Quixote pas de deux (Petipa/Minkus). Gelsey Kirkland
and Mikhail Baryshnikov (photo by Louis Péres)

Le Baiser de la Fée (Neumeier/Stravinsky). Daniel Levans, Bonnie Mathis, and William Carter of American Ballet Theater (photo by Louis Péres)

Don Quixote, Act III (Balanchine/Nabokov). Suzanne Farrell and Richard
Hoskinson with New York City Ballet (photo by Martha Swope)

La Sylphide (Bournonville/Loewenskjold). Natalia Makarova, Karena Brock, and Ivan Nagy with American Ballet Theater (photo by Costas)

The Big City (Jooss/Tansman), Jan Hanniford and William Whitener with City Center Joffrey Ballet (photo by Herbert Migdoll)

"Mistake Waltz" from *The Concert* (Robbins/Chopin). New York City Ballet (photo by Martha Swope)

Stravinsky Violin Concerto (Balanchine/Stravinsky). Kay Mazzo (right) with New York City Ballet (photo by Costas)

Appalachian Spring (Graham/Copland). Left: David Hatch Walker; right: Tim Wengerd and Diane Gray with Martha Graham Company (photos by Martha Swope)

Here and Now With Watchers (Hawkins/Dlugoszewski). Erick Hawkins and Nada Regan
(photo by Nathaniel Tileston)

Rebus (Cunningham/Behrman). Merce Cunningham (far left)
and company (photo by Thomas Victor)

Piano Peace (McIntyre/Williams). Dianne McIntyre
(photo by Nathaniel Tileston)

Nijinsky, Clown of God (Béjart/Henry). Ballet of the XXth Century (photo by Costas)

Quarry (Monk). Meredith Monk (right) and The House (photo by Nathaniel Tileston)

Sticks (Brown). Trisha Brown (second from right) and company
(photo by Nathaniel Tileston)

Sue's Leg (Tharp/Waller). Rose Marie Wright, Tom Rawe, Twyla Tharp, and Ken Rinker (photo by Herbert Migdoll)

Lazy Madge (Dunn). Above: Diane Frank, Daniel Press, and Douglas Dunn;
below: Jennifer Mascall and Dunn (photos by Nathaniel Tileston)

silly when a man cracks his whip. Clytemnestra consciously assumes a kittenish attitude when she's luring Agamemnon to his death. For Graham, a traditional feminine stance can be adopted only as a weapon or a sign of weakness. She seldom found a way for men and women to be equals.

But her view of sexual relationships is not the most important statement she makes as a preeminently gifted feminist. Her dances redo history through a female mind. Almost the entire sum of our intelligence about the world's past has been transmitted to us through the eyes of men, and is pictured with men as the prime movers. I doubt if there's ever been as concerted an effort as Martha Graham's to present a more balanced perspective. She didn't set out to make political statements; one way to see her work is as a manipulation of tradition to reflect her personality or provide herself with starring roles. But even if she has been merely making her themes serve her art, she has told the stories another way around. We all know the agony of Oedipus; Graham describes Jocasta's pain. For her "The Oresteia" became *Clytemnestra*.

The extraordinary thing that this refocusing does is to make the women protagonists human, where before they had been the pawns of gods and men. The Joan of Arc story usually comes to us as a tale of a woman's martyrdom. Joan herself is less important than her religious fanaticism and her temerity in playing a man's role in the wars that are the business of kings. It's fascinating, then, to see what elements of the story Graham chose for her version, *Seraphic Dialogue* (1955). The dance is a meditation on three aspects of Joan's life: her youth and early visions, her decision to take up the sword, and her martyrdom. There are no kings or prime ministers in the dance; no peasants or armies or bishops or judges. Joan, played by one dancer, sees her former selves, played by three other dancers, enact her interior struggles, doubts, and spiritual joy. The only other dancers in the work portray Sts. Michael, Catherine, and Margaret.

Once again, the protagonist is a woman who has to make up her mind. Michael helps her, Catherine and Margaret inspire her, but the decision to defy society and realize her calling is hers. The political intrigues that smolder around her might not touch her at all; she has her eye fixed on God. To this Joan it doesn't seem unnatural or disgusting to dress as a man or not have children. Those are minor terms of the pact. What's hard is that she knows the whole venture will be dangerous; every step is a risk and every success will bring her nearer to death. In Graham's universe, Joan wins her own beatification. By the time sainthood is conferred on her — when she's crowned and taken up into Noguchi's stained-glass-window set — the glory has already happened.

You could see the same attitude toward sacred figures in Graham's very early masterpiece, *Primitive Mysteries* (1931). A white-clad woman and twelve companions enter and leave very ceremoniously three times. Each of the three dances, Hymn to the Virgin, Crucifixus, Hosanna, suggests the elements of praise, suffering, joy that are part of Christian ritual. But the women experience it, they act out the grief and compassion and exaltation without male intermediaries to do it for them or delineate the forms of their worship.

The dignity and power of Graham's women emanate from her sense that women do have an independent existence, as rich psychically and creatively as that of men. Perhaps nowhere did she explore the variety of that interior existence as deeply as in *Letter to the World* in which Graham was stirred by the New England recluse-poet Emily Dickinson to create a dance that has more changes of mood, more possibility for lyricism in a strong female role, than any other I've seen of hers.

The dance begins with a fast, impulsive solo for Emily (the One Who Dances), in which she mercurially flits from place to place, can't seem to light anywhere before she takes off again. Another Emily, the One Who Speaks, walks sedately behind her, telling of New England ways and weather. She exclaims, "I'm sorry for the dead today!" and suddenly the mood turns black — "Looking at death is dying." The scene is transformed into a "gay, ghastly holiday," Emily stiffened and laid out like a corpse, and handsome young men turned into pallbearers, and black-veiled women running all bent over with their arms curving down behind them so you can't tell if they're fleeing or hurling themselves into a battle. Finally Emily works up all her courage and spits at the Ancestress: "The Bible is an antique volume, written by faded men àt the suggestion of holy spectres!" — and prances off chanting, "In the name of the bee — and the butterfly — and of the breeze, Amen!" (These lines were used as the benediction in a Dickinson poem describing an imaginary funeral for summer.) The dance continues in one unbroken stream of consciousness, bringing alive the childlike, perceptive woman who had to sacrifice love for respectability, but who defied tradition anyway, by pouring her rebellion and her appetite for life into the secret poems that formed her letter to the world.

When I saw Martha Graham after the season, I asked her how she was able to find the lines of Dickinson that so brilliantly carried the dance from one luminous state of mind to another. She couldn't say, except that she hadn't gone searching for the words; she'd known Emily a long time, lived with her poetry, and when it came time to do the ballet, the words were there.

I've always thought that one of the principal reasons Graham attained her position in the world's esteem is that, although a dancer, she operates so verbally. Her notebooks, published last fall, attest that she is not only a near-poet herself, but an intellectual, a scholar, who reads incessantly and scours literature for choreographic themes. One of her recent works, *Chronique* (1973), was based on a poem by St. John Perse, and had in its first version an actress reciting lines from the poem onstage. Later, the speaker was placed in the orchestra pit, but now Graham says she wants to omit the words altogether. "I'm not pleased with them being spoken as they are. I only use words if they're an intrinsic part of the dance. The words dance their own dance and the dancers dance their own poetry."

I think the physicality of her presence on stage asserted the dance's integrity over its literary sources. The audience could see that mind and mover were one. When she grew less active and finally retired from dancing, her work became diffuse, more literary, less personal. The poem "Chronique" gets its grandeur from its language. "Great age behold us, and take the measure of man's heart." "Divine violence be ours till the last eddy." Graham translated this into a dance of symbolic, anonymous beings — lovers, contestants, seekers — who do beautiful movement that has no core. The words are contemplative, but there's no one in the dance who contemplates; it swirls and ripples across the stage but doesn't ever really come to rest. Graham told me the poem was an affirmation of life and a diatribe against war, but the dance needs a person who affirms.

The same is true with this season's new work, *Holy Jungle*. In a program note, she describes it as "A fantasy of man's sufferings, temptations, strange visions that attack and surround him on his pilgrimage to the almost forgotten Eden of his dreams," and earlier, in a press conference, she referred to "frescoes in the skull," the memories and legends in man's mind. The figures in the dance are representational. The audience can't connect them with anyone real; they have loaded names like Angel, Celestial Bride, and Lucifer. Graham has a wonderful company of young dancers now, and perhaps she will become interested enough in some of them to make them the motivating characters in future new works, to project onto them the urgency that made her create for herself. At this point her choreography looks imposed from the outside.

I never saw Martha Graham dancing at the height of her powers. All of her pre-1960 works I've seen were performed by other dancers, with the exception of a few on film. So I'm not speaking of some remembered presence shedding invisible wattage on pathetic revivals. Even with other women doing her roles, Graham's theater has magnetism, conviction, consistency.

From the compact, apparently simple but very sophisticated *El Penitente* to the huge, dense, luxurious *Clytemnestra*, her theatrical skill is like one more outlet for the energy that is making the whole dance happen. The props in *El Penitente* belong to the peasant-performers; they might have made them, they're so simple and in the case of the Christ-mask so crudely beautiful. In *Clytemnestra* (1958) the props are immense, like the scale of the dance. Long spears are carried by soldiers and serve at different times as the masts of Agamemnon's ship, the funeral bier for Iphigenia, the sedan-chair on which Agamem-

non is borne home. After Clytemnestra has decided to murder
her husband, two women come onstage with a contrivance that
I'm sure Graham and designer Isamu Noguchi must have invented, a tremendous length of crimson and pink paneled
cloth, attached at both ends to curving poles held by the two
attendants. The cloth, like a gorgeous river of blood, flows
over the stage during the whole murder sequence. Clytemnestra wraps herself in it, winding around her body the awful role
she has chosen. It gets stretched across the stage as a kind of
welcoming carpet for the king. The attendants stand the poles
up in front of the murder-place, pulling them aside just long
enough for us to see Clytemnestra striking the fatal blows.

I can't help contrasting this with the way props are used in
Holy Jungle, where objects stand for life intentions. People
play with globes and candy-cane staffs and toy trees. They
duel with long, metal rods, touch each other with a paddle
sculpted into the form of a hand. The props are used as tools
— they substitute for what the dancers haven't actually done.
The more striking or strange their design, the more they separate us from the dance idea, rather than enhancing the dance
idea.

Graham's is often a theater of polarities, of shocking contrasts or contradictions, but the most telling of these are accomplished by dancers dancing. Oedipus and Jocasta's duet in
Night Journey (1947) is a series of twinings and inversions in
which the dancers lapse from poses of lovemaking into poses of
mother and child; one moment he straddles her and the next
she's rocking him in her lap.

Images repeat themselves with slight differences, gaining in
weight and meaning each time. *Cave of the Heart* (1946) is full
of figurehead shapes assumed by Medea and the rival Princess.
Each time one of them thrusts her upper body forward and
gazes in an arc across the horizon, we are reminded of Jason's
journey and the transitoriness of all the events and relationships that are taking place. After poisoning her husband's paramour, Medea actually slips herself inside Noguchi's brass wire
branching sculpture and reaches out from the waist in glittering
sweeps. Metaphorically she has become a bird, at one with the
sky, where her rescuing chariot is to come from. But literally,

too, she appends the prop and all its symbolic associations to her own body, not just displaying it, but merging with it.

Graham's theater is priceless because it brings all these things together. It's more than a vehicle for her own performing power and intellect, more than her psychological insights or the particular way she developed nonverbal structures. Now that she is not dancing herself, we can see the totality of its impact better than ever. Throughout her career, Graham worked for the moment, put her energies into the dance that was being made, didn't devote her efforts to preserving or restoring works that had already satisfied their purpose. Now I think that attitude is changing. The audiences at the spring season were very enthusiastic, and Graham was not unaware that there's a revival of interest in her work.

I asked her why she thought her dance appeals to people now. "The audience is much more knowable and aware than we ever had before," she said. "The young people identify with young people — dancers — who are disciplined, because they're not. They've shattered all the idols, now they want something they can idolize. The middle-aged people, well, maybe they studied dance when they were young, and they held those days as an ideal period of charm and emotional strength. People today want something that means something. They get everything else on television. They want something which will quicken and stir them, make them feel more alive."

Then she talked about her company, the excellent young dancers who are so obviously making her feel more alive. And she told me something I never expected to hear from her, something that made me extremely happy. "The dance is a legend, but on the legend the next generation builds. Yes, this season it seems there's more of a chance for the dances to live than I thought."

January-February 1975

Art, After a Fashion

I DON'T GIVE a damn about Martha Graham's caftans. Neither do you, right? They're producing the great genius of American choreography with an ultra-upper-luxe veneer that I find really tasteless. Art used to serve our need for escapism and fantasy; now fashion does that. With each new Graham season it gets harder to separate the art from the camouflage that's ordinarily employed when no art is there. Martha Graham doesn't deserve an audience that's interested only in the address of her plastic surgeon.

There were a lot of anniversaries and firsts and mosts — mostly monetary — connected with the month-long Graham season that began last week at the Mark Hellinger Theater, but I forget all of them. I trudged through the razzle-dazzle until halfway through the second night, when Yuriko Kimura gave an unbelievable performance as Medea in *Cave of the Heart*. Then I knew I had come to the right place.

No one can say that the prettification of Graham is entirely the doing of her cohorts. When you look at her new dances, you see a continual enlarging on the outer appearances, a taking for granted or skimming over of the essentials. There's a short piece called *Adorations*, which Graham called "technique" when she introduced it opening night. Actually, it's our old friend the lecture-demonstration, performed in a set made of golden cubist modules. The dancers wear white lamé cummerbunds and hair bands with their flesh-colored body suits and tights. The familiar classroom floor exercises and combinations are gussied up with entrances and exits, artistic groupings of people at different floor levels, and just a bit of counterpoint, so you'd almost think you're watching a dance.

One object of *Adorations* is to show how technique is used in a dance. *Point of Crossing*, a second new work, is given immediately afterward in the same set rearranged, and for all I know it has the same movement combinations. But *Adorations* is already much more artful than the cold, spare ritual of the learning process.

The dancers seemed unsure of how to do this changeling. Is it a performance for the audience, a demonstration for Martha, a warm-up for themselves? What they did — and it didn't look rehearsed — was to smile and react to each other quite spontaneously. In no other Graham work at the moment do the dancers look so natural.

Point of Crossing is drawn from the Biblical story of Jacob and Esau but I don't know enough scripture for that to mean something to me. The dance shows a man (Ross Parkes) who's caught between various people making claims on him — two Messengers, who wear voluminous robes cut to reveal their chests and crotches, and who stand around waving arms that have been extended, Loie Fuller-like, by sticks inside the sleeves; a Brother, Tim Wengerd, with whom he grapples from time to time; the Temptress, Diane Gray, who seems to be linked to the Brother, but who makes a few passes at Parkes too; and a Goddess, Janet Eilber, who disapproves of everything Parkes does and finally presents him with Yuriko Kimura, the Beloved, who tempts him too, but is more refined than Gray. Parkes fights them all off at the end, and climbs a ladder to the unknown, leaving them all behind.

This is no more complicated than the plot of any good Graham dance, but *Point of Crossing* doesn't tell you why these people are doing these things to each other. You remember the dance as a series of setups, tableaux, rather than as the projection of anyone's feelings. The choreography seemed to consist entirely of the dancers manipulating themselves or their partners/adversaries into positions. Graham saw the poses as angular, twisted, the bodies making very ornate shapes. However, the way the dancers get into and out of these shapes is smooth, often curving, and without emphasis. In other words, the shape, the static image you remember, is not the result of a movement impulse. Without this consistency and continuity between movement and design, the dance breaks into tiny unrelated units, with only costumes and props holding it together.

Parkes's encounter with Kimura, which is perhaps the clearest emotional episode in the piece, is accomplished almost without their touching each other. First she lures him by dancing a solo in which she winds a long rope around herself seductively. Then he diddles himself with the rope. Then they both dance with the rope. Engineering it and themselves into different entanglements takes the place of getting physically involved with each other.

Rudolf Nureyev was dancing practically every performance of the first week in *Lucifer*, the piece Graham choreographed for him last spring. I hadn't seen it before, and it seems to be somewhat stronger and less fussy than *Point of Crossing*. There's a wonderfully spooky opening scene in which Daniel Maloney swoops around the empty stage, apparently gloating over the falling Lucifer. Nureyev, lying rigidly on a rock with his arms and legs stuck in the air, didn't exactly create this illusion, but my logic told me that what took place afterward was a flashback, so I helped him a little.

Maloney, I take it, is Satan tempting the angel to his doom. Janet Eilber, in the role created by Margot Fonteyn, models a number of stunning green costumes. Nureyev is goaded beyond endurance by the vision of Eilber — she's really just a hunk of bait offered by Maloney and his henchmen — and finally yields to his desire for her in a few seconds of violent, impersonal contact. That finishes him, of course.

I couldn't figure out how Nureyev conceived the character. He started out at superhigh intensity, as if demented, and stayed that way all through. A ballet dancer sometimes has to project passion through acting because the movement he's doing has none, but modern dance works on the opposite premise. In any case, I couldn't figure out why this guy gets chosen for such an awful fate. And I was rather dismayed by Graham's guilt-ridden, punitive attitude to the sex act. It's her imitators who usually show such aversion and so little sympathy for heterosexual consummations. Or maybe this tendency was there before and is just now surfacing in her.

Cave of the Heart, choreographed in 1947, has a more open attitude to sex. Or perhaps the choreography has more depth. Medea kills in revenge for her husband's infidelity. I used to think this crime canceled out the other, and that Medea was cleansed at the end of the dance. As Yuriko Kimura does the role, she turns into a monster feeding on her own hatred, and her triumph at the end is that she's surpassed all human doubt, compassion, regret. She's become totally without morality. It curdled my blood.

Of the other revivals in the first week, *Acrobats of God* (1960) is back after a six-year absence. It might do as well as *Adorations* to expose the bones of the Graham technique. It is, in fact, Graham's tribute to her company, a circus of dancer-feats including some of the most ingenious partnering she's ever choreographed, with a whip-cracking ballet master and an anxious, proud lady who might be their governess.

Acrobats was one of two comic roles Graham choreographed on herself, kidding her own artistic temper, her advancing age and vanity. Linda Hodes, returning to the company after several years, has taken over the role, and seeing her is a shock, as all Graham roles are when first done by other people. Hodes is a much younger woman than Graham was when she made *Acrobats*, and this is one case where I'm not a stickler for authenticity in a revival. Surely Hodes could do more than flap her elbows together and gesture arthritically — unless *Acrobats* is only a joke about Martha Graham getting too old to dance, in which case it isn't funny.

The perennially gorgeous *Diversion of Angels* (1948) looked and sounded underrehearsed, but the splendid David Hatch Walker, dancing the duet with Takako Asakawa as the Girl in Red, made me feel I was watching the most wonderful, vital moment in his life.

Janet Eilber and Peggy Lyman both did the very early solo *Lamentation* (1930). I saw it on the Graham tour last spring, but at the Hellinger I missed most of it because the audience was permitted to stroll about after the curtain was up and it lasts only three and a half minutes. Nevertheless, it is a giant of a dance. Even today I dare you to find as tough and power-packed a piece of theater anywhere. Graham was not on subsidy when she made it, and I bet the mink growers don't think much of it now either.

December 18, 1975

The Ground Is Where
the Roots Are

ONCE THEY'D LAUNCHED the season with sufficient glamour, and the mink barons had retired to the background, the Martha Graham company settled down to repertory. And what a repertory, and how well they're dancing it now. I don't know what combination of malevolent forces keeps us on this perpetual roller coaster of magnificent Graham seasons and long periods when the whole enterprise seems imperiled.

Martha Graham has been making dance for fifty years, yet it's still necessary for her to put her personality on the line in order to get her dances produced. And we call ourselves civilized. For our sake and the dancers', for the sake of keeping before us the proof that dance can touch the spirit and kindle the mind as well as please the eye, we need Graham dances to see regularly, every year. Nobody should have to make a special campaign for that.

One drawback of these brief, almost accidental seasons is that we don't have a sense of the whole company — what's motivating it and linking it together stylistically. Every season people debate whether the company looks more or less authentically Graham than it used to, but I'm not sure anyone knows what authentic Graham looks like, because we never see the company long enough as an ensemble. The performance we think is particularly effective or ineffective may be the luck of one evening or the influence of one leading dancer or a moment in a process of growth or decline. But most people won't see that dance again for a year or so, and then the personnel will have changed.

For various reasons some works are looking exceptionally good to me this winter. *Cave of the Heart* and *Errand Into the*

Maze because of Yuriko Kimura's performance. *Night Journey* because of the gutsiness of the chorus. *Dark Meadow* and *Letter to the World* because they are monumentally wonderful dances. *Hérodiade*, *Seraphic Dialogue*, and *Diversion of Angels* because they are less monumental but no less wonderful. But there have been too few times when I thought everyone in the cast understood the dance in the same way and worked together to create one dance image.

This happened at one matinee of *Appalachian Spring*, with Diane Gray as the Bride, Tim Wengerd as the Husband, Peggy Lyman as the Pioneer Woman and David Hatch Walker as the Preacher. Of all things, *Appalachian Spring*, the dance of Graham's that seems most accessible and most familiar, that afternoon got one shade clearer to me — the way it is at the eye doctor's when you think you can see everything, until he takes one lens away and you see a little more.

I've never perceived these four characters so distinctly before, or with such depth. *Appalachian Spring*, like most of Graham's works, is a dance of recitative rather than ensemble. People dance their feelings about the event they're all involved in, sometimes in reference to one other character or to the four women in the Preacher's entourage, and at only one point in the dance do the four principals all meet each other, the actual wedding ceremony.

Yet in their many facets, these four embody just about every passion, strength, and vulnerability that might have built an American frontier community. The dancers I mentioned conveyed this diversity, I think, by relying as much on the force of the movement gesture as on their acting skill.

That day I was particularly aware of how different the bride and groom are from each other. Gray's changeableness of mood, her hesitancy about the future seemed almost at odds with Wengerd's solidity. I wondered if they would get along well together, if she'd be able to tolerate his spit-and-polish or he her scattyness. But I saw for the first time that once her fears get focused, once her husband anchors her, this woman is going to be a fighter. The last and most anxious solo, which I've always seen as a fear-fantasy of childbirth, Gray turned into a much bigger foreboding, of war, epidemic, drought, threatening the homestead and the family she was going to plant there. And I saw she was going to defend them savagely.

Appalachian Spring is full of religion and the supernatural, hardly any of it orthodox. The Bride refuses to bow her head when the others pray; she lifts it instead. But — maybe she has a more direct connection to God — her Husband leans on her when he makes his own reverence.

The Preacher has no sectarian trappings. Walker shows him to be a man of the flesh, firmly taking command of the occasion, earthbound in his dialogues with heaven, even a little amused by his own pomposity. The paroxysm of curses he hurls at the bride and groom for dancing at the wedding may even absolve some guilt of his own, connected with how much he enjoys being cuddled by his female groupies.

And the Pioneer Woman is the real source of joy and calmness at this solemn and rather apprehensive gathering. She initiates two little group dances of celebration and adds all the benedictions that the Preacher forgets. And after his most violent outburst, she exorcises the Husband's fears, almost as if she were practicing a ritual of good witchcraft. According to her, not dancing may be an even greater sin than dancing.

December 25, 1975

Another Corner Turned

TOBY ARMOUR'S SOLO CONCERT was long and demanding. I didn't realize until I saw it how that sort of performance is passing from the scene. She did seven numbers, most of them choreographed by herself. After each dance, she bowed and left the room to change costumes. There's an old-fashioned

kind of theatricality implied in this. The performer goes away
and reappears as someone else. But the Cubiculo is too intimate for any but the most subtle transformations, and most of
the pieces Armour did were so brief that it was hard to identify
the distinguishing attitudes of each.

The program opener, *Rattlesnake*, seemed clear and interesting as an exposition of the lowdown, mean propensities of
that animal, with lowdown, mean piano music as accompaniment. Instead of coiling and slithering the way most people do
"snaky" movement, Armour rotated all the big and little segments of her body, tied herself in angular knots, and fired
deadly looks in various directions.

But as the concert went on, it began to seem that the spiky
body and slow burning stare are basic to Toby Armour, rather
than particular to her idea of rattlesnake. In *Last News of a
Morning Cruise* she quietly burlesqued burlesque, Spanish
dancing, and Wagnerian bathos. In a morsel from Lois Gin-
andes' *Winter Pavilion* she postured and looked middle aged.
And in *Heads, Continued*, in a pinpoint of light, she jabbed
and nodded and rotated her head on her neck, always with the
same alternation of piercing eye and withdrawn, slightly secre-
tive smile.

Those strong focuses into space made Yvonne Rainer's *Trio A*
look much more theatrical than I've ever seen it. The steps
were the same, but a lot seemed to be changing. Where Rainer
and other people who've done the dance like to throw away
and smooth out the differences between actions, Armour made
the gestures more isolated and thus more important. Loosen-
ing up is something she works at; it's not a cessation of effort,
not casual.

James Waring — who's spending the year in Boston as guest
artistic director of Armour's New England Dinosaur — has
made a lovely new piece for her, *Moonlight Sonata*. The
dance suggests Isadora Duncan in its elaborate use of the arms,
little skips and hops, its dislocations of the whole mass of the
torso. But it evokes more for me — about the death of Romanticism. Waring's devices are so elusive that to name what
they seem to be is almost to overstate the dance. Armour begins facing upstage, standing in first position with one heel

raised expectantly off the floor. Through the slow first movement she wanders in a kind of balletic-impressionistic disquiet. The music gets faster and she takes little leaps but holds herself aloof from the space. And in the agitated finale she throws herself into big angst-filled jumps. When it's all done, she walks blankly, a-musically, toward the audience making sketchy motions with one arm.

A dancer with any less restraint than Toby Armour would have torn the piece to shreds. Yet there were times when I lost the sensibility of it, when I felt either she or Waring wasn't sure how it was going. I'd like to see it once when it's the only thing she has to do.

The evening ended with *Social Dancing*, in which she seduces a dummy. There was something strange about the piece — perhaps its comparative literalness. And then, it was hard to imagine thin, suave, androgynous Toby Armour as a female who gets her rocks off by massaging a suit stuffed with pillows. I can believe in her hidden sexuality but I can't believe such a crude object would satisfy her.

November 7, 1974

James Waring 1922–1975

JIMMY WARING was a dedicated outsider. Unclassifiable. He made ballets, he made modern dances. He lived the Judson era but he didn't quite belong to the avant-garde. He choreographed for kids in a summer camp and for fringe groups that went out of existence. He could be a creator of nostalgic portraits, a satirist, an impresario of show-biz camp — sometimes all three at once.

In recent years he never seemed interested in the hassle of maintaining his own company, so you had to snatch his works one by one as they appeared in other people's repertories. How pleasant it would have been to see his fine ballets in place of the glop that ABT and the Joffrey often serve, but I guess Waring wasn't built for that world.

Anyway, his ballets were probably too intelligent. They were, like Jimmy, quiet, refined, not always respectful. Seriously witty. A dancer couldn't do his work with half a mind on it. He needed a certain loving irreverence from performers — otherwise his little feints and jibes would have seemed too crude. Sometimes he was so subtle you didn't know if he was spoofing or not. But his dancers understood that playing him for laughs would be disastrous.

He choreographed out of love for the dancer or the dance form — and in perusing his subject matter, if he found vulnerabilities to smile at, that was part of his affection.

No one knew his repertory, I suppose; it was scattered all over the place. I doubt if I ever saw anything of his more than once. And his ballets were even more ephemeral than dance ordinarily is — they went by like clouds, you couldn't remember what had happened a minute after they were over. Except your mood was changed.

There was, recently, a lovely group piece he did for Raymond Johnson's company, *Scintilla*, to Gottschalk. A ballet — really. Not condescending to the company's modern dancers' techniques and bodies as another choreographer might, he gave them steps to do, and made them look wonderful — and like themselves. And an earlier solo for Johnson, *Andante Amoroso*, to Mahler: strange, inward, catching the implied decadence in Mahler and in Johnson's beautiful black body.

There was Beethoven's *Moonlight Sonata*, in which I thought Toby Armour was dancing the death of Romanticism and the hesitant beginning of a new age. And Ze'eva Cohen doing 32 *Variations in C Minor*, also Beethoven, of which all I remember is that it evoked Isadora Duncan.

Jimmy Waring was an aristocrat — though I didn't know him well enough to say that. He was a man of exquisite taste, without a trace of the snob or dandy in him that I could tell. I would see him across some lobby and he would smile that smile of his that never reached his sad eyes, and I would nod and say Hello James — I always wanted to treat him formally, I don't know why. A skinny long-haired soft-voiced middle-aged man with a scraggly gray woolen muffler dangling down over his old tweed sport jacket? I thought he was some kind of a prince is all.

December 11, 1975

Liberation in a Cocoon

THE STAR SYSTEM at best can be a shot of glamour for a provincial company languishing in the acceptance or neglect of its home audience. More often I suspect it's demoralizing to the dancers. The stars blow into town, take over roles nobody ever saw the locals in, grab all the glory, and disappear, leaving unflattering comparisons in their wake. You don't hear dancers saying this very often, because the system is now so entrenched around the country, it's become a substantial factor in keeping dancing alive at all.

Rudolf Nureyev's appearances in New York with the Paul Taylor company was star-time, doubled, in spades. Nureyev could spare just one day for his two ballyhooed performances, and management was tactless enough to let everybody know that Rudi was dancing for free, and the double-price tickets for those two shows were going to float the anticipated losses of the entire season.

It's not quite as crass as it all sounds, however. Nureyev is an old friend of the company, and danced with Taylor in Mexico as early as 1972. I saw them rehearse in the studio just before that trip, and was impressed with Nureyev's interest in modern dance, and with his seriousness in learning Taylor's style. It seemed to me that, given a few more rehearsals and some settling-in with the company, Nureyev would be doing it right.

He couldn't sit still for that kind of study, though. His gig now is international fame, novelty, and don't wait around for the roses to fade. His fans or the ecstatic sponsoring managements turn every appearance into a circus where serious dancing couldn't be seen even if it were being done.

I think Nureyev wanted to give *Aureole* its due but under the circumstances nobody could have expected more than we got — a very self-conscious, tentative, and superficial performance. Nureyev looked small and inadequate in Taylor's role until the fast pace of the finale gave his bottled-up energy a place to go.

I learned a lot about Taylor's style from watching Nureyev try to do it. By now we've seen enough ballet types fail at modern dance to know that the moderns require an entirely different sense of the body's weight. Where the ballet dancer's objective is to make his weight seem to disappear, the modern dancer wants to use it actively. Taylor especially has dealt in refinements of weight: softly pressing or sinking into the floor, suspending, swinging, flinging out into space are all part of his vocabulary. It's not that Nureyev is incapable of sensing his weight but that he can't produce the range of subtle variation in it that the choreography needs.

What was also missing, that I hadn't even known was there, was Taylor's strange, internally focused but not narcissistic sense of himself as a performing presence. He dances as if inside a cocoon, from which he peeps out every once in a while — an upward gaze into the wreath of his arms, a glance along the line of a kick, a swift grin at the audience. With Eileen Cropley in the *Aureole* duet, he looks not so much at her as into her, seeming to draw her inside his capsule of air. It looks utterly sexless, seraphic even. But it also makes the choreography more interesting; the dancer is neither in nor outside himself *all* the time so he forces us to wonder why his attention goes out or in at the particular moments that it does.

The original dancers in *Aureole* — Taylor and Dan Wagoner, Elizabeth Walton, Sharon Kinney and Renee Kimball — all danced that way. Succeeding members of the company have tried to imitate it with varying results; it can look stupefied or merely smug. But Nureyev couldn't find any way to be in the dance — no performing attitude he's familiar with quite fits the occasion.

Aside from Carolyn Adams, who's always wonderful in her own way, it was Taylor himself who danced the season most fully. Taylor, looking heavy and out of condition after a series of illnesses, gave the choreography the nuance and dynamic fluctuation that it needs to avoid smarminess. The senior members of the company look tired now, and the newcomers are forcing a theatricality that doesn't seem appropriate. They have balletic bodies, these younger dancers, long and pointy-footed, and they don't use their torsos expressively at all, and they do a lot with their faces. Trouble is, Taylor choreography falls so distinctively between modern dance and ballet that extra technique doesn't enhance it. As it does in the case of Alvin Ailey, for instance.

Taylor was one of the best of the post-Graham choreographers, but he also anticipated the current trend toward balleticism in modern dance. His dances were orderly, musical, at a time when dance was supposed to be independent from music or make its own. Early in the 1960s we saw him crystallizing a movement vocabulary, formulating a language that wasn't to vary much over the years as it served a wide variety of choreographic purposes. If most of the modern dancers were expressionists, in the sense that they were seeking to translate their feelings into appropriate movement, Taylor was a classicist. He was more concerned with form than messages, even in his most explicit pieces. His dances often had a presentational style that seemed odd in a period of introversion. And he was witty and clever at a time when anything funny had the volatility of a cement balloon.

All these qualities have now been adopted by the most popular dance companies, but the Taylor company, ironically, can't seem to cash in on the balleto-pop success that it foreshadowed. To audiences saturated with Ailey/Falco-type spectacular entertainments, Taylor choreography looks formalistic and empty; the dancers straining to put it across. I think some of the old confidence in their own idiosyncrasy has gone out of the dancers. Only in the season's new work, *Sports and Follies*, did the company look as if they were generating an energy, creating the piece for itself.

The dance, set to orchestrated theater music of Satie, is very much like several others — *Public Domain, Foreign Exchange*, and *Piece Period* all come to mind. Taylor can make dance comedy more fluently than almost any other choreographer, and in all the dances I mentioned the comedy comes from what the dancers do rather than any prearranged plots or situations. Yet the dances are all different from one another; you never have the feeling Taylor is ripping himself off.

His fund of American vernacular dance material is enormous, and in *Sports and Follies* the dancers break into little bits from a beer hall chorus line, strut the loose-limbed but precise cadences of drum majorettes and cheerleaders. Carolyn Adams' first solo, a semivaudeville set, reminded me of the American Girl in *Parade*. By contrast. Massine took a similarly disjointed musical idea and duplicated Satie's sound effects by giving the girl a long succession of pantomime gestures taken from machine-age, Prohibition America. Taylor's dance is also fragmentary, but it's all dance, and what specifics there are in it refer to the American stage, not the American street.

American Genesis, Taylor's big, Biblical-historical-allegorical evening-length dance, is almost an encyclopedia of dance idioms, from Colonial times to the present. Taylor tries to use period dance styles to evoke period behavior, and he's almost successful. The hillbilly Eden and the bouncy cakewalk and minstrel dancing in the final section, The Flood, convey to the audience something of the innocence of Adam and Eve in the Garden and the spirited irresponsibility of Noah's children. In Before Eden, Taylor sets up an air of seductiveness and sexual intrigue within the contained manners of a minuet.

But you can't just look at the dancing in *American Genesis*. Its excessive layers of logic force us to consider it logically, and that's where it breaks down. Except for the title, the program makes reference only to Biblical sources and characters, but the props, costumes, and situations refer to various cherished items of Americana, like the landing of the Pilgrims. It's almost impossible for the audience to keep both these sets of symbols in mind, together with all their ideological connections, and at the same time follow the action of the dance, with characters turning up in new guises and familiar stories twisting into new endings.

Taylor takes some very unusual — you might say liberated — views of sex in *American Genesis*. Women play male parts — or the parts of angels with male names. Adam and Eve try a *ménage à trois* with a fellow called Jake; then, after each one is left out in the cold while the others duet, they all decide to go their separate ways. Some early Americans are caught wife-swapping. As often as there's a character who goes naughty-naughty at some sexual innuendo, there's another character who's touting the benefits of Sin. Fun-loving Lilith's Child appears to inherit the earth after the Flood, but stalking off close behind her is Lucifer, who first introduced Adam to her mother and, in the guise of Noah, later banned her from the Ark.

The strangely balanced way Taylor presents these curiosities has a lot to do with the feeling of decadence they give me. He proposes various attitudes but doesn't take a stand on any of them. In West of Eden, the most problematical section of *Genesis*, he presents an orgy of lust, rape, and fratricide, with Cain and Abel being comforted impartially at the end by one Elder while the instigators — two other Elders who've previously been identified with Good and Evil — wash their hands of all responsibility. The fact that this part of the dance is choreographed in Martha Graham style just adds to its burden of unresolved morality.

More graphic in its sexual indifference is *Churchyard*, which could almost be a version gone haywire of the famous Dance of the Dead Nuns from *Robert le Diable*, precursor to *Giselle*. What disturbs me is not the conversion of these saintly beings to raving sex fiends whose overactive hormones have produced lumps over their bodies and kinks in their spines, but the fact that their dance is as symmetrical and carefully patterned as if they were wearing tutus.

I don't know why an idea that would look modish and just slightly raw in the hands of another choreographer and another company gets under my skin when Taylor does it. I think it has to do with the ambiguous message I get from him now — that something deeply personal is being treated in an impersonal way. This is no doubt part of a phase that all modern dance is going through. And Taylor is so much better a choreographer than most of the other moderns, it may be harder for him to make the passage.

December 1974

Blissed-Out Burlesque

AT THE BEGINNING of Erick Hawkins' concert at the Whitney Museum, a young man without any clothes on walks ceremoniously into the space carrying a prop that looks like one of the fertility symbols in Martha Graham's *Dark Meadow* — a rock with fronds growing out of it. Except that instead of having rounded contours, this prop is a stylish white cube. The young man squats down, keeping the cube modestly in front of him as long as he can, then places it on the floor. When he stands to go, we see that his genitals are concealed in a little white case on a G-string. But no matter. Hawkins probably knows that in certain branches of show-biz, it's better, if you've got it, you should hide some of it.

Ruth St. Denis brought polite pornography into the concert dance at the beginning of the twentieth century, but I suppose it's one of the oldest cons in the world. The people who are doing it tend to get increasingly righteous, too, the more successful they are. They really believe it's the mysticism or the beauty or the classic grace of what they're doing that hooks the audience. Maybe it is — or maybe it doesn't matter.

I try not to let myself get bothered by the mutually exploitative number that's so much a part of Hawkins' act. If the
women enjoy bouncing around naked under filmy accordion-
pleated nighties, and the audience enjoys pretending they're
digging Greek nymphs instead of Playboy bunnies, it shouldn't
do anybody any harm. Where I lose my resolve is in considering the artistic side of Hawkins that is supposed to elevate his
work above the pretentious narcissism it appears to be.

Hawkins developed his theories of dancing in reaction
against pain and stress, and I think also against the graphic
sexuality that was propounded by Martha Graham in the 1940s
when he was her partner. To dance without fear of pain or
injury is a most admirable goal, and Hawkins' easy, flowing
technique has an enormous appeal for refugees from the shin-
splint-and-broken-crotch schools of modern dance.

When I see his dancers for the first time in a performance,
I'm pleasantly impressed by their serenity. Not a furrowed
brow or a pursed lip among them, no strung-out, quivering
limbs, no sweaty dislocations of shape. But after a while the
serenity turns to syrup. The thing of it is, they don't really *do*
much.

Working from their flexible hip joints, they ease themselves
into the ground and out of it with a nice placid rhythm. The
arms float up and into big pliant curves around the body. They
jump softly, not far off the ground; push off into a turn or two;
tilt prettily but never dangerously out of the vertical. Their
dance is not about feats of any kind, or about compositional
structure, or about speed, contrast, excitement, strength; most
especially it's not about change.

I don't say all dance has to have these things, but in the
twenty years or so since he's been working this way, Hawkins
have failed to develop anything further with his tensionless
movement. It has remained what it was in 1957, when he choreographed *Here and Now with Watchers* — a means of calling
attention to the human body in a rather pristine state. *Here
and Now* was supposed to be revived in toto at the Whitney,
but only four of its eight sections were seen. At the end of the
agonized fifties it was pretty daring to say we didn't have to do

anything with our bodies, we didn't have to make psychological justifications for our physicality, we could just be sensually alive. In 1976 we've got sensuality to burn, and Hawkins' prim allusions seem a retreat rather than an advance.

Here and Now with Watchers was originally a duet, and its extended length — an hour and a quarter — made it something of a tour de force for Hawkins and his partner. The sections done at the Whitney were performed by Hawkins, Robert Yohn, Cathy Ward, and Nada Reagan. The dance is a cryptic love-play, Oriental in the sparseness of its gesture and its drawn-out methods of getting to the point.

There's a long procession of greeting — a man and a woman holding shields in front of their bodies, taking the measure of one another, stepping and bending in tentative synchrony. There are individual display dances in which Hawkins parades the space, falls carefully, holds himself in poses close to the ground; Yohn makes little sliding steps and big unspectacular jumps; Ward walks sinuously with her knees together like a Geisha, undulates her arms and hands; Reagan promenades with one hand over her breast, one covering her abdomen, at length revealing black cutout designs on her leotard where we thought the no-nos were. Various pas de deux lead up to one where Hawkins and Reagan touch each other in unexpected places — his foot cradles her head, he butts her gently in the stomach, that kind of thing. She appears to think this over and leaves. He dances a solo that ends with a long, imperial pose and a noble gaze sweeping across the ranks of onlookers.

The more recent *Greek Dreams, With Flute,* which filled out the program for the missing parts of *Here and Now,* seems even more chaste and conservative to me. It seems almost regressive. Besides the diaphanous women hippedy-skipping around Isadora Duncan style, there was Robert Yohn wearing very little more than body make-up and a laurel wreath, striding and making declamatory poses. He reminded me of a film I once saw of Ted Shawn imitating Greek statues.

Tad Taggart played the flute selections that accompanied this dance, and Lucia Dlugoszewski played her score for *Here and Now with Watchers.* Dlugoszewski is a dance all by herself as she bangs around inside and outside the piano with a variety of mallets to create wonderful unheard-of textures and tones. I guess Hawkins figures she supplies the dynamics and he the aesthetics. Strange separation, that.

January 29, 1976

Grotto

ALWIN NIKOLAIS' new dance, *Grotto,* has an archeological feeling to it. You might be looking down through layers of fossilized rock at several civilizations that disappeared long ago — or that could evolve eons from now. Nikolais is a great master at using sound, light, motion, and the utensils of every-day to create imaginary worlds, and the denizens of *Grotto,* which was premièred during the Nikolais–Murray Louis season at Brooklyn Academy, are certainly not of this world. At least I hope not.

The ten dancers, who rise from underneath sail-shaped silken shrouds, are dressed in identical white tank suits, tights, fright wigs, and face make-up. They have no gender and no personality. They present themselves to the audience two-dimensionally, with frozen expressions and a dry predestination about their energy.

In a series of episodes they act out fragments of what might have been a life-style, but with the vitality gone. They glide along, lean against each other, bounce and sway, with their bodies in one solid piece; they work in partners, slowly pulling each other from one pose to another. They jabber and yell but no sounds come out of their mouths. It's anybody's guess what these roly-poly robots might have looked like when they were alive, before they lost the ability to articulate, to touch or be touched.

These beings are only one element in the total scene Nikolais has excavated for us. The sails that covered the dancers at first are long tapering triangles with big circles sewn on them. They're hung on tracks and can be moved around to create different designs or screen parts of the stage. Sometimes they're piled up at the side like icebergs. Nikolais lights these versatile shapes in candy colors — raspberry, grape, lemon — so they don't look forbidding at all. In fact, the entire dance has a rather lurid decorative appeal, like a Victorian valentine or theatrical poster.

Using highly contrasting planes of light, Nikolais slathers one image upon another. Three female dancers downstage do a provocative dance in an amber light. Three men wander in behind them, lit in a dim greenish blue. They appear to see the other group but are mystified by them and eventually they leave. In another section, the dancers are lit by blue projections with white lines, while on the cyc is a sketch of yellow and orange flowers on a black background. Other projections show literal heroic figures, gladiators, knights in armor, sheriffs and cowboys, in photographs with curlicues and doodads drawn around them. There are a couple of elephants — a building that resembles Brooklyn Academy.

The use of all these wildly different kinds of images in stratified areas of the stage gives the effect of overlapping time. At one point, two dancers did an acrobatic duet, curling and stretching around one another, and two other couples did the same thing, each completely encased in a tube of elasticized material. I wonder whether the rounded blobs in the sacks represented an earlier, or perhaps a later stage of evolution than the emotionally bland but recognizable beings out in the open.

Finally, with the stage in silhouette, the dancers lie on the floor where they began, and black cutout doubles of them rise out of their places and float upward, like the fumes from an oil refinery. Yet even this marvelously contrived effect couldn't entirely transform the dance into metaphor for me. Nikolais' desexed, posturing humanoids kept reminding me of dancers, and my regret was stronger than fantasy.

March 19, 1973

Index

IN HIS RECENT WORK Murray Louis seems to be choreographing two dances at a time — one for himself and one for his company. His new dance, *Index*, premièred during the joint Louis-Nikolais season at Brooklyn Academy, is a prime example. *Index* is subtitled "(. . . to necessary neuroses)", and it opens very effectively with a lone girl on a dim stage, red and green lights flashing on her alternately from opposite directions. It's an optical illusion: her image jumps sideways as the light blinks red — green — red, and she seems to be two people, except one of them is always invisible. (Lighting for the piece was created by the master magician, Alwin Nikolais.)

From this, and from the Rorschach-like double-image photographs projected on the backdrop, we infer that the dance is going to be about psychological hang-ups. But it's not really, until Louis appears. His three solos constitute a kind of progression. In the first he's rooted to the floor, tugging and pushing at gravity but unable to get up. Between these exertions, he gestures compulsively, jabs back and forth through his folded-up legs, scratches, reaches his hands around his back toward some impossible joining place. Finally he squats like a chimp and plays "wipe that face off your face" at the audience.

Next time we see him he's wandering irresolutely like a specter through the empty stage. He faces upstage a lot, where two sets of railroad tracks are projected onto some red squiggly lines that turn out to be drawings of a family. In his last dance he seems to have been freed, and he explodes all over the stage in a fast, jazzy mania. These three scenes are scattered among sections done by the other six dancers, and the whole piece ends with the group dancing to a raga, with bugs projected on the cyc.

Since the solos are what makes sense to me now about the

dance, I've concluded that the group sections were the interludes and the solos the main event. But you can't really perceive this from Louis' construction of the dance. Its moment-
to-moment logic, the sequence in which people follow each
other on and off, isn't particularly leading, nor does the group
make interesting statements of its own. Mostly in unison, the
group does explorations and repetitions of small ideas like
bouncing up and down on both feet, swinging the knees back
and forth, one dancer falling backward across another dancer's
forward-curving body.

Louis doesn't dance with the group ever. Sometimes they
seem to be giving him a fanfare, but their exits and his entrances don't quite coincide. The group might, of course, represent the crushing mass of conformity from which Louis is
trying to break loose, old-fashioned as that idea sounds. But
nothing about him, actually or stylistically, really links him to
them in the first place.

Louis' distinction as a dancer has always been in the ingenu-
ity of his articulation. When he's dancing well, and he is this
season, he seems able to induce any part of his body to move
with any desired dynamic quality and in any sequence or combination. He prevents himself from looking like a puppet because there's such a strong identity controlling and organizing
the total body.

The six dancers in his present company have Louis' gifts in
varying degrees, but he seems to count less on their individuality than on the sheer weight of their numbers. All three men
have the same kind of beards. The girls wear their hair alike.
The movement looks mechanical on them — in *Index* at least.
Louis seems to want it that way.

March 19, 1973

Growing Old in the Land
of the Young

DANCE IS OBSESSED with youth, like all the narcissistic en-
claves of our society. Dance as sport, dance as glamour factory
— a passion compounded of physical mastery and an idealization of the human form. Other cultures use dancing as an
outlet for pent-up emotions, as a celebration of the natural and
supernatural wonders of life, as a means of teaching the society's rules, announcing its codes. Western ballet and its twen-
tieth-century relative, modern dance, have minimized these
functions or turned them into vicarious experiences. The
greater part of society, the audience, doesn't get to do the physical part of dance or its mystery-making either. We sit and
watch while the dancers do it for us. We're shown its physical
prowess, and though we feel twinges of kinesthetic exhilaration, we suspect that we couldn't possibly achieve any authentic physical charge of our own. Grown-ups in our society don't
ordinarily run and jump and bend and wave their arms, any
more than they make magic.

Mechanization has severely curtailed our opportunities to
use our physical resources. The suburbanite may travel many
miles each day but the only exertion required is a few steps to
the garage, a few twists of the arm and hand, the micromotions
of foot to gas and brake pedals. We're so out of touch with our
bodies, no wonder we're satisfied with the faint reverberation
we feel from a dancer's leap.

In leaving physical expression to dancers — and sports players and rock stars — we've given away part of ourselves. We've
assigned them not only our potential for moving, but our hopes
for physical perfection. The more divine their tricks, the less
we can identify our own physicality with theirs. However thin

or sexy or agile or coordinated or beautiful we are *not*, we know dancers will be. We've made them our so much riper, grander, more potent alter egos that we've caused them to become almost totally separated from us, another race altogether.

Dancers believe it too; they have to. We constantly hear of good dancers retiring in their early thirties or leaving companies they've been associated with long enough to carry major responsibilities. A few years ago Erik Bruhn, probably the greatest danseur noble of our time, retired at forty, then made a comeback — but he plays the villain now instead of the prince. It's not that these premature dropouts can't dance anymore but that the reality of what they are doesn't measure up to the ideal of what they've trained themselves to be.

From a very early age the ballet dancer externalizes himself, tries to become a superversion of himself. This image comes from what the audience wishes for, from what teachers put into young dancers' heads, from the romanticized words of past and present writers, and from the way they see other dancers — in a fairy-tale glow of bright lights and make-up and tulle. When Pavlova was eight, she saw her first ballet, *The Sleeping Beauty*. "When we left the theatre, I was living in a dream . . . That very night I dreamt that I was a Ballerina, and spent my whole life dancing like a butterfly . . ." "The lights and warmth made me think of Paradise." (Karsavina) Butterflies don't have wrinkles or arthritis. I don't think we can underestimate the power of that prince or butterfly that dominates the strivings of a dancer. The dancer's goal is not only to become a more than perfect being but to remain there once having achieved the identification. The first place in a ballet company goes to the ballerina, the princess, not to the friend, the older sister, or the wise confidante. Seniority in a ballet company does you some good only if you can conceal it. This means that a dancer's experience and maturity have no value in the coin of his profession. Older dancers make good teachers, coaches, choreographers, but they cannot use their years on the stage, except in lesser roles.

I was noticing last fall during the Eliot Feld Company's season at the Public Theater how little he was using the older members of his company, John Sowinski and Elizabeth Lee, who left Ballet Theater twice to dance with Feld, and Naomi Sorkin and George Montalbano. Two of them have now left the company. Christine Sarry, another Feld stalwart, still dances major roles, but the new work he choreographed for her, *Excursions*, styles her as a rip-roaring tomboyish teen-ager rather than the gifted grown-up artist she is.

Like many choreographers, Feld wants to challenge his dancers' highest powers. This seems to leave no place for the dancer who's no longer at peak speed, strength, and flexibility, or who has to work too hard to achieve them. Most companies, including Feld's, look like a high school senior class. Ballet sometimes sneaks around this imagery but not often. Feld once choreographed a stunning solo for a woman that required her to be neither virtuosically fast nor classically beautiful nor flirtatiously young, in *At Midnight* (1967). As danced by Elizabeth Lee, it became one of the more profound moments in ballet — a comment on the isolation and despair of the woman who is different in precisely those ways. The solo was choreographed on Cynthia Gregory, who never did it as well as Lee, perhaps because she couldn't escape her own perfections.

Ballet technique does set up goals. It's not just a question of dancing well, but of getting your leg up to there, of turning to the exact spot on the diagonal, and when a Baryshnikov comes along with a higher jump, the goal immediately adjusts itself upward. Virtuosity isn't the only component of ballet training, but it's stressed more than ever today, even in Europe where a greater range of excellence is conceivable if only because older dancers get tenure there and have to be given things to do. The ever-increasing dance audience is impressed by feats, by flash and even distortion. I find some new ballets exhausting to watch because they're so high-pitched all the time, but I think a lot of the audience can only feel by feeling used up.

Modern dancers at first denied all this glamorizing of the physical capacities, resisted the confinement of a technique so narrow and exacting. They made room for the dancing person with other qualities, for the high priestess who danced on into her old age, for the mimes, the eccentrics, the earthbound. Without one technique as a norm, modern dance developed in several different directions based on the movement preferences and perceptions of its leaders. You could say it was egocentric but I think it wanted to be — and was — more in tune with human life.

Initially most modern dance choreographers wanted to make dance that expressed themselves. They didn't have to stop dancing early, because their dance was about whatever age or condition they were in. Martha Graham made herself a bride at fifty — in *Appalachian Spring* — because she was a bride then, a great artist and supremely powerful woman marrying for the first time in middle age. I feel sure that the depth of Graham's choreographic achievement has everything to do with her longevity as a performer. She created roles from the inside, with her own huge dimension; ultimately she had to dance them.

The time of individualism passed in modern dance. The drive to see oneself dancing, once satisfied, expanded to include other dancers, and then there came the question, Why not let them do it? I think this question has determined the present character of just about every middle-generation modern dance company. The companies formed in the last decade don't appear to have considered the question at all. Or haven't had to.

Alvin Ailey was the first to stop dancing, when he was around thirty-five. Like Paul Taylor, who's the same age but who continued dancing until a year or so ago, he had to face the question of how to project his vision through other dancers. Ailey had made intermittent charismatic "soul" pieces but his company mainly does a repertory of other choreographers' works, dancing in a relaxed, all-purpose balletic/Broadway style.

Taylor struggled with the question in *Esplanade* — a dance to Bach in which there are almost no dance steps, just arrangements of walking, running, and falling that have been given the intensified dynamics of dance. *Runes*, new this winter, recovers much of the old Taylor vocabulary, but the movement emphasis seems to be on changing the shape of the body, particularly the upper body, rather than traveling. *Runes* is an oracular, incantatory dance; it reminded me of some films I'd seen of Mary Wigman. Something about the dancers' self-possession, self-absorption makes me think they're projections of a sedentary, contemplative Taylor.

Some choreographers have turned much of the repertory over to young dancers but have continued to dance themselves. In a kind of reverse sublimation, Murray Louis choreographed a piece for Rudolf Nureyev, then later danced the role himself, to almost universal acknowledgment that Louis did it better. Erick Hawkins has developed a whole technique and repertory of soft, pliable dancing that demands no more stamina or pyrotechnics than can be comfortably pulled off by a man of sixty. His dancers look as happy in it as he does.

Merce Cunningham has handled the problem differently. He's kept his company working at a technical fever pitch, taxing their speed and rhythmic sensitivity to the utmost. Cunningham's movement vocabulary makes use of the articulate footwork of ballet, plus an active, differentiated torso. His dancers can get across the floor with more complicated steps in less time than anyone — and the steps are always embroidered with changes of direction and force. His choreography has lost the fragmented look it used to have; there aren't so many disparate things going on at one time. The dancers do a lot but they're more likely to do it in unison or in small ensembles working in counterpoint or succession. They also work with the idea of support, teaming up fleetingly to lift, hang, fall, carry, then splitting off to another partnership.

Although Cunningham may link up with these groups briefly, he presents himself as a different order of stage being. Cunningham has often set himself apart from the rest of the company. His works are not dramatic, but they become so when Cunningham hovers in the background like an anxious chaperon, walks into the middle of an active ensemble and taps someone on the shoulder to break up the sequence, or paces a difficult meter by clapping out the time. In the last few years he has allowed himself to move differently from the group too.

He gave himself a solo called *Loops*, which he often performs simultaneously with some group activity. Standing in one place, he describes a long rope of curlicued hand gestures. As his hand squiggles, loose-wristed, out, up, over his head, meets the other hand, gives it the gesture to continue, you get involved in all kinds of fantasies; sometimes the hands are separate creatures living a life of their own, sometimes they hold objects or perform tasks, sometimes Cunningham seems acutely aware of them, sometimes he seems to wash his hands of them.

He did studies for himself in which he would drop into a particular spot on the floor or along the walls, perch in a peculiar position, and immediately become still, as settled into the place as if he'd been there for centuries. And he did a short dance called *Solo* (1973), in which he came out, crossed the stage, stood in one place, moved a few steps downstage, lay down, got up and left. Using a very limited number of body parts at a time, and moving those very minimally, he managed to suggest a whole jungle full of animals and birds.

I find several pretty amazing things about Cunningham's doing this, not the least of which is his honesty. No more is he trying to remind us that he was once buoyant, fast, engaging. These dances admit that he is an older man, and that what he can do now is not less than what he could do before, but of a different variety of genius.

As he's been so often during his thirty years of choreographing, Cunningham is once again out in front showing us new possibilities for dancing. This time it's the weightiness of age that he plays with — the sense of solidity and mass, of the earth not as something to resist or to celebrate but as something with which he is in intimate contact. And also the idea of economy — I think *Solo* must have become a dance about animals because, like a wild creature, he wastes nothing. His repose is complete, but never so deep that he can't come out of it easily. He moves only what he needs to move, looks exactly where he wants to see and nowhere else.

This latest cycle of work has brought Cunningham back to very simple ideas, and in that he now reminds me of some of the earliest modern dancers. Although his intention is still as objective, as nonexpressionistic as it ever was, the simplicity of his design, the purity of his concentration has the same kind of basic feeling as Graham's 1930 *Lamentation* or Doris Humphrey's 1928 *Water Study*.

Cunningham's *Rebus* (1975) may be, like all his dances, only

about movement. But it is about both these kinds of movement — his own — pulled in, solid, preoccupied with essentials, and that of his dancers — active, spreading out, spend-
thrift. It's remarkable for a choreographer to underline the
difference between himself and his company this way, to dram-
atize it.

At the beginning of the dance he's alone on stage, dressed in
a sleazy pair of slacks and a sport shirt that's cut long and
straight and is buttoned at the neck. He looks like a retired
night watchman in Sioux Falls. He's standing in profile in the
upstage right corner, feet flat, one hand extended from the
elbow to touch a clothes rack with a few garments hanging on
it. After a long time, he turns toward the audience and begins
a sort of warm-up, very carefully and slowly sliding his feet out
along the floor, then gradually working up to more vigorous
action and expanding his attention from the serious business of
his body out to the stage space and then the audience. When
he speeds up and uses more of his body, he has to push himself, and the spurts of energy are quickly used up.

Ten dancers enter and begin their warm-up, and Cunningham goes back to standing by his clothes rack, this time on
one foot, and holding the rack for support. As the other dancers move in ordinary classroom patterns, reposition themselves
in the space, stand and wait, Cunningham moves around the
periphery, sometimes initiating sequences that they copy,
sometimes drawing one or another of them aside to work with
individually.

This has all the elements of a dance class though it isn't a
dance class. Cunningham is undeniably, indispensably there
— the inventor, leader, prime mover, guru — and yet he fades
out. He sketches a fast combination for the feet, then walks off
and leaves the dancers to finish as soon as he's sure they've got
it. He stands behind a man who's lifting a woman, shadows his
movements — or is the man following Cunningham's lead?
While the group holds a difficult balance, he works with a
woman in the background, holding one of her hands and drawing her lightly across the stage as he makes little excursions
around her. He's guiding her but he's doing his dance at the
same time. Later he crosses with another woman, walking

backward so he can face her and pat her arms, shoulders, waist, just so. Suddenly she's gone, back working with the group, and he's left there with his hands touching empty space.

While the group is busy, he goes behind the clothes rack and takes off his pants and shirt. Underneath he's wearing red leotard and tights. He steps into the middle of a group that's been standing facing away, they fall, disperse gradually, and he's left alone. He dances his solo, faster and more eccentric than anything the company could do, but also full of effort, even rather desperate. Then all of a sudden he's back posing by the clothes rack, as if some signal interrupted his revels and called him back to the land of the bewitched.

Rebus is the most personal dance I've ever seen Merce Cunningham do, sad, ironic, and hopeful all at the same time. It states the case of Cunningham and every dancer, not only the poignant case of his age and his dilemma of what to dance, but his relationship to the dancers who carry out his work and will carry it on. This is the first time I've ever seen Cunningham speculate about the future, and his view is ambiguous; the dancers need him and he needs the dancers. He will leave them and they'll leave him. The work will go on somewhere without him, in some form that neither he nor they can be sure of.

Rebus is a parable about the fundamental duality in this whole system of Western dancing. The young dancer is full of energy and power, expresses the fulfillment of the art's possibilities, and is at every moment subject to replacement by someone coming up behind. The old dancer is past his technical power but wise as a performer. The young dancer's technique gets used in great displays of brilliance but his qualities as an individual are submerged. The old dancer has learned who he is and how he dances, but the dance is passing him by. And both of them are poised where the audience can't quite put itself, doesn't quite want to be, in a state between mystic intelligence and sweat.

Summer 1976

The Candid Art of Time

WE HAVEN'T HAD a good old-fashioned succès de scandale in so long, I wonder if anybody cares passionately about art anymore. Something is more likely to get booed as a bad investment than as an aesthetic mistake. The closest thing to a scandal in the 1971–1972 dance season broke out at the opening of Jerome Robbins' new piece, *Watermill*. The shocker was that *Watermill* had virtually no dancing in it. New York City Ballet star Edward Villella was required to strip to his jockey shorts and spend the rest of the dance as a spectator to a long chain of extremely slow, droning events. There wasn't a pirouette in the package.

Not that these desecrations didn't exist before — anyone with the mildest interest in experimental dance, or even pop ballet or the commercial theater, had certainly been exposed to nudity and nonlinear, minimal action by that time — but the dignity of Lincoln Center and its patrons is vast and easily affronted. You don't expect to find these goings-on in this place. Clive Barnes promptly unfurled the Masterpiece bunting over *Watermill*'s eager head and the furor subsided, but something still bothers people about the piece. What makes *Watermill* daring, what pushes its viewers beyond the entertaining, pleasantly excited point where they want to go, is also the one element that to me is most characteristic and most interesting about the ballet: its distortion of time.

Dance, of course, is very much *about* time, and we expect ballet to contain fast and slow movement, to stimulate us with abrupt changes or delayed resolutions. As long as it stays within the musical beat and doesn't let either the quickness or slowness get out of proportion, we can accept dancing of near-eccentric timing. Violette Verdy's phrasing — the way she draws out the upbeat in order to pounce on the beat — fascinates us even when it becomes almost too emphatic. Edward Villella initiates with an extremely powerful and quick impulse, often using a lot of busy little motions to get himself going and then slowing down dramatically at the end of the phrase, and these harsh spurts and intakes of energy allow him to jump higher and turn more times than almost any dancer in this country. *Watermill* cheats the audience of all the thrills we get from accelerated or retarded motion on stage. Its time is evenly distributed, slow, monotonous as a ticking clock, and, to many people, frustrating.

Of all the intangible forces of our existence, time seems to preoccupy Americans most. Space contracts or opens out around us without our noticing. We ignore the weight and tensions of the bodies we live in, and we make ourselves oblivious to all but the most overbearing sounds and smells. But time seems to be always pressuring us with its deadlines and anniversaries. When we're not doing time, we're killing it, or saving it, or making it, or borrowing it, or trying to catch up with it when it gets ahead of us or bring it back when it's gone.

The idea of doing something to time has intrigued choreographers for almost fifty years. Perhaps it was the German expressionists, perhaps it was Martha Graham, but someone decided that time in dance didn't have to be only a matter of speeding up and slowing down depending on the tempo of the music and its permissible rubatos. Theatrical time has never been the same as literal time, and the drama's various devices of narrative condensation and heightening had taken hold early in the history of ballet. But Graham departed radically from these conventions by introducing flashbacks, memories, and the simultaneous visualization of more than one time at a time as a character confronted events of the past — not in a dream but in a "real" action.

In a Graham dance it's not always possible to tell where in time a character is — past, present, or future. The narrator figure can be at one moment telling how she feels now, in her old age; at the next moment she may be acting out events in her past. Graham can show a whole war, a love affair, the development of a personality by introducing characters or events consecutively or together that are really spread far apart in time. The fact that some of these characters are real people and some are symbols, that some events are shown as the narrator actually lived them and some are as she imagines them, doesn't make the audience's orientation to time any clearer. However, by deliberately taking her narratives out of time, Graham gave them a quality of universality, a sense of transcending time and so existing for all time.

In Germany Mary Wigman and her disciples were working in nonnarrative forms, and were experimenting not only with the actual drawing out or compressing of the time it took to do a movement, but with the subtle effect that other elements like sound, light, or a restructuring of space could have on the feeling of time. Working at the level of sensation and perception, rather than the more artificial, presentational area of consciousness, they could effect a feeling of timelessness by making time go away — by repeating an action, like a trance or dervish dancer, until both performer and viewer became engrossed in the physicality or the emotion of it. They explored how great masses of people in motion could alter the audience's experience of time and space. The fantastic multimedia creations of Alwin Nikolais, applying the time-and-space-changing possibilities of technological devices to dance, are a direct product of this branch of experimentation.

In recent years we've seen people in both the extremely avant-garde and the extremely popular dance using time as a factor equal with or more important than movement idiom or narrative content. Instead of being something that's supposed to enhance or vary the look of movement, time can actually convert the movement into another thing, or can impose an entirely different stylistic gestalt on it.

Possibly the most far-out work in all of dance — and at this point the most unadorned with theatrical business — is being done by Stephanie Evanitsky and her Multigravitational Experiment. This group works off the floor, in a trapezelike arrangement of six inner tubes hung from the ceiling. But they don't swing, balance, or do acrobatics in the tubes as you might expect. Carefully keeping their bodies nearly weightless, they move with a slow fluidity as they continuously progress through the tube-sculpture. They change their shapes, transfer their weight to new supports, reach, slither, suspend, mold, make contact with each other.

It doesn't look exciting or dangerous; in fact, it hardly looks like anything at all. But after a long time you begin to see an overwhelming sensuality in this movement; the dancers seem to be pouring themselves through space, wrapping every inch of their bodies around the palpable air. I think it's the slowness that makes you especially aware of their ability to hang in grotesque or unnatural attitudes for the longest time without going dead or posing, the gradual way they change to new configurations, the lingering, melting images they create.

One reason *Watermill* seems terribly long to the audience is that it uses this same held-back sense of time — except that where Evanitsky's concern is with pure movement, Robbins portrays a quite realistic narrative situation. We get the feeling that someone is deliberately keeping the dance from going at its normal pace, as indeed someone is.

But also, *Watermill* is in fact a long dance, about an hour. The simple fact of duration is important to Robbins' theme, which is nothing less than the totality of a man's life. Robert Wilson, from whom Robbins derived major inspiration for *Watermill*, creates epic-length productions; to him an hour is just a start. His most recent work, *OVERTURE for KA MOUNTAIN AND GUARDenia Terrace*, was given in two parts, from 6:00 to 9:00 A.M. and 6:00 to 9:00 P.M. Wilson called this work "an introduction" to an even larger piece he was planning for performances in France and Iran. Meredith Monk too is fond of lengthy pieces in several installments. Her Joan of Arc piece, *Vessel*, had three segments of about an hour and a half each, in three different locations in downtown New York.

These choreographers have specific reasons for making extremely long works; it's not that they are unable to edit themselves. Something happens to you as audience when you stay involved with the same group of performers and the same theme for such a long time. The formalities begin to break down. You get relaxed and comfortable with where you are, you get to know your neighbors, you may chat quietly, smoke, go out for something to eat and come back. It's like a baseball double-header, with much the same attitude of familiarity toward the players, of not having to pay close attention all the time. You are free to do this because you're in an informal space rather than a proscenium stage, which focuses your attention and limits your means of responding to a work.

Both Monk and Wilson lead semicommunal groups of people who live and work together, and their theater-pieces stress the continuum of lives in that kind of community. You are meant to be aware of their growth, of the pasts and personalities that have contributed to the theater event. You're meant to feel that you've grown somewhere with them while you've been visiting.

In *Ka Mountain* a girl builds a small cairn of rocks, placing them one by one in a pile, with a branch of juniper on top. Later the juniper bursts into flame. Still later a little girl dressed as an old woman laboriously lifts the rocks and the unburned twigs one by one into a basket and drags it all away. This could be done much more economically — and it would be in the conventional theater. Dance is full of stylized work movements, like the peasants' hay-cutting dance in *La Fille Mal Gardée* or the chain gang swinging its invisible heavy hammers in Donald McKayle's *Rainbow 'Round My Shoulder*. There are scenic transformations and things that grow or get built by magic. A hundred years' worth of vines and cobwebs creep over the castle in *Sleeping Beauty*. Hilarion puts the finishing touches on a cross to place on Giselle's grave in the woods. The toy Nutcracker turns into a prince.

What Robert Wilson is saying is that work is *not* magic. When he substitutes real work for stagecraft he's not only making the audience more aware of the task that's being done, he's also calling attention to the other lovingly fashioned artifacts that are part of the production — a pyramid made of wooden boards mortised and doweled together — the very doorposts of the room we sit in, made of cement poured into wooden frames, with smooth, striated rocks mounted on them for decoration. This is no stage set. This is the life of the people who make this theater.

*

The idea of showing how long it takes to make something instead of taking a theatrical shortcut is related to the idea of endurance. Rather than skip over or disguise the effort required to do something hard, some people want to emphasize the effort. Kei Takei and William Dunas have circumvented the almost universal attitude in dance that certain physical reactions are unacceptable in performance. They don't pace their dances so that they can catch their breath, or duck offstage when their legs get rubbery from too much running. Both of them, in fact, have worked on extending a movement sequence to the verge of exhaustion. The resulting physical depletion makes its own dramatic point.

Dunas' recent solos have been made up of many variations on a calculatedly few dance themes. In *The King Is Dead* he examined at least fifteen elements of traditional jazz dancing, building a little dance around each element — a rubber-legs dance, a knee-lifting dance, a mooching dance. In between these sequences he stopped — composed at first, gasping toward the end — and transformed himself into another character, a rigid, clothespin doll of a man who made slashing gestures with his arms and issued strangled commands. The dance lasted over an hour, and although Dunas produced no changes of intensity, no "acting" clues that would develop these characterizations, as time wore on the jazz dancer seemed to be suffering intolerably while the angry puppet grew oppressively more cruel and irrational.

Kei Takei's *Light Part* V presents a monolithic arrangement of three bodies, Takei and two men — one person holding the other two up until they all topple, lie on the floor gathering strength, and slowly pull themselves up again into a new position. That's the whole dance, except that sometimes Takei stands with her face to the ceiling and her eyes closed. You are forced into an intense awareness of these bodies, their shapes and mass — Takei, built like a twelve-year-old, with the tenacity of a fierce hunting animal — the men, neither of them young, one tough and highly strung, the other heavy and obdurate. You note the different ways they support each other, the points of weakness and tension, the first sign of collapse, the lack of resilience when they come apart and fall, and at the

same time you feel the permanence of the image they are creating — that the structure will survive because they have an
endless capacity for restoring and re-creating it. Is it courage,
is it madness? Is it blind evolution?

Takei, Dunas, and the rest are certainly not making conventional theater, but in every important sense of the word they
are theatrical. More theatrical, I think, than a piece like Glen
Tetley's sometimes-nude ballet *Mutations*. Here only the *idea*
of the ballet was theatrical. Dancers were going to cover and
uncover their bodies — with clothes or paint or grotesque costumes. Tetley extended the time it took to accomplish all these
changes and filled it with a lot of motion of no particular origi-
nality or focus. The audience feels suspense because we have
to wait so long for the promised exposé, but our response to
what is happening *during* that long wait is anything but
heightened.

Not only the most experimental choreographers use time to
reshape the immediate event. The second act of George Balanchine's *Don Quixote*, which is about as bizarre and unconventional a story ballet as has ever been made, takes place in
the court of a sadistic Duke and Duchess, who have brought
the befuddled Don there as a kind of jester. 'The Don thinks
he's being rewarded at last for his brave and noble qualities.
The people of the court wear stiff, heavy black and gold costumes, and they move with exaggerated slowness. The steps of
their procession and sarabande are portentous, oblique, mock-
ing. Their cruelty is prolonged and deliberate, and the Don's
martyrdom at their hands is dwelt upon as if it were a cherished
thing. I got the impression the whole scene was taking place in
the Don's self-pitying mind. It was as if by slowing down the
action in his imagination, he was savoring and magnifying the
wrongs that had been done to him.

We're probably more aware of slowed-down theater time
than speeded-up time, because American life, especially American life in cities, is fast. Once I was in Montreal at noontime
on a working day. I wasn't in any particular hurry, but the
crowds seemed to be moving at a crawl; I could hardly keep

myself lagging along at their pace. We pick it up right away whenever a theater action decelerates, but extra speed on stage fits in unobtrusively with our own racing rhythms. We're impressed with speed, we even crave it if we don't have to do anything to achieve it.

Gerald Arpino, chief choreographer of the City Center Joffrey Ballet, has been gradually modifying the classic ballet style with this jet-age infatuation in mind. Arpino has always known the spectacular uses of fast dancing and the dramatic effect of changes of pace, suddenness, and gradualness; and allegro dancing accounted in part for the success of such works as *Viva Vivaldi* and *Confetti*. With his rock ballet *Trinity* Arpino seems to have decided on speed as a primary method of operating.

Everything in *Trinity* is pushed just a little faster than it should go. The ballet opens with dancers running across the stage, taking giant leaps that change direction in midair. This propulsion comes from nowhere. There's no development of tension, no time for revving up the motors; it's just a natural resource that can be turned on at will. Tap water. Later there's a more subdued, romantic section where the man lifts a girl high above his head with one arm. Having hoisted her up there, he's not content to simply stand and admire her, or carry her off in triumph. He runs with her. And other running couples fill the stage — the girls backbending down over the men's supporting arms, with their limbs streaming out as if in a fast current. The final section begins in a salvo of urgent punches and ends with a visual image of calm: all the dancers placing candles on the floor and going away as the music recedes from a roar to a heartbeat. Yet the ballet's drive doesn't let up — the walking is formal, the energy contained only by the pulsating rhythm. And we find, with the curtain falling to that rhythm, that it's been driving us too, all along.

After *Trinity*, Arpino refined this idea of speed-ballet. He quoted from other ballets and hyped them up — a solo that might have come from *Giselle* done at double time in *Kettentanz*, for instance. He crowded so many steps into each musical phrase of *Chabriesque* and *Reflections* that he had to develop a kind of platoon system, sending in new groups of dancers every few bars to spell each other. Gradually you could see the dancers in his ballets losing their classic line without losing their virtuosity. Arpino's pace forced them to omit details — they were good at covering a lot of space, but small changes of position like foot beats or arm adjustments were blurred out of existence. They could spin like demons, and they almost always exited in the air so your last impression of them was of human cannonballs. To the ballet-goer these dancers look unbeautiful, but to the general audience they're a replica of the nervous expertise of our times.

For the visual satisfactions of balletic style Arpino substitutes a sort of Hollywood-romantic illusion that softens the contacts between the dancers. Men hold the women tighter than is necessary for support — they grab and snatch in a facsimile of modern passion, not the sissified, delicate handling of classic ballet. The women don't merely lean on the men's shoulders or arms, if possible they twine their arms around the men's necks, they hug instead of merely touching.

Arpino-ballet is kitsch, but so is *Watermill*, with its pretty, pseudo-Oriental demeanor and the importance it lends to ordinariness. Robbins never quite makes a case for the characters in his ballets — I wonder why I should be interested in them since they are always just passing through my field of view, acting out dramas that have neither beginning nor end. But I usually am interested in them, because of the compelling way Robbins puts together the dynamics.

Changes of speed in his *Dances at a Gathering* provide the dancers with a wide range of possibilities for expressiveness and interaction with each other and with the music. You don't need a lot of elaborate staging or literal acting-out to tell you that these characters are real. They describe their own feelings; they chase each other, daydream, rush ahead of the beat, walk slowly arm in arm, race, reconnoiter, stop. Deprived of these time changes, *Watermill* seems much less human, more pretentious. The central character's banality is exposed and even emphasized as the unexceptional events of his life trail across a carefully detailed scenic canvas. I don't think this is at all what Robbins intended, but the audience can hardly be blamed if they misunderstand.

Fall 1972

If a Rock Could Float

PHOEBE NEVILLE'S DANCE is very slow and deliberate. Things go on for such a long time that they begin to gather solidity, weight. In spite of that, the work never seems static, it keeps moving inexorably on. It holds me to its progression of events until someone does something — not too different from what has gone before — that uproots the whole thing. What has been prosaic and maybe even plodding is revealed as metaphor. Or sometimes many possible metaphors.

In *Ladydance*, one of five pieces performed by Neville and company and beautifully lit by Nicholas Wolff Lyndon at Riverside Church last weekend, she enters wearing a long velvet dress and walks in big circles, stepping onto a high-arched foot, then dipping into plié. She interrupts herself with sudden, emphatic gestures. She turns in smooth, sensuous spirals, then builds up into paroxysms of stamping both feet and shaking her fists. This recedes, and soon she twists up her loosened hair and goes out the way she came, contained, imperturbable, aware, her potential for fury suppressed.

At the beginning of *Cartouche*, a man (John Dayger) squats for a long time by the prone body of a woman. I can't think of any literal reason for him to be hovering over her that way, and when he finally rises to stand on her back it's even less comprehensible. He does a slow series of arm and hand gestures, all slightly the wrong shape for naturalism, and the music, a Purcell fanfare for brass choir, has been altered electronically, just enough to create odd dissonances and echoes. I begin seeing the man as a fascist politician in some silent movie.

For no apparent reason, he jumps down, and as he continues gesturing the woman (Neville) squirms around his feet, grasps his ankles, tries to climb up his legs. Finally he falls and she mounts his back, where she squats and makes faces until the lights go out.

I always thought this dance was about some type of revolution. Now Neville has made another version of it, *Unamed* [sic], in which, instead of gray jumpsuits, she wears overalls and Dayger a business suit and tie. The music is one of Bob Dylan's diatribes against the proprietors of the world. The dance goes faster this time, because of the music, but it's essentially the same thing again, only with different characters.

Neville's dance is gestural. There usually seems to be only one thing happening at a time, and if the phrase is made of a longer group of events, it's often drawn out so that as you keep looking at it, it hardly seems to change. It doesn't lead to its own climax, it just comes to a stop, at some point.

Arms are extended, folded, scrunched up close to the body, left to hang from the elbows. These aren't functional gestures, though they haven't the consciously artificial look of dance gesture either. Sometimes they lead the body into spiraling turns, falls, or spurts of locomotion, but what I remember is a succession of very grounded, clearly oriented positions.

In her new dance, *Mosaic*, four women cross the stage, one or two at a time, opening their arms, closing them, turning once, standing still. The shapes each one makes are distinctive enough so that you can recognize them when they're repeated by another dancer. The gestural motifs don't follow a clear pattern of development. Neither does the piano score by Meredith Monk, a sequence of arpeggios played in different registers, or broken up in different rhythmic ways.

Neville works a little apart from the other three dancers, and her actions are slightly more literal. She seems to trace letters or numbers in the air, she looks inquiringly over her shoulder at the audience from time to time. She reminded me of the character in *Ladydance*.

While a woman stands at the back of the stage, her head and upper body dangling from one reaching-up arm, Neville is motionless in a darkened foreground. The lights reverse and Neville clutches her skirt, drops to her knees, falls sideways, and pulls herself along the ground. In the last section, all the women step backward cautiously toward the center of the stage, and Neville works her way to the back where a picture frame hangs in space — one of the other dancers posed in it at the beginning of the dance. As Neville passes behind the frame, two of the others peer at her and the third woman looks away.

I didn't get to study this enigmatic pose long enough before the lights went out, but the dance seemed to have to do with some unspoken bonds between women. The dancers never acknowledged each other's presence except as onlookers, even when their actions momentarily coincided. In fact, Neville's dancers are always kept apart by the formality of their movement designs. They may touch, wrap themselves around other people, or, as in *Oracle*, work for long periods of time in synchrony, but I never feel they've ceased to be isolated individuals and become a group.

Oracle is in three parts. First a woman in black stands, stoops, bends on a box, her arms pulling her in all directions, while three other women in white sit among some other boxes. The woman in black leaves and the others rearrange themselves into angular new positions for a long time. Gradually they all leave their boxes and advance one step at a time, covering their eyes. One goes back to her box and the other two pose down center.

The woman in black returns and, after squatting and beating her fists against her thighs several times, she climbs onto the back of the woman sitting on the box. The woman gets up and starts walking. The bearer is as steady as she was, unencumbered, earlier in the ritual, and the woman in black roosts on her shoulder, arms spread, like a statue of a bird about to leave the ground.

April 1, 1976

Planned Pandemonium

ROBERT WILSON'S WORK has never been what you'd call transparent. His latest production, *The $ Value of Man*, on view last weekend at Brooklyn Academy, is the murkiest of all. And not just because audience and players are enveloped in smoke for most of its two and a half hours.

Like all Wilson's pieces that I've seen, *The $ Value of Man* is first of all nonlinear. You can't hope to make "sense" of it by following its action along from moment to moment. Wilson uses every device in the book to distort the anticipated flow of events: repetition, slow motion, cutting up and rearranging the parts of a scene, removal of the natural dynamics of speech and movement, simultaneous but unconnected activities. Adventurous theatergoers nowadays have probably experienced this phenomenon; it's only an exaggeration of the perceptual anarchy we live in most of the time anyway.

You get the message of Wilson's theater from visual and audible images that take shape amidst this seeming confusion, not from any specific information conveyed to you. Maybe message is too strong a word — attitude might be better. *The $ Value of Man* is about materialism, if you have to know. Wilson is against it because it oppresses and compartmentalizes people. There's nothing startling about this premise, except how Wilson arrives at it.

He's become increasingly interested in words, and for *The $ Value of Man* he's chosen to collaborate with Christopher Knowles, a student of his who has been described as autistic or brain-damaged or various other imprecise terms that indicate his mind doesn't work like the rest of ours. I wouldn't bring it up except that Knowles's thought process seems to replicate the scrambled yet highly patterned effects of Wilson's nonverbal theatricality.

Wilson works with only a few basic dramatic motifs here, but most of them are present in every scene. A chorus of black-coated, cigar-smoking plutocrats who stage stickups on each other; men and women in black evening clothes who throw small talk across gambling tables without expecting to be heard — "100 songs together!" "It could be some of . . ." "It could be special"; dancers in pants and T-shirts who I guess are the innocents; pairs of people on stilts who shout monotonous, meaningless dialogues above the voices of the others — "A!" "B!" "A!"; characters in melodramas like a woman standing over two prone bodies intoning, "It's so sad. But why did I do it?"

None of these characters interacts as a group with any other group, nor individually with their companions except in pro-grammed routines. They file in, take up their positions, speak their lines. Knowles, standing at a mike, picks up phrases of their dialogue and repeats them. A man with a tape recorder threads his way through the action, instant-replaying lines in the same way. From time to time Wilson bends over a micro-phone and speaks very quietly. He may be explaining the whole thing — "That seems to me to be the most . . ." or ". . . the first hour and a half . . ." But his words get swallowed up in the din and I never do find out.

The proscenium frame of most previous Wilson epics gave him a great deal of control over disparate elements like this. More important, it gave the audience control. You were free to focus on a pleasant composition or an intriguing event, or to let the actors drone on incomprehensibly for long stretches, like muffled radios in the next apartment.

Now Wilson is working in the open Lepercq Space at Brook-lyn, partitioning it in different ways so that more than one play can be going on at the same time. With the audience seated on risers on all four sides but free to move around, the space is dense with people. Instead of feeling more free and flexible than a traditional theater setting, it became crowded, claustro-phobic, as each scene built to a climax of noise and activity.

It got smokier and smokier as machine-made fog rose from inside the lighted green boxes that represented gaming tables. Michael Galasso's fiendish violin music played on and on in

minimal repeating phrases. The room became a kind of in-
ferno, lit in green and red. Everywhere you looked, above,
around, across, there were half-hidden, animated figures moving on errands with neither beginnings nor ends. It was quite
beautiful. It gave me a headache. It *was* hell.

May 15, 1975

The Storm Is in the Eye

MEREDITH MONK WORKS with very down-to-earth materials
to create very extraordinary effects. There's not much illusion
to her theatricality. Transformations take place in front of
your eyes, not behind scrims or out in the wings somewhere.
She invests spectacle with a sort of workaday homeliness that
often weighs down my imagination, but in *Quarry* I found the
actuality of her theater as interesting as the metaphorical vistas
it suggests.

Quarry, an opera in three movements — not acts, isn't constructed that differently from her last big piece, *Education of
the Girlchild*, or from the larger epics that came before. But it
gives me a greater feeling of unity. Things happen that involve
the whole space, affect all the participants, instead of illuminat-
ing pinpoints that I don't know how to locate or connect.
There's a progression and a consistency that I haven't seen in
Monk before. She is also beginning to infuse the staging and
the individual movement of her performers with the emotional
energy that has become so highly developed in her music.

Quarry seems to be a projection of a child's universe — the
close, familiar world of her family and the outer world that she
only knows secondhand. The piece takes place at a temporary

lull in the child's life; inactive and slightly spacey because of an illness, she passes in and out of consciousness. Real events and companions begin to merge with mysteries she's only half aware of; nastiness dimly perceived grows menacing enough to turn the commonplace into holocaust.

With the audience seated along the sides, the space at La Mama Annex is first divided into five little islands: a small dining table set for three, a parlor, a writing desk, some Oriental-looking mats and a scroll, and in the center a pallet with a patchwork quilt, and a night table nearby. A maid putters around the set while the audience is entering, then settles down to read a magazine and listen to the radio until the show is ready to start.

The lights go down, and before they come up again we hear Monk's voice in the dark, repeating plaintively, "I don't feel well. I don't feel well. I don't feel well." Pause. "It's my eyes. It's my eyes. It's my eyes. It's my hands. It's my hands . . ." We first see her in the bed, wearing flannel pajamas, lying very still only calling out over and over.

A tall lady in a 1940s print dress comes and tries to comfort her by telling her stories of a family picnic they went on together. Having quieted the child, she leaves, and the people in the corners of the room come to life. An elderly couple talk over the events of the day; three young women have dinner silently but with large communicating gestures; the mother sorts mail at the desk; and a foreign couple in long robes and head cloths pursue their domestic occupations.

Gradually these characters become more animated, begin to edge over into unreality, as the child is stimulated by the passing day, by things she sees and hears and remembers. The mother, a somewhat flamboyant character to begin with, seems to be rehearsing lines for a play, trying out different ways she would read them. Her motions get more melodramatic. When the maid flips the radio dial to amuse the child, it's the mother's voice that's heard announcing the news, the weather, doing a soap opera. Clouds pass overhead — people dressed in black, holding fluffy white sculptural things high in the air on sticks.

People pass by as if on the street — bicycle riders, a strolling couple, a photographer in a dirty-orange jumpsuit. The old man complains to his wife that his scholarly research can't be completed because his rivals are trying to wreck his career. The photographer snaps a flash picture of the Middle Eastern couple, and they immediately roll up their mats and all their possessions and run away as if being chased. More cloud people pass through, except this time the clouds are in the shape of airplanes and a droning sound fills the space.

The child sings a shrieking solo and half runs, half dances around and around her bed, with the maid agreeably following, trying to join her. But the child gets dizzy and the old man picks her up in his arms, puts her back to bed, and tries to soothe her. When he leaves, the maid turns on the radio again and, high overhead in a booth with a glass window and a clock on the wall, the mother appears.

She's dressed in black sequins and she acts wilder than ever, gesticulating in front of a microphone, although the voice that comes out of the radio is Monk's, singing. At the other end of the space, bathed in the same greenish white fluorescent glare as the radio studio, sits a tall sinister man in a gray flannel suit and tie. He's watching the woman in the booth. He's fixed and intense, truculent; you can tell she's in his power somehow.

The lights go out on this tableau, and as they come up again the old people are raising a toast to each other, and so are the young women. Many people in white advance down the space, singing canonically and interrupting their procession to do short, increasingly agitated individual movement phrases. This is the first of three big choral scenes. It's called Wash, and it does wash across the room with a polyphonic, polyvisual texture. Before the tail end of the procession is gone, attendants are rolling a wide red carpet down the center of the room in its wake.

Now a parade of eccentric megalomaniacs called Dictators arrives. A turbaned, fur-coated woman who eats imaginary oysters with obscene gusto and babbles about intergalactic messages. A tidy woman in glasses and a beige sharkskin suit. A white-haired man in a wheelchair who tells a pornographic story about Donald Duck and guzzles gumdrops. A military officer with an eye patch and a chest plastered with campaign ribbons and the voice of a petulant child. A diva in black velvet cape, jewelry, ostrich fan.

They all meet violent deaths, with the man in the wheelchair succumbing last — to a flash from the photographer's camera. This photographer, it now appears, is the hired gun of the man in the suit. His motions are watchful, furtively quick, brutish. After the assassination the man in the suit goes up on the stage at one end of the space and, with his henchman on guard, gives a speech.

It's a very harsh, stentorian speech, amplified through an echo chamber, and it has no words that you can understand. But you can see that this dispatcher of dictators is more psychotic than any of them. There's a thrill of spasmodic violence underneath his flat, automatonlike gestures, but he's always in control of it. You can also tell that he's not explaining or exhorting, but simply giving orders.

When he's done, the space has been cleared and a film is projected on a screen behind his rostrum. We're looking at a pile of all different shaped rocks left over from the quarrying process. The film is shot straight on, so you can't tell the size of the pile until antlike people dressed in white begin to inch out from behind the rocks. First one, then another, then the rocks seem crawling with people, who climb carefully over the rocks and disappear again. I doubt if this takes more than five minutes, but it's a stunning image of people in hiding. Then the camera drifts to the center of the quarry, which is filled with still, black water. People dressed in nightclothes are floating in the water, clinging to pieces of timber. Their eyes are closed and they don't move at all.

During the film, you've become aware of real people crawling into the darkened room, and when it ends and the lights come on, a tremendous activity shatters the deathly calm. As if answering the mad dictator's commands, people in gray shout a cadence: Ha! Ho! Hup! Hup! as they do fast calisthenics on the floor. Another group marches among them, singing to a martial beat. Still a third group snakes through, arms linked and held shoulder-high, like members of a chain gang or some grotesque hora, singing above the others in a guttural rallying cry.

Sometimes the marching group splits in two, going opposite ways around the perimeter of the room until they meet on the other side. They collide and fall to the ground in a heap, still singing. Characters from the home scenes we saw earlier pass through. The Middle Eastern couple reappear, only they're dressed in black modern clothes now and they look like inhabitants of a ghetto. They run back and forth, trying to get out of the way, but they're caught between two armies and knocked over.

The three young women enter with some luggage on a hand truck. They pass down the room, distributing bags to people. You hardly notice this amid the symphonic pandemonium that's going on, but gradually you realize that a silence is spreading across the room. As each person in gray is handed a suitcase, he or she stops marching or doing push-ups, stops singing, and drops to the ground. The next minute the whole space is still, and what you're looking at is a yard full of refugees, huddling together in groups of two or three, slumped over their belongings.

After this, the vision subsides. The ghetto couple and the old man and woman come forward and slowly throw their valuables on the floor. All the victims are herded away. The child and the maid appear, dressed for a journey, and while the child runs almost frantically in a circle, the maid calls out in French to someone we can't see that it's getting late.

Then the child begins a walking song, a final chorus. Everyone returns, now in street clothes, and there's a big procession with the group singing canonically. As the chorus continues, the child and the maid sit on the bed and, still with their coats on, leaf through a picture book. The chorus dies away and Monk/the child echoes their firm, measured refrain. Only she sings faster and faster, her voice rising and breaking almost out of control into nearly hysterical sobs or screams. She's still pointing at the picture book and she still hasn't quite lost the tune when the lights go out.

There's much to think about in this wonderful work. Monk

isn't old enough to have known the comic-strip terror that World War II represented to children growing up safe and sound in America, yet she captures it amazingly. Does she refer to another war? Did children feel that way in later wars?

Her theater techniques are almost faultless in this work — the attentiveness to light, sound, costume, scenic detail; the contrasts between motion and stillness, between language and song and gibberish and silence; the gradual evolution of the characters from loving protectors to the bringers of cataclysm; the shrinking of the child's circle of security in an immense world to one tiny spot, her own bed, and maybe even that is tippy.

The older members of The House by now play versions of the same roles in all Monk's work: Lanny Harrison, tall, lanky, always a bit exaggerated, is the mother; Ping Chong, who can carry off the role of a superstraight so well, the stage manager or boss or dictator; Coco Pekelis, the perennial peasant, the Sancho Panza of a maid, the only one of the child's familiars who doesn't betray her by secretly being someone else; Lee Nagrin, the earth mother/grandmother, steady and impervious to unrest; Monica Moseley, the independent, bright young woman. The others include Gail Turner and Mary Shultz as Moseley's working-girl companions, Tone Blevins and Daniel Ira Sverdlik as the Old Testament/ghetto couple, Pablo Vela as the persecuted scholar, husband of Nagrin, Steve Clorfeine as the photographer/body guard/hit man, and thirty-odd beautifully disciplined chorus members.

Quarry is a feminist statement in some ways. In the child's world, men are either absent or ineffectual. She has no father, but there's a picture of a sailor on her mother's desk. The three young women are single and on their own. The elderly uncle and the man from the Old Testament are bookish, unworldly, victimized. All the other males are predators and madmen. It's the women who do the work, hold together the homes, offer what rare emotional support the child receives. And it's a woman, Monk, who enacts the visionary, the vessel, the innocent who passively takes in the world and issues it out again in disembodied, transfigured images. A woman, Monk, who articulates the great lone cry of fear from the heart of repose for all of them, for all of us.

April 22, 1976

Ritual as Life

POPULAR THEATER FORMS, no matter how stylized or virtuosic they are, need at least one very evident and immediate connecting link with their audience. It may be low comedy, universally known songs, stories or dances, excursions into the supernatural. The audience, coming into the theater, recognizes a part of its own experience in the actors.

When the Kerala Kalamandalam Company performed here three years ago, it seemed to me I was encountering the ultimate theater art. Kathakali, the marvelous theater from South India, made such a deep impression on me that when it returned, I seemed to know every scene by heart. Two other formally structured, panoramic theater forms also appeared here Thanksgiving weekend, the National Chinese Opera Theater and Meredith Monk's The House, but neither moves me as Kathakali does.

Kathakali is a danced play with musical narration. Its stories and characters are taken from the ancient Sanskrit holy books, the Ramayana, Mahabharata, and others, but its actual texts and its theatrical form were developed in about the seventeenth century. This is the period of the building of the Taj Mahal, and Kathakali reflects the spatial clarity and the detailed workmanship that marked this high point in Indian art.

At first sight, Kathakali actors hardly seem to resemble human beings, with their faces painted green, red, or gold, elaborate designs traced on their foreheads and cheeks, delicately shaped paper beards and false noses, their eyes tinted dark red. Their costumes feature voluminous wide skirts and leggings; carved gold bibs, bracelets, bells, epaulets, earrings; long silver claws on the fingers of their left hands; towering headdresses of intricate design; and additional decorations and accessories for each individual character.

In their introductory scene, instead of jumping up and down or displaying their costumes or making some big show of force, they merely stand there in their huge magnificence and do a dance with a tiny, hardly visible portion of their faces. Elbows jutting wide, knees splayed out, clubbed feet digging into the floor, they wiggle their eyebrows and dart their eyes from side to side with faint, fixed smiles on their closed lips. That radiant glance, drawing even more power from the body's imposing stillness, seems as if it could melt buildings or save a man from death.

Kathakali characters are gods, heroes, and demons, capable of fabulous energies and transformations, and the Kathakali actors can portray subtle generosity, titantic rage, and everything in between. They can articulate parts of the face we don't use separately — the nostrils, the brow, the upper part of the cheeks, the jowls. They talk to each other in mudras — gesture language — often making simultaneous facial displays in a faster, vibrating counterpoint, or adding accents with the feet or voice.

A great deal of Kathakali's distinction comes from this multiplicity of techniques, this piling on of riches. There isn't much pure dance, but in another way, it's all dancing. Musicians and singers keep up a constant recitation/accompaniment, in which the rhythms change in accordance with the intensity of the story. The actors use mudras, dance, facial gestures, realistic pantomime, and even some improvisation in playing each scene. They don't move around on the stage much, gravitating instead to one of four or five central locations, and usually facing at least three-quarters to the audience. But their attention to the space that they're in can make them seem to be traveling great distances, or can create whole environments out of a few red boxes and a bare stage.

Kathakali storytelling takes place on many levels that are inaccessible to Westerners — we're not familiar with the lives and morals of all the characters, for instance, nor can we follow the mudras or the singers' words. But it's not through pure pantomime that we can understand so much of it.

I especially love the long duets where two opposing characters confront each other. In Kathakali the battles and seductions aren't realistic; they're more like studies concerned with the nature of the contest rather than the blow that ends it. When the villain Kichaka tries to seduce the virtuous Malini, the scene extends beyond realistic length — in any natural sequence, either Malini would run away or the old lecher would seize her. But he keeps grabbing and she keeps shrinking away from him until you see that they are both engaged in saving face. She's afraid of his fury, and she delays the moment of rejection, hoping to find a graceful way to escape. He restrains himself from taking her by force, apologizing and getting more and more frustrated, because he doesn't want her to think him a brute.

Similarly, when the two monkey brothers, Bali and Sugriva, get together for a fight, they hurl so many preliminary insults and challenges at each other that they eventually settle down comfortably on the floor to continue their shouting match, and you realize they don't want to kill each other at all. Sure enough, when Bali is shot by Rama's arrow, Sugriva collapses in grief.

I think it's the dynamic variety more than anything that makes Kathakali so close to life. That and the many-sidedness of the characters: the villains can evoke our pity, the heroes are capable of brutality, the gods make mistakes. Laden with conventions of costume, narrative, staging, and movement which could by now have emptied of everything but symbolic content, the actors manage to energize the forms, to activate feeling.

In the Chinese Opera the spectacle comes from masses of people parading through in gorgeous costumes, or from equally inexhaustible numbers of acrobats tumbling and flying through the air in precision-timed formations. These displays of brocades and giant masks and physical virtuosity may represent contending armies, but they don't in themselves have any emotion, character, or morality.

Chinese Opera — or Peking Opera as the form was known before it was forbidden in China itself and salvaged on Formosa — became codified a hundred years or so after Kathakali, and takes its texts and morality from very old sources, much as Kathakali does. The characters are legendary generals, demigods, animal-folk. But the theater is ceremonial, stylized; it's all prescribed gesture and movement and elaborate vocal style.

Dynamically, the Chinese move in a limited range. There are few points of extreme excitement or intensity; climactic moments are built up through an increase of speed and numbers of people, but in fact even the dramatic peaks of this theater are moderate. The actors seem to be pacing out their energy in measured amounts, carefully, neither too much nor too little at a time. You remember them gliding about with even, skimming strides. This careful husbanding of energy is what seems to permit their acrobatic agility and their maneuverability in large groups. They attack movement with a sudden lift of the body and a gradual settling back into place. It's the soft pouring back down that makes their acrobats look so bouncy to us, I suppose. Western acrobats do it the other way around, pushing off to spring up into the air and coming down all in one piece.

Not that the Chinese are incapable of fine detail. Far from it. Their vocalizations are very ornate; each speaking character has a particular stylized vocal range, within which he or she achieves great facility — slurring and sliding into quarter tones, glissandos, and odd intervals. Their bodies don't echo the sinuous quality of the sounds, though; in fact, they can isolate the vocal technique so successfully that they can move around and even dance with little perceptible change in their singing.

Meredith Monk also cultivates this ability to do virtuosic vocal things without changing the body. In fact, I'll venture the hypothesis that one sign of a high culture approaching dissolution is the development of very refined skills that have little interdependence or connection to man's physical being. Monk is up in her head — it's a brilliant head, but the principal way we can relate to her is by intellectualizing. The people who dig

Monk the most seem to get at her through their reading, their past experience, their knowledge of myth and religion, their asethetic sensibility, but hardly ever though their viscera.

Monk's theater is not popular in the sense of appealing to a mass audience. In fact, this fall her audience seemed more homogeneous than ever, mostly twenty to twenty-five-ish middle-class men and women. I'm sure Monk is aiming for a wider segment of the population. This is implicit in her refusal to call her works dances — *Education of the Girlchild* is subtitled "an opera"; in her attempt to create mythic substance out of a huge range of social and historical information, and in the whole ratty-funky-Everyman ambiance of her productions.

Yet she keeps her audience at a distance. Deliberately, I think, she holds back, or holds out, on us. Monk's performances are always late. The audience is forced to wait on windy sidewalks and claustrophobic staircases. The reservations are always mixed up, and when the doors finally open, we are pressed into an overcrowded space that is badly arranged for seating and visibility. Monk has been giving performances long enough to have learned how to make the audience comfortable, so one can only assume she wants to alienate it.

Possibly this extended buildup is some kind of showmanship — a girl behind me in line this time compared it to getting into a rock concert in Hartford, Connecticut. Or perhaps it's part of Monk's desire to take us away from the real world — if she makes the surroundings unpleasant enough, we'll be only too eager to leap into her fantasies.

The problem, I find, is that she's asking me to leap so far. All I can find for her walking abstractions is admiration, never empathy; interest, never excitement. Monk's symbolic figures are as strange to me as the characters in Kathakali. But where Kathakali figures exude life signs, act out life processes, Monk figures are dead artifacts that *represent* life processes. Her naked, blue-painted Death woman, with dolls sprouting from its head and fingers, is fantastic, but the figure does nothing. It's a grotesque, not a dramatic presence.

Monk limits not only the characterization but the movement itself, to very simple shuttlings back and forth or circlings of one body part while the rest of the body holds a pose. These little repeating motifs are like a rhythmic ground bass in music, and they sometimes serve as underpinning for a vocal solo, but sometimes they merely give a sense that the static group you see — a family seated around a table or building and taking apart a brick pile — is in a condition that will continue for a long time.

Whenever the movement threatens to get out of control, as when the characters appear to rebel against an authority figure and go into wild, flinging fits, she cuts off the phrase and makes the sequence start over again. A spiral is never connected to another spiral, never leads the dancer into space; it's quickly brought to a stop as the dancer gathers her momentum in to the center of her body, then has to start it going out again.

At the end of Part I of *Education of the Girlchild*, Monk is ceremoniously dressed as an old woman by the others in the cast, and is carried to a platform that has been prepared for her. There, like a marble statue, she sits in a chalky light while the audience mills around during intermission. Later she comes to "life" — a drained, spare life, a shadow of a life. The character gets younger and the motions get bigger but Monk is eerily weightless; she's so light she seems transparent, even when making the motions of work and assurance and firmness. The dynamics are so remote, so unvarying that the solo, and the rest of the work, seem pale and washed out to me for all their conceptual vitality.

January 1974

Shenyang Acrobats

WHATEVER MAY HAVE been accomplished in the way of cultural exchange, the Shenyang Acrobats certainly reveal something about the brave new world in the People's Republic of China. The Acrobats, the first mainland Chinese cultural team to visit the United States since 1949, opened a five-day run at City Center last night.

From the opening tableau, with the forty members of the troupe stacked in human pagodas, circling a maypole, and riding bikes atop twirling parasols, you know this is going to be spectacle in the grand manner. It's not only big as spectacles go, but curiously beautiful. The production is costumed in clear pastel colors and Chinese red, and each number is backed by a sky-soft cyclorama with clouds or delicate landscapes projected onto it.

The performers run on and off with airy speed and lightness. They connect their feats of dexterity with pretty poses and stylized little steps resembling ballet that seem to be derived from ancient Chinese fighting rituals. Though their routines frequently call for immense strength, these are no muscle-bound heavies. Like most acrobats, the Shenyang company are masters of tumbling, juggling, balancing, and pinpoint accuracy. They can do boneless backbends and create impossible, towering pyramids while smiling confidently.

What they excel in, though, is their acuity in space and an ability to separate their bodies into two or more systems performing very different tasks simultaneously.

For example, they keep three or four plates spinning on long rods in each hand by establishing a constant rhythm of the hand and arm. This never varies, and the plates never fall off the sticks while the acrobats are doing slow shoulder stands, head-to-head stands, and even flips. The torso makes big changes, but the arms stay steady.

In the traditional "swallow game," men dive through hoops the width of barrel staves, upended close together on a table. Curving and somersaulting in and out, they can control their speed and direction so precisely that they don't touch the hoops, but they never stop moving either.

The other unusual skill of the company is its balancing feats. Together with physical strength, the performers have an uncanny sense of placement, of where to find the exact perch that puts the least stress on the supporting object or person. They don't do pyramids with brute force, kneeling on each other's shoulder blades until the bottom row gets squashed. Instead, they carefully place a foot just so on somebody's thigh and lean out at a precise angle.

In the wildest of these flirtations with the laws of physics, a man rotated around in the air while doing a one-hand stand on top of a table, four glass pedestals, four chairs, a stool, and six bricks.

The company achieves some of its effect through an overall fluidity of movement and sequence. But even more, it can multiply: the extent of the danger or the number of times something can be done or the number of people doing it. I kept seeing those pictures of the millions on parade in Peking, happily waving and all alike.

January 4, 1973

Trucking Through the Spheres

THE COMPUTER BROKE DOWN at Hunter College a couple of Saturday afternoons ago, and it took a flustered box office half an hour to get the audience in to see the religious and ceremonial dances given by the Tibetan folk opera, Lhamo. Twenty minutes after curtain time a young man in a Western suit and tie, who later appeared in some of the dances, came out and announced that the program would be delayed ten minutes, and that they were cutting four numbers originally scheduled. He assured the audience that we weren't missing anything — the dances were pretty much like some others we would be seeing and they were kind of boring anyway.

The Tibetans have that kind of charm. Nothing inscrutable or humble or high-flown about them, they just do their dance. They carry their rich costumes and headdresses casually. There are no provisions in the dance for posing or showing off.

The program I saw was a mixed collection of sacred dances, folk dances, and dance/drama episodes from the Tibetan folk opera. Yet in terms of movement it was very consistent, and the most spectacular things the dancers did, toward the end of the afternoon, seemed to me a logical development of the same things I'd been watching.

Just about every dance begins with the dancers shuffling on one at a time or in a line. They keep a basic bouncing rhythm with their soft mukluk boots, and their bodies ride along easily on top of the beat. It's a propulsive thing, this beat, not aggressive or stagy. It's a means by which the dancers establish themselves and stay together with others in the group. The emphasis or accent can change, as well as the tempo, but there's never a harsh attack. In some dances the men stamp down forcefully on the beat and the women stay in unison with them, keeping their rhythm more smooth.

Out of this rhythmic continuum there come two tendencies — one for going into the air and one toward the ground. But again they preserve the idea of going on rather than stopping to show off. Most of their jumps and plunges are circular in shape — hopping in a ring, barrel jump-turns, whirling spirals up and into a fall.

In fact, the circle seems to be their main spatial alternative to the straight line. There are no intricate floor patterns or ornate body shapes to decipher in this dance. The dancers, usually working in equal numbers of men and women, or in groups of four or five men, move in linear paths across the space, back and forth toward the audience, or in squares or circles. The men and women occupy separate areas but they're usually doing the same steps, and they frequently address each other or work in otherwise complementary patterns.

Their bodies are quite simple. The torso isn't differentiated into its various segments like shoulders-chest-ribcage-pelvis, but moves as one unit. Nor does the torso make designs of its own; it bends or twists in response to the downward or upward thrust of the legs, or to the outward pull of the arms. Their arms are constantly in play, often waving symbolic objects from side to side, knives, wands, scarves, hand bells. In several dances, the arms are extended a couple of feet by long sleeves.

In their arms and hands these dancers make the most developed use of space, enlarging the flat circle into a three-dimensional spiral or sphere. I have a feeling that the comparative complexity of their arm gestures is related to the work tasks they execute with their hands — some of the dances incorporated mimed references to sewing, dispersing seed, milking, churning butter, and molding the butter into cakes. Unfortunately, two of the dances they omitted were about other kinds of work; I'd have loved to see them.

The most exciting moment of the afternoon for me came in the Shamba, or executioners' dance. The four men in the dance wore ferocious masks, skeleton bones painted on their red costumes, and long fingernails that they wiggled to make their arms seem longer. From the same side-to-side waving and bending motion that we'd seen several times, they enlarged the gesture until with both arms they were sweeping through huge curving diagonals across the body, from low and to the side of them, to high on the other side, and back the other way. The very same gesture forms' one of the main motifs of the dance of Death in Kurt Jooss's *The Green Table*. I was amazed.

The dance continued with variations on this taking-in-the-whole-globe idea — the dancers twisting halfway around to the back in following the path of their arms, making the same gesture while kneeling on one knee with the other leg extended forward, hopping in a tilted circle, jumping while gathering up and throwing out armfuls of space.

Other dances included Sha Cham, the dance of the sacred stag, one of the few solos. The dancer, wearing a deer's mask and antlers, did choruses of hopping in a circle and dropping to a prayer rug to do a bouncing dance on his knees while making small spiral gestures with his hands. In Yak Tse, a scene from the Tibetan folk opera, there was a great yak dance — two men forming each animal like the lions in Chinese opera, but much more shambly and lovable — and a wife who milked the female yak and later made butter with the help of her husband and the yak driver.

December 4, 1975

Far-Eastern Baroque

DECORATIVE IS THE WORD for the Dancers and Musicians of the Burmese National Theater, who made their U.S. debut last week at Carnegie Hall under the sponsorship of the Asia Society. Their dance is a dance of embellishment. They don't just turn themselves into beautiful ornaments, they cultivate the act of ornamentation.

There's very little that is static about this dance. Shifting rhythmically from foot to foot, the dancers keep their energy flowing, their smiles alive. Although their serpentine body lines remind you of the Cambodians or of Japanese women dancers, the Burmese seem to be in motion all the time. They show you the process of developing a line, rather than try to make the line look finished even as it's evolving. Sometimes they get themselves into rather inelegant situations — entangling their feet in a complicated twisting design near the floor and sitting down with a bump — but there's always a quick recovery and a reassuring grin to follow.

The Burmese dance is all S-curved paths and swishy lines. The dancer's body almost always seems to be in opposition to itself. If the arms undulate out to one side, the head will tilt to the other. If the lower back is contracted and the buttocks push back, then the chest is thrust forward. They never give your eyes the indulgence of a symmetrical shape or a line that's stretched as far as it will go. The dancers draw attention to themselves by staying in a rather small sphere of space around the body. They're constantly folding inward and opening out again, but only to lead back to another part, not so far out as to draw your eye away from themselves.

But theirs is not a lulling kind of fluidity. The line may be broken — something is held flat while everything moves around it — so that you'll notice the flatness. They make extensive use of their hands in a long straight shape, often drooping or flapping loosely from the wrist, with the pinky out and the thumb pressed into the palm. It looks imperial, or vaguely ecclesiastical. They make little punctuating jabs of the head and arms for emphasis, and the women may also accent this way with their hip or shoulder.

Rhythmically the dance is quite simple — the meter is regular and repetitive, but it accelerates into climaxes of turning or other feats accompanied by great clattering crescendos from the drums and gongs. Their costumes too are quite simple — in contrast, for instance, to the many-layered, intricately cut and specialized garments of a Kabuki dancer. The Burmese wear a sort of basic body-shirt and wraparound skirt or knee-length trousers. But draped around this, or tacked on or hanging or protruding from it, is a fantastic array of beads, panels, scarfs, epaulets, collars, cuffs, trains, and heraldic emblems.

If you look at a map, you'll see that Burma is kind of pinched in the middle of Southeast Asia between India and Pakistan, Indochina and Indonesia, and China on the north. Its dancing seems to have borrowed elements from all of these — the dramatic flair of the South Indians, the filigreed delicacy of Malaysia, and the acrobatic skill of China. This latter could be seen in the Zawgyi dance, in which a sorcerer portrays superhuman feats by agilely jumping over and under his own bow.

The Burmese dancers differ from their South Asian neighbors in their more equal presentation of the sexes. I found it interesting that neither men nor women dominated the company, or played the roles of the other sex. You could see from the set of exercises demonstrated at the beginning of the program that men and women get very similar training and can do most of the same things.

The second half of the program consisted of four excerpts from the Ramayana. They seemed very brief to me, hardly more than introductions to the characters, in comparison to the exhaustive meditations on the same events and personae that other Asian companies like the Kathakali of India have presented. Again I had the sense that the object was to elaborate on a very minimal set of actions.

The heroes — Rama and other members of his clan — dress in dazzling gold and silver with gold headdresses and stiff winglike decorations hanging from their waists. They stand on a narrow base, a sort of low fifth position, legs turned out with knees bent and feet close together. When they walk they take about three little rocking steps for every one they need to get ahead. Or they make curving passes at the spot where they're going. They hold their arms out to the tips of their flaring aprons, fingers delicately curled, pinkies out.

Dasagiri (Ravana), the villain, wears an animal mask with a snarling mouthful of teeth. He takes bigger steps, but he doesn't make a direct approach either, slicing at his objective with one shoulder forward, the other pulled away. Dasagiri is the only character who breaks into the even-tempered rhythm by throwing a stamping, shaking fit to an irregular beat, when he's defeated in a contest by Rama.

When people fight or when two lovers dance a duet, they don't usually come into frontal contact. Instead they circle around, back to back, eyeing each other over one shoulder. That way the audience hardly ever sees the back of anyone; the body, especially the front of the body where the decorations are, and the face get shown to their greatest advantage at all times.

October 9, 1975

Perennially New

MERCE CUNNINGHAM never seems to go out of style. He's been choreographing for thirty years and has had a recognizable company for twenty, which is no short time in the annals of modern dance. Although the basic ingredients of his vocabulary were established long ago, his dances always look different, and interesting, to me. Two of his three new works, shown during the winter season just completed at Brooklyn Academy, involved a minimum of pop-art gadgetry, and they looked so bare and complete that I got really involved in them. Bizarre décors and sonic environments lend theatricality and sometimes fun to Cunningham dances, but his unadorned works are as starkly satisfying to me as a tree against a February hillside.

Landrover was the big work of the season, almost an hour of encounters, events, and explorations done in near-silence. I could assign the piece an atmosphere of vague, nonhuman menace by putting together the title with the score — John

Cage warbling a few nonsense syllables into a mike, a constant high-frequency ticking like that last sound you hear before going under an anesthetic, and a distant bombardment of electronic thuds — with Richard Nelson's no-color lighting and a huge, pale orb fading in and out of a murky sky. But the dance action wasn't really specific enough to support or deny this impression. Besides, I didn't need a metaphor to sustain my fascination with the piece.

Landrover is about speed and weight and tension. It's about people holding each other up by leaning and people hanging together by pulling away. It's about flying through the air by pushing off from another person, and being caught just before the end of a fall, and groups toppling under their own dead weight. And it's about slow togetherness and sudden dispersal.

The piece is in four sometimes overlapping sections. Part I opens with Cunningham soloing all over one half of the stage while a close group of five dancers waits in the other half. When he exits, they burst out vigorously into the whole space, like the splash that follows a diver, and then, just as suddenly, they're lined up absolutely still against the backdrop, spaced evenly across the width of the stage.

Carolyn Brown does a solo that begins slowly, pensively, as the group stands in a tight, inward-facing circle. She makes a tour around it on one flat foot and one half-toe, then gets faster and farther away and is gone.

In Part II a new group crosses the stage doing individual combinations of arm and leg gestures, occasionally bobbing up and down together softly, like jazz improvisers hitting the refrain. Douglas Dunn and Susana Hayman-Chaffey do a slow duet of opening and closing, rising and falling movements and then make a big circuit of the stage in a pattern of stepping and sitting that gets progressively slower.

All the people in the first two parts come in and out during Part III, except Chris Komar, who will finally return in the last part. Cunningham does a duet with Carolyn Brown in which he stalks her, copies her, is ready to hold her up, but hardly ever touches her or takes her weight.

Gradually the personnel changes until the original group of five plus Cunningham is assembled — except for one girl who wasn't there before. Then two men carry her out horizontally and come back a minute later with the right girl in the same position. They group themselves as we first saw them, Cunningham solos off, skittering and punching the air, and the curtain falls.

If *Landrover* is about ten people together, *TV Rerun* is about ten separate people. The piece is a variation on a dance class, beginning with slow stretches, bends and balances, progressing to little jumps, turns and arabesques, high skips across the floor, and finally a long phrase of big sideways jumps and a long-held balance on half-toe.

But it's not the least bit academic, since all the dancers do the class in their own ways, at their own tempos, and they're allowed to drop in and out whenever they feel like it. There's virtually no physical contact among them. They're concentrating on their own bodies; the presence of others only raises the temperature of each one's workout.

TV Rerun has two gimmicks. Photographers wander around the periphery of the dance taking pictures. And there are three telemetry belts that the dancers take turns wearing. The belts transmit wireless signals as the dancers move, and the mix of all three signals — controlled from a console in the pit by composer Gordon Mumma — constitutes the score for the dance.

You don't have to bother a bit about either one of these effects. I did find, however, that the belts drew my eye even more closely to the individual dancers' movements. I usually couldn't discover whatever it was about the movement that changed the sound, but I didn't mind because the company looks so fine now that it was nice to be able to pay each dancer particular attention.

Borst Park, the last of the new works, seems of lesser importance, containing less dancing and more tricks than I care for. Christian Wolff's score was played by three musicians onstage and three in the pit, all twiddling away pretentiously, fabricating unusual, disconnected sounds with musical instruments, wine bottles, sticks thrown on the floor, and so forth.

This technique is at least ten years old — Cage did almost the same thing in "Atlas Eclipticalis," which accompanied Cunningham's *Aeon* (1961) — so I didn't see why the six dancers had to sit down in chairs facing the wings and make us listen to long chunks of it. Maybe it would be more fun performed by ten orchestras, which is supposedly possible.

There is some lovely comedy in *Borst Park*, among scattered sequences of playground-like games. Cunningham is one of the great clowns of our time, a role he doesn't display as much as he used to. Hints of it show up, though, in his dancing with Sandra Neels, who is not so cool and perfectly placed as his usual partner, Carolyn Brown.

Early in the dance they do a little off-beat-ballet duet that ends in a sort of polka. As they two-step off together, Neels ties a scarf around her head and Cunningham pulls a cap out of his waistband and puts it on. Suddenly there's a whole period and character established for the dance; the music starts reminding me of Charles Ives — the clashing holiday moods of his turn-of-the-century tone pictures — and the dancers look like they've come out of a more innocent age.

March 26, 1972

Human Events

ICONOCLASTIC as he may seem, Merce Cunningham has clung to the basics of Western theater dancing. There's just enough tradition in his work to deny us the complacency of snubbing it. You can be subjected to Cunningham under the most severe conditions — endure blacked-out stages or spotlights piercing your eyes or demonic sounds — what makes you angry is not the dance, but your inability to see the dance. I think this is what makes Cunningham such a powerful force for change in our dance thinking.

In the past ten years, when he made his biggest theater works, *Winterbranch, Place, RainForest, Walkaround Time, Canfield, Landrover,* he would build in variables, to be decided before or during each performance by chance. No Cunningham dance was ever exactly the same twice. Each section of the choreography, sometimes even each dancer on the stage, was seen in a different sequence or with different things going on around it. This made each moment, each performance unique, and shifted our perspective as well.

We found our attention sharpened. We learned to appreciate changes rather than similarities, to keep readjusting our standards and finding new pleasures instead of trying to recapture old satisfactions, and most of all we came to value that very evanescence that was supposed to be dance's biggest liability.

You get the feeling that for Cunningham there's always dancing going on someplace; his dancers are just tuning in on some cosmic process that they convert into a momentarily useful activity. The transformation of energy may be incomplete, fragmentary, interfered with by static in our consciousness, but whatever part of it we can focus on is the part he'd like us to see. It has no more need to be selected or organized or embellished than rain or interplanetary dust.

Now Cunningham doesn't do dances anymore. He does Events. These usually consist of parts of Cunningham's dances presented in more or less familiar sequences, together with new choreography and peripheral behavior that may or may not catch your eye. Last year Cunningham made a dance called *Changing Steps* that was never shown as a single entity. Parts of it have appeared in most of the Events I've seen since then, and some of them I always recognize. Other parts never got fixed in my mind because they crossed the busy thoroughfare of the Event and were gone before I could identify them.

The steps of *Changing Steps* are an Event. Maybe Cunningham made it to show us he thought of his dances that way all along. Maybe that's why he still calls the parts of an Event by their original names. For the audience, it's like getting some clues in a treasure hunt to be told you're about to see parts of *Changing Steps, Loops,* and *TV Rerun.* Yet you're apt to go right past the prize that's lying in full view, because all its original trappings are gone: the costumes, scenery, sound, spatial orientation that you knew it by before. I'll bet it wouldn't be that easy to tell the *Don Quixote* pas de deux from the Auber *Grand Pas Classique* either, without the music. Somehow, having those teasing titles to go by — and nothing else — can become a distraction, almost a burden.

What I do with an Event now, I realized at the one called #90, in Brooklyn Academy's new Lepercq Space, is to make a dance out of it.

Most Events take place in open spaces. I've seen them in a sports arena in Athens, Ohio, and the Cunningham studio at New York's Westbeth artists' housing project, for instance. The various musicians, poets, video makers he invites as accompanists provide a gray, unobtrusive texture against which the dancers work, far from the screeches and clangor that surrounded his earlier pieces. Every Event is different, not just because of what's in it. The place where it's given shapes and orients the dancing, becomes tailor-made for that dancing in fact. So does where the audience sits, and how the seating is arranged. What you see and hear from your angle and distance becomes very much your own to get involved in.

Well, why isn't all this just a Happening? What's its claim to Art? Or is just any old thing art? I think Cunningham has gone way past the stage of calling attention to ordinary things, as the Happenings did. He may want to wake us up — to keep us focused on the here-and-now instead of using his dance as a springboard into our own fantasies. But it's not just everyday occurrences he's showing us; he doesn't, I think, expect it all to pass over us like our encounters with grocery clerks. Cunningham is working with tremendous finesse in a rather small territory. He keeps his lens on the same thing but discovers a new world every time he changes the focal distance.

A prime example of this is his solo, *Loops*, which slipped into his repertory a couple of years ago. I don't know whether I've ever seen the complete dance, or if it is a complete dance, but there's a sequence that begins with a very fast twirling of one wrist, the fingers loosely extended, the vibration spreading into his whole arm and shoulder. It's a gesture that doesn't quite look like anything you recognize — it's too intense to be just shaken-off tension, but if it were a practical action it would have a more definite path in space, the fingers would conform to certain imaginary shapes.

On different occasions I've seen him make a whole unspecified pantomimed world with this gesture: he lets it carry his hand around his body and up over his head, transfers it to the other hand, slows down, speeds up, notices it, follows it with his eyes, reacts to it with other parts of his body, forgets it's there, lets it tug at him, lets it seem to drift away as if it would take him — hand and all — off into the blue. It looks silly, funny, sad, crazy, and all the time he's just a man standing there with his hand shaking.

Event #90 contained almost the same movement material as Event #83, which I'd seen only a couple of weeks before at the Cunningham Studio. At the studio, sitting on the floor right on the edge of the dancing space, I was very conscious of the way the dancers used weight, the way their contacts with each other were reflected in their faces; I felt I was a part of the intimate act that performing must be for them. At Brooklyn, up on the top of some bleachers, I looked down on a continual redeployment of forces, a touching off and sustaining of energies and a gradual modulation into other energies, a breaking apart and coming together of the group.

Eleven dancers filed in and spread out over the floor, evenly spacing themselves, as dancers do, to allow just enough room for moving. A few turns, stretches, and shakings-out in place and they began a series of solos, most of them variations on this warming-up process, body-centered, not traveling much. Then a long trio, and everyone was in the center again, swaying, pivoting in arabesque, slowly circling their arms, their upper bodies, until Cunningham with a few hand claps set a faster tempo for the group but continued moving slowly around the edges.

The Event kept expanding this way, almost mathematically, with duets and quartets; then unison; trios and larger ensembles; then unison. It was as if something in the air was suggesting bigger ways to combine individual forces, but the company as a whole still held. At the end Cunningham, who had been

quietly going about his own complicated business since the beginning — trying out inward rotations of the shoulder or leg,
sliding one clubbed foot into the place of the other, putting a
hand to his face and intensifying the pressure till it pulled his
head around — finally rejoined the group. They went into a
fast combination of traveling jumps and turns that ended with
pirouettes and a balance on half-toe. The combination repeated itself six times in different directions, in a great bravura
show of energy still in reserve after an hour of dancing, and
then the dancers filed out as the room went dark.

The sense of the group is strong in the Cunningham company. In other years you could see it in their aliveness to each
other, in their skillful timing and maneuverings around each
other in space. Now this sense is less intellectual, more physically dependent. In one double duet, a woman would lock her
body in one piece and lean full tilt against a man; one person
would mold herself into a rounded shape and another person
would curve his limbs around her. A quartet linked hands and
lowered one member at a time to the floor, supporting and
giving at the same time, like a big sling. Susana Hayman-
Chaffey and Brynar Mehl clasped hands, nailing each other
down to earth, and soared out into space as far as their limbs
would stretch.

Maybe because I wasn't close enough to see tiny relaxations
of tension, the company looked rather brittle to me at Brooklyn, not having fun in any carefree sense. Not excited by the
movement as they sometimes are, but investing a lot in controlling it, containing it. You saw the sharpness of changes,
from straight pushing-up legs to bent legs, breaking to send the
body toward the ground. You felt the slow concentrated positionings of arms and torsos get shattered by fusillades of running and turning. And hovering around it all, taking it all in,
was Merce Cunningham, who seems to have let go of everything superfluous, only to become wiser and more wonderful.

June 1974

Bostonsnatch

1965: LINCOLN CENTER with the wraps scarcely taken off is about to be defiled for the first time. Merce Cunningham's *Winterbranch* is having its New York première at the brief spring season of American Dance Theater. The audience is puzzled, then annoyed and sullen as dancers in black sweat suits slowly gesture and fall, sometimes flattened by harsh lighting, sometimes swallowed by complete darkness. Hideous sound suddenly rips through the theater. Outrage. A spotlight glares straight into the audience. The dancers fall faster, run until they vanish. Some people are furious. Others think it's beautiful.

1966: Cunningham sets *Summerspace* on the New York City Ballet. It doesn't work.

1968: Cunningham company's residency at Brooklyn Academy. They've toned down the lights on *Winterbranch* and if you sit up very close you can almost see all the dancing. The sound still smashes into the pit of your stomach.

1973: Cunningham does *Canfield* and three Events at Brooklyn Academy. The audience is contemptuous. Hoots, jeers, bands of teen-agers running through the balcony, an undertone of conversation.

1974: Boston Ballet does *Summerspace* and *Winterbranch*. Half the audience pretends it's a joke, the other half submits.

Boston's confrontation with Merce Cunningham in November was notable for several reasons. Cunningham revivals are rare — even his own company has stopped doing repertory — and *Winterbranch* (1964) and *Summerspace* (1958) haven't been done in their entirety by anyone in years. Since neither one, to my knowledge, has been filmed, they were as good as lost until now. The fact that Boston Ballet artistic director E. Vir-

ginia Williams invited Cunningham to stage the works, and
that Cunningham agreed, is extraordinary, but the impact of
the works on the Boston audience interests me even more.
Cunningham's work doesn't seem that advanced to me or to
New York dance fans, I suppose, because we've seen so much
of it and its offspring in the past ten years. But far from here,
plopped in the middle of a standard ballet repertory, it appears
in an altogether different perspective.

As an opener the Boston Ballet did Birgit Cullberg's *Medea*, a
balleticized modern dance that might have looked impressively
stark in 1951, when it was made. To the staging formulas of
Martha Graham it adds the equally restrictive vocabulary of
classic ballet, and in Boston, without the slightest benefit of
sets, backdrop, decoration, or decent lighting, it looked dreary
and repressed.

When the curtain opened again after this stoic ritual — at
the second performance the program began with George Balanchine's more interesting but no less formal *Allegro Brillante*
— there was nothing there but Robert Rauschenberg's pointil-
list backdrop. A space, dotted with pastel.

In silence a girl runs in from the wings and circles the stage
several times before two other women join her. Here, in the
very first phrase of *Summerspace*, is Cunningham smashing
convention. The girl runs. She isn't *preparing* to do anything,
like leap or pirouette. She claims our attention by doing what
other dancers throw away. And this running in a big circle
clears the space, neutralizes it, opens it up. The girl completely avoids that coveted spot in the middle that our eyes are
all set to zero in on the minute anything important seems
about to start. She's saying any place is a place for dancing,
just watch us and see.

Once you've recovered from all these preconceptions being
broken apart, you can see that *Summerspace* does have a form
and a continuity. Instead of building excitement in a curve by
introducing one character after another, piling one effect upon
another, Cunningham makes a series of discrete events that
please you by just continuing to happen. Energies aren't arranged for cumulative impact, but to touch off other energies.

Summerspace is very much about changing tempos. This

not only keeps the dance moving, but gives us another way to see the movement. At one point all six dancers are leaping across the stage, all at different speeds. Often a dancer picks up a gesture and carries on with it at a different pace after the first dancer has left the stage. You begin to see after-images, to hear reverberations.

The dancers in *Summerspace* are solitary — separate units like the isolated bursts and cascades of Morton Feldman's aleatory music that accompanies the dance. There are a couple of almost trivial encounters — a man follows a woman who's leaping around the stage, several times trying to lift her but reaching out just a second too late, and finally getting the jump on her and carrying her off surprised. But more often the dancers seem to create ensembles by sensing the others' location and energy in relation to their own, rather than overtly positioning themselves or acknowledging the others. They use the space without getting in each other's way, but without sharing it either as they do under the gracious codes of classical ballet.

The Boston dancers handled Cunningham's difficult movement quite well, but they tended to line up their bodies with the single-minded, picture-oriented clarity of ballet, defining one particular space but closing themselves off from the overall space. Cunningham's inclusiveness in space is part of what makes his dancers look so alert and alive. The Boston cast seemed more manipulative, more dramatic, and less into the movement. They had trouble, too, finding the calm mobility in the upper body that is part of Cunningham's style. The dance in general looked tense and expectant, which I think Cunningham characteristically likes to stay away from. But who knows how long it takes a Cunningham dancer to achieve serenity. Certainly longer than two performances.

Winterbranch is another story. Like *Summerspace* it has six dancers but that's almost the sole resemblance. Instead of opening up space, *Winterbranch* closes it down. Closes it off. The dancers are alternately confined by deep darkness and exposed by glaring light coming from sharp angles. They're like insects or some other helpless creatures beating out their existence against inexorable, uncontrollable forces — or like man living under the hand that stays the Bomb.

The dancers work often in groups and pairs, but ineffectually. Their actions cancel each other out, or lead back to where they started, instead of resulting in real change. A woman wheels across a man's back, leaning back on him, wrapping her leg around his legs. In taking her weight, he collapses and they both fall to the ground and begin again. A girl initiates a fall by flinging up an arm, then the other. Teetering on her toes she starts to fall backward. A man behind her supports her as she sinks to the ground and a man in front of her holds her feet and scoots them around until, all huddled up in a ball, she faces the other way. Then the first man walks her hands around fast till she's facing in the original direction, where she rises, flails, and starts falling again.

Winterbranch seems to be almost all about resistance — about falling so slowly the dancers might be tempting gravity, or getting up so slowly they seem to have heavy loads on their backs. Sometimes they succeed in their determination, as when they start to do slow backbends and just before their hands touch the floor they wrench themselves upright. Sometimes they seem defeated from the start — a girl clasps her hands together high above her head, slowly brings them down in front of her, and pulls her body over double. When her hands touch the floor, she stands and walks away.

People do extremely simple things extremely slowly. A man and a woman lie face down on the floor, side by side. She begins to push her upper body off the floor with her arms. After about two minutes she's sitting facing the audience with her legs stretched out sideways. The man gets up and pulls her up by the arms, then lets her down in the same position on the other side. Her legs have done nothing but anchor her. It's an agonizing buildup to nothing — why are they working so hard to accomplish so little?

Or they rush through things that are complicated and dangerous. A group, hanging on by clenching hands in the center of a circle, comes barreling across the stage. One person falls backward, pulling the whole machinery down with him. They scramble up and do it again. Again. When they've gotten to the other side, they lie in a heap. A girl comes and throws a cloth over them and the whole pile drags itself off.

Although the dynamics are more extreme than *Summer-space*, the dancing in *Winterbranch* is not really violent. It's minimal, laborious, tortured sometimes in its futility. In fact, you wish the dancers would be aggressive, would explode in fury against the elements that are so cruelly infringing on them. But they don't, they do their tasks doggedly, they're resigned.

Perhaps more than he knew, Merce Cunningham was giving us back a metaphor of ourselves in *Winterbranch*. When it was first done, I didn't like it either. After a while, when I learned how to look at it, it seemed to open the whole world of modern art to me. In that way, I think of *Winterbranch* as a latter-day *Sacre du Printemps*. Scandalous, offensive, extreme. Crucial. But its power lies in its ability to make you mad, to shake your equilibrium.

It's deliberate, all that ghastly noise in the second half, following after the ghastly silence in the first half. The viciousness of the one heightened by the self-consciousness of the other. The lights going on and off are more than disconcerting, sometimes they obliterate the dance completely. Sometimes they flash on us. Perhaps even the audience's hostility is a necessary prod to mobilize the dancers' energies, to make them grit their teeth and keep going.

What I've noticed lately about novice Cunningham audiences is that they don't let it get to them. I suppose the Bostonians felt cheated not to see any "dancing" — and perhaps they had a right to that. Orchestra seats to the Boston Ballet cost $12.50, and not much of a young audience is enticed in at $7 student rush prices. If Virginia Williams wanted to expand the consciousness of the purple-haired Brahmins in the brocade dresses, I wonder why she picked the most radical of all Cunningham's works, instead of, say, *Place*, which is dark too but more conventionally structured and produced.

What the audience did in Boston wasn't a protest so much as a rejection. People chattered and giggled, held loud sarcastic conversations, took their time about getting up and leaving. When the ear-splitting soundtrack began, the audience's jamming rose to a din. They were not going to hear/see/feel this message. So, I imagine, did the world go larking in the last days of the Weimar Republic.

Near the end of *Winterbranch*, the stage is empty and a piece of sculpture makes an entrance. It's probably put together each time the dance is done, from things they find backstage, and it always comes as a shock. It trundles across the darkness, an amorphous hulking shape made of metal and cabling and with lights blinking inside it — infinitely mechanical and somehow disgusting. The dancers come back and continue their desperate running, struggling, collapsing. When they are all lying on the ground, the curtain falls.

After that, in Boston, they did *Graduation Ball*.

January 1975

Repertory Is
an Out-of-Town Tryout

IT'S BEEN ALMOST four years since Merce Cunningham's repertory was seen in New York. For his own inscrutable reasons, Cunningham prefers to dole out his dances in mixed-up smorgasbords of movement called Events, and he leaves it up to us to call slices of this movement *Canfield* or *Part of Landrover* or *Everything But the End of Winterbranch* if we want to.

Now I like the Events a lot, especially when they're set in dazzling proximity to the audience at the Cunningham Westbeth studio. But a dance is a very different entity when it's contained within the space and time frame we call staging. Merce Cunningham's dances — even Merce Cunningham's — all say something when they're seen that way that they don't convey when they're blended into the kinetic contours of an Event.

Cunningham's touring repertory got a tryout last week at the McCarter Theater in Princeton, and the two performances convinced me all over again how important the theater side of Cunningham is. There was, officially, one new dance, *Torse*. Also one revival, *Rune* (1959); two New York area premières, *Sounddance* and *Rebus*; and the fairly familiar *Signals*(1970), *Solo* (1973), and *TV Rerun* (1972). But material from all these choreographies has been steadily on view in the Events, in more or less intact condition.

It's not particularly surprising that the people around Cunningham call his stuff "material." Seeing it in the Events, it is material, great gobs of it. The company now is full of dancers with strong legs and feet and backs, and Cunningham is choreographing up a storm for them, infatuated with their power. *Torse* on stage is like a perpetual motion machine. A curtain goes up on the New Jersey Turnpike and goes down on it several minutes later. Maryanne Amacher's droning mechanical noises, like the all-night sounds of a distant superhighway, contributed this sustained image to the stage version. The ten dancers in the piece don't all move at the same time, and not always at high speed, but the dance itself is relentless. There isn't a moment when everything comes to a stop. Cunningham is using almost all traveling movement here, and it's very complicated. Working in turned-out positions, the dancers run, hop, jump, beat foot to ankle, dip into plié and immediately go up on their toes, make tiny fast detouring steps and big fast, in-place stamping steps, lunge forward and pull up into precipitous balances. It looks like a balletic tap dance on roller skates.

Although *torse* is the French word for torso, the center of the body, arms, and head are not really stressed or exploited in *Torse* the way the legs are. The dancers will kind of heel over sometimes to come closer to the wind, or throw their upper bodies down toward the floor as if trying to prevent their feet from getting away from them.

The Cunningham company now has all kinds of dancers, some technical and tight, some loose and ungainly, some spitting energy, some smooth and assured. In *Torse*, they all move together a lot of the time, unified by their dancing rhythm and by common agreement that they're doing desperately serious business.

When I saw the *Sounddance* material in Events it seemed to have a lot of wild rhythms and a lot of evolving configurations of people holding each other up in strange ways. David Tudor's score — electronic blatts and buzzes often amplified to excruciating levels — is the kind of noise I usually cross the street to avoid. Trapped there, I could just watch it obliterate the dance's music.

They did *Sounddance* immediately after the revival of *Rune*, and nothing could have been a more graphic illustration of how differently Cunningham is choreographing now. The older piece employs Cunningham's now-familiar balletic body attitudes, which must have been pretty outrageous in the days when modern dance was militantly antiballet. But instead of piling steps on steps, *Rune* seems to have a lot to do with stillness, with condensing energy instead of spilling it out.

Cunningham likes the idea of establishing things in the eye — a long balance, a preparatory pose, a stage layout repeatedly returned to — and then breaking them, often with something unexpected. The archaic, almost desolate mood of *Rune* was reinforced by Christian Wolff's score, half-uttered piano phrases with long intervals of silence.

It's to this gravity and intensely concentrated energy that Cunningham has returned in choreographing for himself. *Rebus* (1975) is heartbreaking, sardonic, funny, uplifting, because Cunningham dances what it means to be himself at fifty-plus with a company of young firecrackers.

Wearing a limp sport shirt and trousers, he spends long periods of time standing still at the back of the stage near a clothes rack. He begins the dance with a meticulous warm-up of foot and leg exercises, building his energy and his awareness of the audience. Dancers enter as if for a class. He works among them, leads them, sometimes beginning their much more taxing combinations, dropping out while they continue, joining in again. He's out of that league now, he hasn't got stamina to burn — but he can make them all disappear with a turn of his head.

He draws various dancers out of the group and works with

them apart, master and pupil, Svengali and victim, high priest and acolyte. But always they get drawn back to their companions. He stands behind a man who's beginning to partner a woman; places his arms and legs in the same supporting shape; walks alongside empty-handed for a few steps. Finally, he sheds his elderly uncle clothes, emerges slim and terrific in red dance clothes. But the dancers all walk away. Alone, he dances eccentrically, demonically, then retires to his corner dressing room.

It will take me some time to find words for *Rebus*. It will take me some more viewings. Maybe if I go to Berkeley in March . . .

January 22, 1976

The Authoritative Gamble

IT'S WONDERFUL to keep new choreographers company in the first stages of their careers. Before they find a success formula or use up a too-small inspiration. Some start almost obscurely and gather assurance and force. Some have a quiet mastery from the beginning. With Douglas Dunn, every new piece bursts out like a celebration.

Since he left the Merce Cunningham company a couple of years ago, Dunn has given himself a series of challenges, all different kinds: he's done environmental things, body-improvisations, films, theater pieces, and just plain dances. They've all looked odd and convincing. He takes risks, not cautiously but with gusto.

In *Lazy Madge*, an "ongoing choreographic project," which he showed a couple of weekends ago, he's working with a sizable group of dancers for the first time. What I loved most about it was the wholeheartedness of the dancers' energy. All eight of them (nine including Dunn) moved unreservedly, as if they weren't afraid they'd put in something that would upset the effect. They moved as if the piece depended on their personal contributions, and of course it did.

This may not seem unusual in an age when the avant-garde is philosophically committed to the individual. But what you actually see most of the time is a group of dancers trying, if unconsciously, to look like Lucinda or Trisha or Twyla or Dan. Not that Doug Dunn's group didn't do his steps; but each dancer emerged as a very distinct dancing presence. They came out looking possibly even stronger than they are, instead of homogenized in the service of a style, or made beautiful by it. Maybe Dunn hasn't been working long enough for anyone to know what his style is.

Since the work was all dancing, serious dancing at that, each individual simply showed us his or her way of doing it. Dunn gave the dancers some leeway — possibly they could make their own decisions, within some general limits, about when to enter and leave, and where they'd work in the space. Even better than that, he let each dancer be seen for a nice chunk of time, and he gave everyone some things to do that no one else shared. The audience could really sense them, find out how they operate. There was a lot of overlapping too, but when several things were happening simultaneously, they all seemed to have their own character; nothing quite became a faceless activity.

Except for the extended time things were allowed to go on, *Lazy Madge* seemed compositionally similar to a lot of the dances Merce Cunningham did in his most free-for-all period. Dunn's kinetic line seems to consist of one gradual or sudden change of body shape or location followed by a repeat or another, unrelated phrase. These movement events are not only discontinuous, but they seldom coincide with the events of other dancers, even partners. Dunn's duets have a certain detachment — they even look accidental at times — which somehow makes me see the points of potential contact all the more clearly.

But contact is a big factor in his work — or impact. When it's not there you notice. Dunn has the same acute sense of time that Cunningham does, but where Cunningham is also particularly clear about the space the dancer uses, Dunn combines time changes with a sense of the body's weight and an unexpected use of parts of the body. I think this is one reason you don't lose track of his dancers when a lot of them are doing different things at once.

His dance is emphatic, surprising, dangerous, contradictory. People smash into the air, fall and spring up again in one motion, slam down from a jump, stomp over other people's prone bodies, land heavily on both feet in relevé from a flying leap, run with one foot dragging. Dunn engages in glancing combat with Michael Bloom or Daniel Press. Grappling, they push or pull against each other, snap apart, then one is suddenly carrying the other. Jennifer Mascall rolls on her back, legs extended, holding her ankles; she goes heavy and thuds into the ground each time she changes sides.

Christina Grasso Caprioli begins a long series of balletic enchaînements, fast and posed for flight. Sometime later you notice her slowly unfolding her torso and rippling her arms, with legs planted sturdily and wide, as if she'd stay there indefinitely. Ellen Webb does a lot of almost-vague gestures that start out to be one thing and change into another before they finish. Later she takes little jumps forward on her toes, digging them into the floor, but each step is cut off, as if she'd bumped into a wall partway.

Dunn does a duet with Mascall where he sort of fits himself inside the shapes she's making with her arms and legs, partnering her almost fortuitously. He shoves Diane Frank around roughly while she keeps her composure, and they leave holding hands, she balancing calmly on the balls of her feet and he skittering in erratic circles. Bloom and Ruth Alpert do a long, amusing dance that looks like some peasant pas de deux from which parts — the yearning and the virtuosity — have been erased. Webb, Press, and Dana Roth make a mysterious game of getting themselves into a slow tangle, one move at a time, and suddenly all whipping free.

Dunn's presence can be felt throughout the dance, even

though he's not dancing all the time. He doesn't dominate or manipulate his dancers in quite the way Cunningham does; it's more as if he's lending them things — his collapsing falls and slides, his big free-swinging leg gestures, his determination to balance in unbalanced positions, his intelligence, and his commitment to the moment. It seems as if his example gives them courage.

May 6, 1976

Coming Closer

SOME PEOPLE automatically struck Twyla Tharp from the rolls of the experimentalists when she started doing ballets for Joffrey, but it seems to me what she does in that setting is no less valid — and perhaps more daring — than any revolution in a loft. If there *are* any revolutions in lofts nowadays. A decade after Judson, experimental dance is healthy and productive, exploring not one but many ideas, feeding into the more conservative forms, and making contact with audiences at many points. With experimental art, as with other aberrant elements of this manic civilization, the cycle from intolerability to acceptability seems to have speeded up.

We're still in a relatively freewheeling phase of government support for the arts. Bureaucracy is beginning its inexorable drift toward norms and categories already known, but in these first years of subsidy a great deal of very extreme work has been funded, and some very radical people recognized. Some companies that started out as experimental have gotten to act like the more traditional modern dance companies; under the NEA touring program and other funding arrangements, that's almost the only way a company can survive. But perhaps this is a

pattern that modern dancers typically follow anyway, from rebellion and independence to stability.

What's interesting to see is how far out of the ordinary the
work is that these companies are presenting in conventional
concert situations or to uninitiated audiences. Dan Wagoner,
James Cunningham, or Gus Solomons may not be making
breakthroughs choreographically, but they are presenting
dance in a very advanced form to *their* audiences, and the
audiences are accepting what they do.

Merce Cunningham, with whom almost every discussion of
experimental dance has begun for twenty years, is still trying —
harder than some of his alumni — not to capitulate to the rules
that chain success to artistic stasis. After his initial break with
compositional procedures, when he had established the particular look of his movement, Cunningham continued to question
the rules in two areas: the operation of his company and the
form of dance itself.

Cunningham's recent layoff of his company for half a year
put into action a discontent with the circumstances of touring
that he had expressed often. He said he didn't like the routine,
and he wanted time to rethink his direction. Now the company is back and planning to brave it out in a brand new arrangement: teaching and giving weekend concerts in their own
studio at Westbeth.

At the first of these (Event #83), the reassembled company
seemed as secure as ever, doing a lot of leaning and falling
against one another with trust and even sensuality. Cunningham has shown a growing interest in the uses of body
weight in the past few years. At Westbeth he spent long sections of the Event taking odd poses that were both settled and
alive, or he patted parts of his body lightly. It's as if, having
worked out there in time and space for so long, Cunningham is
at last coming nearer to himself, giving and asking his company
to give more to the movement.

More than two years ago Cunningham began the conversion
of his repertory from dances to be repeated intact and virtually
the same way, into segments of movement for individuals and
groups that can be put together any which way and performed

without intermission, notes, titles, or other aids to the audience's understanding. Moreover, he now just about refuses to do these Events in proscenium theaters. His audience can be an intimate group at Westbeth, or thousands in a sports arena. It seems to me that this is as exposed as any way for an artist to present his work, especially as famous and long-standing an artist as Cunningham and one with a company of eleven dancers to support.

Even though they aren't breaking ground in the ordinary choreographic sense, Cunningham's Events pose very important questions for me about the nature of dance and of a dance. Cunningham's disruptions of the choreographic process and the flow of movement changed the way we looked at all dance, brought our attention back to the substance of dance from wherever it had been meandering among plots, character, and histrionics. But even a Cunningham dance had unity, rules, internal continuities by which we could recognize and follow it.

Now he seems to be saying none of those dances need to be taken as dances either, dancing just needs to exist. Just when I was getting comfortable with some sequence of events, or with various events in various sequences, before I became inordinately fond of that experience he called *Landrover* — or *Borst Park* or *TV Rerun* — he took away everything by which I could identify something called *Landrover* except the dancing. Now what am I to think about the original series of sequences called *Landrover?* Was it a dance? Is it still a dance? Can I pick out *Landrover* sequences from the other parts of an Event, and if I can, are they still *Landrover?* Was the accumulation of weights and tensions, appearances and disappearances that added up to *Landrover* any more significant than the sum of selected *Landrover* sequences plus everything else in an Event?

I believe in repertory, in preservation, in being able to renew a deeply moving experience — especially since so much dance that I see is not moving. But the experimental choreographer has a right to deny us the safety of predictable enjoyment, and to demand that we look and organize and react to dance freshly every time. Merce Cunningham is doing this, not only to us, but to himself and his company at a time when they might be enjoying more comfort themselves.

A great many people are working for an even more fundamental change in the dance process. I've seen over forty individuals or groups in the past year who would probably consider themselves experimentalists. They seem to be exploring three main facets of dance making and dance performance, but there's less cohesion among them than there was among the Judson group of the early 1960s.

Antivirtuosity has been with us for some time, and except for Tharp, Cunningham, and some modern dance alumni we might say all experimental dance today disavows dance technique as a primary instrument of performance. For some people this opens up the whole area of nontechnical or "everyday" movement as a performance gambit. Others have taken the removal of technique as an invitation to probe the implications of movement at its deepest and simplest level. And still others have started developing new stylizations of movement — including deliberate distortion of technique — to express theatrical ideas. I don't set these up as strict categories, for there is a great deal of overlap among them, as well as a great deal of other thinking that's going on. But they do seem to represent the main trends of work over the past several months.

I feel there's also a strong message in a lot of this work, but the messages aren't doctrinaire; in fact they're personal and sometimes pretty arcane. Several years of attention to process have accustomed us to see the means and the structures quite clearly and be satisfied. Maybe we're due for a swing back to content.

The "everyday" movement people have, in various ways, been developing structures, or "dances," that don't require dance vocabularies, or that use the dance language as only one of several ways of moving. The group can open up and become more inclusive; it can hold nondancers, and dancers of a greater range of technical proficiency, age, and body type than we usually see in one group. The dancing-ground that these diverse individuals can find together thus becomes more life-like, less limited than a conventional dance scenario has to be. Yvonne Rainer pioneered this whole area of investigation, and her *Connecticut Composite* (1969) was almost a textbook of the kinds of structures that were possible within it, from semiacrobatic, semimilitary maneuvers, to group games, choreography meant to be done by anybody (*Trio A*), and improvisations around various predetermined tasks or problems.

Improvisation — in the theater-games sense rather than the more free-form sense of a group exploring movement together until it "works" — has been a mainstay of this wing of experimental dance, and the Grand Union took it over when Rainer went on to other things. The group makes a problem for itself; then, working out of an awareness of each other's movement styles and a sensitivity to each other's signals, they solve the problem. Sometimes, as with the Workgroup, the problem is rooted in movement or dance phrases, and the dancers make individual variations, borrow ideas from each other, pick up and send cues. The Workgroup's concentration is on the changes occurring within the group, and they've managed to let a lot of their feelings come to the surface.

The Grand Union improvises more freely, though I felt at the Dance Gallery last spring they weren't completely dependent on the inspiration of the moment. A prop, costume, or situation might have been decided on in advance or worked with before. The Grand Union was developing theatrical situations, often comic ones, by taking off from a springboard one member introduced, and using movement, sound, music, words, and some approximation of their own personalities, called "Nancy," "David," "Steve," to pursue each idea. Second City stuff, but with the important and potentially serious addition of movement.

Trisha Brown cares less about the psychology of the members of her group and more about how each individual can contribute to the working out of a movement experiment. She starts with a movement problem — usually a rather simple one — and works until the group gets good at it. It's not mastery they're aiming for but an understanding of what it takes to do the problem in various elaborations and ramifications. The dancer doesn't try to be another character or intensify his or her feelings, but Brown's work demands the utmost here-and-now concentration from her dancers. Brown has a special quality of plainness and unexcitability that always makes her work seem extraordinary to me. Her pieces are unusual, sometimes to the point of incongruity, because at first glance they blend so well into the scenery. You come upon a group of people of assorted shapes, dressed in jeans or sweat pants, moving around a plaza or a gallery in not-too-strange ways. But then you see that they're stacking up huge blocks of twenty, thirty, forty movement elements by adding one piece at a time to the end of each repetition. Or they're standing on the roofs of fifteen buildings, relaying movement in a steady stream to the one person in the chain who can see them.

I think Trisha Brown's work is concerned first with the subjective experience of the dancer, then with the vicarious experience of the audience. Presentation, or how it looks as a theatrical show, comes pretty low in her priorities. When Rebecca Fuller did her own version of Brown's *Roof Piece*, at Mills College in California last summer, the dancers were stationed around the outside of the dance building, rather than on roofs. Once you'd stood in one place long enough to see that the movement was being passed from person to person, you could walk around, getting very close to the dancers, sighting along their sightlines to the senders and receivers. What you were meant to understand, I think, was the process, not the outward shape of the piece. Later on Fuller moved the whole sequence inside, where it was performed in a greatly condensed space. By this time I was so attuned to the act of transference, the flow of the sequence, that I focused on that again when everybody was close together, instead of seeing a whole group doing a canon.

Douglas Dunn, who left the Cunningham company in the past year and has started showing his choreography frequently, represents a kind of bridge between the probers of pure movement and the people who are working toward theatrical formulations. Dunn's most potent material that I've seen so far lies in his weight studies, shown at his loft this winter in *Four for*

Nothing. With three other dancers, Dunn did a number of explorations into sensing, mobilizing, working against and giving in to weight.

The men lay prone on the floor and the women found different positions on top of them. With each position the woman would distribute her weight along the man's back, he would adjust to her slightly, and then they both would rest, sinking into their weight and feeling the mass and flow of each other's bodies. This looks rather static, and in fact sinking into your own weight is a good cure for insomnia, but it's also very sensual, and calls on all the accommodating, trusting, yielding, and supporting facets of the relationship between people.

From the pure state of weight and flow, Dunn's studies progressed to adapting the weight to external shapes; supporting other people by absorbing their weight rather than pressing or pushing against it; developing momentum by gathering up the weight out of a fall; working against the weight for such long periods of time that high tension would develop; and gripping or releasing tension, letting go or taking hold of the weight at will. The flower generation, with its do-what-you-like and let-it-all-hang-out attitude, made weight acceptable, but dancers' new preoccupation with weight is something else. For them weight is not just an inert quantity but a force that can be sensed and used for contact and commitment. I predict when this awareness reaches the traditional dance companies, we'll get much more authentic revivals of early modern dance.

Kei Takei has carried the act of delving into a movement impulse over to the realm of theatrical metaphor. The moment or the means of crossing this line is very slight and subtle with Takei; I'm not always sure how she does it. This winter during Clark Center's festival of solos she added a section to her monumental work *Light*. This is the eighth part — as far as I know all the parts have never been done on one program or series of programs. The new section recalls some of the earlier ones in the extremity, even violence, to which it pushes its premises.

Maybe we're forced to adopt substitute reasons because we sense her verging on some ultimate pole of possibility. No one, not even a dancer experimenting with the factors of balance, weight, or the increasing speed and force of a falling body, would cross the room in such an agonized frenzy of scrambling, staggering, slamming into the floor as Mal Pate does. His desperation, his pain, even his blood the night I saw the dance, are real but surreal — too painful to consider without the intervention of another persona, mankind, perhaps, or a man on some hideous but necessary journey through life.

Takei's own solo in *Light Part VIII* had her jigging with outspread feet and arms and a maniacal grin on her face around a pile of misshapen garments. From time to time she would half put on, half knot herself into a piece of this troll's clothing, until she was all trussed up, bent over and squatting, and now toppling over, righting herself, still dancing her worship-of-the-clothes dance or whatever it was.

William Dunas, whose earliest works were as violent as Takei's but less fanciful, has become much less intense, less personal, and more concerned with creating a message or a lesson of some kind. Appropriately enough, he achieves his theatrical images through a very reduced but recognizable dance vocabulary — already at one degree of removal from "real" behavior — or through repeated patterns of restricted everyday movement. His phrases are segments lifted out of a larger movement context, lacking a beginning or end or any of the expected fluctuations of energy.

Dunas also limits very severely the other components of his medium: the path he is to travel through the space, the allowable range of facial expressions when his face is visible; and his function as a solo dancer is further defined by the lighting and sound that accompany him. What little he does, he does for a long time. To change anything, he begins again, in coordination with sequences of music or spoken narrative. Each new portion of movement-sound-light adds a bit more to what we know of the situation, until at the end we may have a whole idea. No one sequence, and no one element by itself, even the dancer, holds up alone. Each piece of the puzzle is fragmentary but specific; if there's an ambiguity, it's not in Dunas but in our clumsiness at putting the pieces together.

*

Like Takei, only at the other end of the performance scale, Dunas creates images beyond the reality we see confronting us. Her intensity is too high to be "real," his is too low. Most of the other main figures in the experimental scene place an increasing emphasis on the image and a reliance on the dancer as a vehicle to create the image. Both Meredith Monk and Robert Wilson place their dancers at the service of ideas through movement that is less and less mundane and more stylized, more controlled, movement that disguises the dancer to some degree.

Wilson hopes that his works will represent the members of his group, and even his big pieces seem to be catalogues of information contributed by all of them from their own life experiences, and unified by Wilson's skill as a visual artist and showman. Andy de Groat's dancing in Wilson's work takes the detached, semiecstatic form of whirling, a state of timeless flow across which specific events can occur without leaving an imprint. This in effect is what Wilson's work as a whole does. The continuousness of the action and the other-worldly sensibility with which it is presented allow many things to happen but few to crystallize. It's almost impossible to remember any one moment or stage picture from a Wilson work, because everything in the picture is always changing. What you remember is how it kept going on.

Meredith Monk's work is very different in several ways, although she has often been compared to Wilson. Both are developing nonrealistic visions based on actual experience — parables or modern miracle plays. But Monk's sources seem to be entirely of her own devising, her pieces are much more uniform in style and content, the individual performers move the same way, conform to the same standards. Wilson's complexity is found in the total organization of his stage; Monk's complexity is smaller, more specialized, and is exhibited by her own very detailed and articulated vocal style, and by small but significant changes in an otherwise static scene. The people all put on glasses, or move one seat to the right.

Monk's theater pieces stop and start, change abruptly rather than gradually, stay with one idea until it's finished before going on to another one. The work demands that you pay attention; you can't slip into that dreamlike province of the mind from which it's so advantageous to view Wilson. I think Monk wants us to follow her thought process, see her implications. Wilson wants us to assemble our own conclusions and organize our own perception of what he's offering.

If I have been looking at some kind of spectrum that runs from realism to abstraction, from natural to stylized movement, I think Yvonne Rainer is now working at this end, having started at the other. In the last piece of hers that I saw, *This Is the Story of a Woman Who . . .*, she had succeeded in so objectifying her own movement style and surrounding herself with the devices of fiction that her very presence on the stage, though determinedly untheatrical and direct, seemed to be entering our consciousness secondhand. It would be too easy to assume that this Woman Who is Rainer herself. All the tokens of verisimilitude that she grants us are veiled, often many times over. Memos typed on note cards are projected on a wall, scripts telling of past incidents are read by an actress into a microphone, Rainer dances her *Three Satie Spoons* to show us how she danced it once. The woman's experiences are conveyed with the extreme literality and exaggerated pathos of soap opera — "A nameless grief swept through her . . ." — yet the emotions are all vague, without objects or reasons. None of the characters have names and none of the conflicts are resolved. Yet, at the end, "Now that she knew her true feelings, she was free to love again."

In this piece Rainer achieved almost a complete inversion; though she seems to focus on the most personal, intimate experiences of an individual she actually shows us the struggles of any or all of us. The very concreteness and overabundance of words and actions releases us from any one actuality. There's been a decided increase in the verbal content of dance generally. In other recent experimental work I think of Dunas' cryptic verses recited by narrators whose faces you never see; Grand Union's comic dialogues, often carried on while the performers wrap themselves around each other or hang by their knees from a pole; Kenneth King's taped monologue that details in punning, labyrinthine language his discovery of *Inadmissle-*

able Evidentdance; and even those Day Glo advertisements of identity being splashed across the backdrop in Tharp's *Deuce Coupe.* None of these words are used in a literal, functional, or descriptive way. They have become devices for broadening the inference of the dance or preventing the viewer from making a realistic interpretation. This may be the first time in the verbal society that so many words have been placed in the service of movement.

Two of the most interesting experimental efforts don't really belong to any of the trends I've mentioned. They both strike me as being close to conventional dance although they probably look less like Western theater dance than anything I've described. They are the work of Laura Dean and of the Multigravitational group.

Multigravitational, under its director, Stephanie Evanitsky, works in the air, in a high steel scaffolding with suspended harnesses, swings, and stationary bars, platforms, and wires. This imposing structure suggests acrobatics, of course, but that's just what Multigrav has avoided. The first couple of years they learned how to move smoothly from one aerial support to another, keeping their bodies in motion but their weight withheld. They undulated through their big environment like fish in a tank, hypnotically sensual and sometimes beautiful, but seldom more than that.

Recently, however, their work has become more dynamic. The Jungle gym has grown sleeker and more sophisticated, with narrow flexible trapezes and other specialized hardware replacing the old inner tubes. The performers have their medium so well under control that we actually stop seeing the trapezes, we begin to imagine for long periods of time that these people actually inhabit the air they move through so fluently. In *Silver Scream Idols* two dancers float in space, languidly lean out to blow kisses at an adoring public, suddenly plummet down like Icarus spurned by the sun, recover unhurt, swim narcissistically back up again.

Carry, their new work, premièred at the Space in December, made me aware of ways we earthlings can never move, the many relationships we don't ever find ourselves in because our world is flat, squared-off, and everybody walks on one level or in one direction. In *Carry*, one person passes another with his head about at her waist level. People lying down encounter people walking. You become conscious of parts of the body that are seldom articulated, like the back of the shoulders, and parts that aren't used for supporting other people, like the hip. People spread or fall out into undiscovered parts of the space around them. All because, as its name suggests, Multigravitational has found alternative means of supporting the body.

Laura Dean sees dance as a unifying activity, a way of strengthening the kinship of a group and minimizing its differences. Rather than impose on the group members a set of standard body attitudes, shapes, and line, as ordinary theater dance does, she dictates a rhythm. Compared to stage choreography, Dean's dance structures are ridiculously simple. All the performer really has to do is keep track of the counts; the other parts of his task probably get registered internally after a while, so that pivot-turn-step becomes almost an automatic corollary to the stepstepstepstepstepstep AND STAMP . . . The interval between accents, the tempo, the path of the dance, the simple gestures, must all become nearly unconscious factors too.

If I've described this right, you're beginning to think of folk dancing, and that seems to me very similar to what Dean is doing. The limited but mandatory rules that Dean's dancers follow give them a common goal, and the regular pulse of the rhythm draws them together in feeling. I wonder if Laura Dean has ever tried out one of her dances on a mass scale. I bet they would look like Laban's movement choirs.

Whether all this discussion of all these people really defines the avant-garde today I don't know. I've always had trouble understanding what people mean by the term, other than to outline the general vicinity of whatever they think is new. The word seems to change from time to time in its particular references and inclusions. In some periods various artists — poets, painters, dancers — work together to extend the existing boundaries of art. Sometimes the avant-garde is intentionally destructive, smiting tradition with no plans to replace it after its hoped-for downfall. I sometimes feel cut off from the avant-garde, snubbed by it, as if it's all taking place somewhere I haven't heard of yet. But I think the experimental dance today cannot be explained in any of these terms.

We can't even fall back on the catchall assumption that nothing *really* new is acceptable to the general audience. Fortunately in some ways, we are in a time of cultural ambiguity. The audience, particularly the dance audience, doesn't know what it's supposed to like or not like. Its loyalties gyrate from one company, one choreographer to another. Careers rise and fall in a season. Style is not sacrosanct; quality is not imprisoned in Lincoln Center. I think this is why we can see Twyla Tharp's ballets cheered by the Joffrey audience; it's not that Tharp has sold out her art to become popular.

I like to think of the avant-garde as a force that's always at work somewhere, nourishing dance and me even when we're not aware of its existence. Like nitrogen or a free press. It's always changing and always asking questions of itself. When it stops doing that and goes into business with a predictable product, it's no longer the avant-garde. Some very nice dance is being done, for instance, by people who are reiterating what the Judson avant-garde was doing ten years ago, but it's not dance that changes anything now. Maybe what I'm saying is that the avant-garde constitutes a position of risk for the dancers and the audience. They're not sure ahead of time what they're going to do, and we're not sure how to look at it. There's a lot of audience willing to take that risk right now. And, no longer on the defensive for the moment, the avant-garde is despising us less and trying to tell us more.

April 1974

Up from Minimalism

IT'S FUNNY HOW we keep looking at dance and thinking it isn't changing much. When Nora Guthrie did Meredith Monk's *Break* (1964) last summer, the dance was as clear to me as a narrative ballet — maybe clearer, because although there were lapses, there were no contradictions. Now, *Break* in 1964 was a very bizarre, even outrageous dance. Not only did it represent a break with Monk's modern dance training and, I assume, aspirations, it fragmented the actual dance event in so many ways that most people took it as a collage or a surrealistic exercise if they could take it at all.

Nine years later, its pieces didn't seem puzzling. I don't know if *Break* was "about" an auto accident or some other crash that affected the choreographer so much she had to separate and disguise its parts in order to recollect them. But it might have been about that, and anyway I'm sure what matters is that we absorb it as an entity despite its apparently miscellaneous parts. And then, Ping Chong's *I flew to Fiji, you went South* this fall hardly looked strange to me at all. As befits the times, *Fiji* was colorful and decorative and entertaining where *Break* was stark, but it must have been constructed from the same set of plans.

After the first eye-splitting change, we go on seeing as if we'd always seen things that new way. Further changes and developments are so much easier to take in that we hardly notice them. Which is why my immediate reaction to Lucinda Childs at the Whitney Museum December 7 was to wonder where she'd been for the past five years. When she and Judy Padow and Danny Tai came striding out across the floor for the first dance, barefoot, dressed in cream-colored leotards and maroon velvet hip-huggers, I thought, why this is Old Rainer. Childs even had an old Rainer haircut, short, straight, and close to the head, with little swatches of hair in front of the ears.

Untitled Trio was choreographed in 1968 at Judson Church and revised this year, and it looked like a throwback. The three-part piece was all walking briskly first along two diagonals and then randomly in the space, lunges that pulled back into a sit, rolling the back down to the floor and getting up again by pushing the pelvis forward. In one variation the dancer would swing over onto her stomach from a sitting position and continue rolling until she was sitting again. There didn't seem to be a strong rhythmic pulse, but the group worked in teams of two against one most of the time. Exaggerating the thrust of their step and the disengaged swing of their arms, they seemed to be trying to reproduce the athleticism that was natural to Rainer.

At one time it seemed awfully important to make dances this way. Movement had gotten so complex, so technical, so loaded with meaning that we saw only the embellishments, the significances. A step was so lowly and mechanical in this hierarchy of accomplishments that it wasn't even noticed. So Rainer and the others stripped away the decorations, gutted it all down to the step. I think she not only wanted us to see the step again, but she wanted to feel it again herself. I think Rainer wanted not only to find the basics but to restore meaning to basic activities, to invest as much conviction in the essentials of movement as her contemporaries were investing in the luxuries.

When we looked at Rainer's *Trio A* we saw activity. Plain as that. Dancers, nondancers — stepping, falling, rolling — muscles adjusting themselves to bone structures — each person's system of joints and nerves operating in its own particular pattern that you could see because that's all there was to see. The energy and the presence of the moment were all.

After only a couple of years of this, we could see that these bare elements carried implications of their own. Without going back to conventional theatricality and virtuosics, the performers could move on in several ways: improvisation and games, big political and social statements, literary or narrative structures. Yvonne Rainer and various associates — Trisha

Brown, Steve Paxton, the Grand Union — ventured into all these. Now, principally because Rainer freed performance from technique and made us concentrate so hard on that least little thing, lots of people are dancing and improvising and exploring movement who never would have tried it before, and lots of new challenges are being offered to the audience's perceptions.

Into all this stepped Lucinda Childs, her new pieces scarcely less austere than the older one. *Particular Reel* was a solo in which Childs walked, mostly backward, back and forth until she'd covered the space like a sweeper, changing her arm positions, making very slight excursions into space by twisting her torso or leaning off-center. As she progressed at an even pace, I wondered how someone could be changing all the time and still manage to look always the same. In *Checkered Drift*, Padow and Tai fell forward from lunges that slowly tilted into the ground or King Kong struts that leaned backward and then pitched forward. And in *Calico Mingling*, Childs, Padow, Janice Paul, and Susan Brody strode backward and forward continuously to a silent count of six, making intersecting semicircles all over the space.

In 1973, Lucinda Childs looks intractable, even reactionary. Instead of digging for sources that could lead to new ideas, she seems to be burrowing into work that's been done to find what's at the bottom of it. Excavating planted ground rather than exploring fallow ground. What bothered me more was the dancers' matter-of-factness, their look of near-boredom, and their determination not to vary their dynamics or show any particular enjoyment in the task. Maybe this was the authentic performing style for this kind of work. But I missed the comradeship and spontaneity that's allowed to come through now in today's more relaxed work.

Laura Dean's concert at NYU's Loeb Student Center the next night brought me back to the present. Dean is as rigorous and pure about getting back to basics as anyone at Judson Church ever was, but she's taken the essentials in her own direction, into structures of considerable complexity. She's definite where they were almost sloppy, high-strung where they were cooled-out.

Dean's unit of movement is the weight shift, with variations limited to stepping, stamping, small jumps, and pivot turns, and, at NYU, one choreographed gesture: clapping. Her dancers don't fall, sit, or make any arm designs, to name a few things that the early minimalists permitted themselves. Dean's bodies are upright, purposeful, not a thing wasted or added. I think they have to be, because Dean sets up such demanding assignments for them.

For each dance the performers create a geometric floor pattern and a rhythmic framework by their extended repetition of the step. In *Stamping Dance*, which looks like a refinement of Lucinda Childs's *Calico Mingling* except it was made two years before, four women walk, with pronounced emphasis on the outside foot, first in one large circle, then in individual smaller circles. Every so many steps, they change direction.

Ten people walk with tiny shuffling steps in four concentric circles that change directions one ring at a time, in *Circle Dance*. The interval between changes gets smaller until the group is pivoting on every step, then it lengthens out again, and at a certain point the rings start breaking up and the dancers spin very fast out into space.

In *Jumping Dance* twelve people jump together, straight up in place, expelling a forceful "HA!" on every push-off from the ground, until they get tired. Then they stop, recover, join in again. *Changing Pattern Steady Pulse* divides the group of twelve in half two ways — they face each other in lines of six, and, as a musician keeps time with claves and the dancers clap, every other person goes into the center, where they spin in a big circle that ends one place down the line from where they were. This shift makes the whole group move gradually across the room.

Dean's work is extremely mathematical and calculated, and we're meant to see that; the structure is not just a device of choreography. The look of it is also extremely flat — military almost in its insistence on unison movement, in the inviolability of the programmed floor designs, and especially in its repetition. To dance for thirty minutes may be tiring, but to do the same step for thirty minutes, with only your counts for comfort, as in *Circle Dance*, seems excessive.

Yet it doesn't become deadening, either for the performers or the audience. The gradual evolution of visual patterns and the overlapping, shading, falling away of sounds have a continuing fascination throughout a piece. Besides, you can look at individual dancers. They do the same thing over and over, so in a short time you get to know them rather well — how they attack, sustain, let go of movement, whether they have good balance, which ones are tense, which ones are having fun or working too hard.

Nor, despite the choreography's lack of variety and spatial challenge, does it isolate the performers from each other. The dancer's body may be limited in its specific directions and shapes, but it is very active as a whole. The pace is fast, and something — perhaps the constant necessity of keeping track of the sequence, perhaps Dean's own driving rhythm — keeps the concentration very intense and alert. Every time the weight shifts, the dancer renews his or her impulse; Dean builds enough change into the movement so that people don't become spastic or sink into trance. I'm sure these are the very same elements that keep the Australian aborigines and the Africans dancing all night. Maybe Laura Dean is inventing folk dance for Americans.

February 1974

Dancing in the Celestial Orchestra

I ADMIT IT. I got payola. Somebody at Deutsche Grammophon sent me the three-record album of Steve Reich's "Drumming" and other pieces, and I listened to it for three weeks before seeing Laura Dean's new dance at Brooklyn Academy.

Three weeks was not nearly long enough to explore the rhythmic and harmonic vitality of "Drumming" — it's a feast for listening and moving to. Watching it is another experience again.

Maybe you wouldn't think eight dancers, ten musicians, two singers, eight drums, three marimbas, three glockenspiels, and a piccolo playing a twelve-count pattern at the same tempo could keep your interest for over an hour. But you would be wrong. By severely limiting his tonal choices and giving up the emotionally, aesthetically loaded compositional techniques of Western music, Reich shifts our attention to what seems like an infinite variety of rhythmic changes and sonic textures that are possible for this scoring.

Dean has a different problem, since her instruments — the dancers — have to create their own limitations. The human body is capable of so much more nuance, more complexity of tuning and attack than a drum. Just a person standing before us is a statement, and the person hardly has to move at all before we start making interpretations.

So when you first look at Laura Dean's dancers, standing very straight and squared-off to the audience, arms at their sides, and when they begin a quick stepping to the drums, they seem unnaturally restrained. They look stern, almost military. Later the dance gets more active, but never what you'd call ego-centered. I think all that suppressed performing energy parceled out evenly helps provide Dean's dancers with the endurance to keep up a rhythmic pulse for the whole span of the music.

She rings her changes on this plain, clog-dance body attitude by increasing the complexity of foot steps — there are sections of skipping, running in place with the feet kicking out forward, jumping up and down with both feet together — and by adding a limited number of arm gestures — rotating the fists very fast is one, flinging both arms out behind the shoulders is another. The floor patterns are very clear, simple lines and circles, with the dancers in unison most of the time.

Having established this rather didactic attitude, Dean later has some fun with it. Facing the audience in a nicely spaced formation, the dancers do a whole series of combinations in place that incorporate ballet steps — entrechats, ronds de jambe — in canon and with different rhythmic accents. There's a glimpse of a tap dancer's time step. Suddenly they look as if they're doing some kind of balletic Hungarian folk dance. At another moment they're gliding around on bent knees like Balinese court dancers. The rond de jambe becomes a Charleston kick.

The dance usually follows the rhythmic emphasis of the music, but at one of several phasing interludes — where the musicians go a beat out of phase with one another to change the rhythm — half the dancers are stepping on the beat and half off the beat. During another phasing section, the dancers keep the original beat while the musicians slide off, into the cracks, then back onto the beat again.

Someone was telling me recently that there are differences between visual and auditory perception, and I find polyrhythms easier to pick out with the ear than with the eye. But we're also very conditioned to regular rhythms on the stage, another habit of Western art. Rhythmic consonance makes the emotional impact stronger.

With my Western eyes and my lingering Romantic need to comprehend everything, I often wished there was less going on in *Drumming*. But there came one moment of transcendence, when, during the second — marimba — section of the music, Dean abandoned rhythmic compliance altogether. Listening, perhaps, to a sustained ringing created by overtones in the percussive sound, the dancers spun in different tempos, in two concentric orbits around Dean. As they whirled and lifted their faces and palms to the resonating space above them, I thought of some great celestial orchestra made up of vibrations, energies, a universal pulse, not any single artist's tune at all.

April 10, 1975

I Went With Him and She
Came With Me

IT's HARD TO EXPLAIN William Dunas as an officially sanctionable, supportable phenomenon. But in another way, he may be the most important dancer we could support today. Dunas is the kind of artist who is his own justification. He isn't "relevant," he doesn't have students or imitators, he doesn't reach a large audience and doesn't appear to care, he isn't giving a significant amount of work to anybody else, and isn't looking to expand his own avenues of work. He is, on the other hand, the most consistently creative person in all of dance.

Since 1968 Dunas has been making solo dances, sometimes only one or two a year, now much more frequently thanks to a Guggenheim fellowship. His modus operandi is to work with the same movement material, constantly reorganizing and modifying it, until he has extracted all the possible implications from it. Years ago I asked him why he wanted to keep remaking the same dance all the time, and he answered, "I haven't run out of things to say yet." This remark drastically changed the way I looked at all experimental dance.

Dunas makes you aware of the way small, subtle adjustments can totally alter what you thought were predictable forms. Or, as a student of mine said the other day, "Maybe he's trying to lower my threshold of differences."

The present works comprise Dunas' third cycle. In the first, he used virtually the same dance themes over and over again in collage form. By changing his appearance and style of moving slightly, and by adding new movement, props, and sounds, he created a different characterization each time. The second series, perhaps a transition, seems to have attempted to involve the audience in an environment that was different and particularly appropriate to each dance. Now he's working with live sound and narration toward making a single statement, usually a political one. He gets at the statement obliquely rather than literally, and the dances achieve their unity through his extraordinarily controlled and stylized use of words, sounds, movements, and images. Dunas' primary concern now is to be simple, though he says the simpler he tries to be, the less people understand him.

I Went With Him and She Came With Me was, on the surface, an hour-long piece in which Dunas merely walked around a space. Following straight, diagonal, or slightly curving paths, he slowly lifted one foot, then the other, going on continuously except for brief rest stops.

John Smead, upstage, played brief passages on an electronic organ, usually setting up an ostinato texture — of melody, chords, or single tones — and then varying the loudness or other qualities electronically.

Carolyn Lord sat motionless in a chair downstage center. Due to Edward Effron's lighting, which consisted of one candle behind a pillar, two old-fashioned ceiling fixtures, and partly concealed lights under Smead's and Lord's chairs, you couldn't make out any of the performers' faces, except in vague outline. It didn't matter, as they purposely had no expressions on their faces, or, for that matter, in their bodies.

Every few minutes Carolyn Lord would recite a line in a rather high-pitched but husky voice with odd, rhetorical inflections. She seemed to be thinking aloud about some important event — a flight, evidently, that she and some other people had made from their home in order to escape attackers. Sometimes she would mention things that happened on the trip or before they left. Other phrases referred to how she felt about leaving. The verses weren't sequential; they were more like the occasionally audible parts of a bad tape, or the phrases people blurt out when they're dreaming.

The verses were written in a strange, mannered style that barely rhymed or scanned, and that confined itself almost exclusively to one-syllable words: "We had to flee so we could be free." "He wanted her and I needed them." "They drove us away with fear and might." The narration was like the affected and almost romanticized way we sometimes talk about a very painful event in order to keep from showing our emotion.

On an immediate level, I never lost interest in the piece. There were the actual events to keep track of — Smead's musical inventions, Lord's fragmentary story, Dunas' one or two variations in step. Besides that, I enjoyed examining Dunas' movement, which is very complex as to the way he distributes his weight, rearranges his tensions, contains himself in space. Since the step itself changed so little, I could pay full attention to its ingredients, and discover new aspects of it as he moved through the room. Each slight shift of the angle of light, of his direction, of his location relative to the other performers created another way to look at the same thing.

In addition, the piece had meaning as metaphor. The narrative suggested exile and war to me, specifically Vietnam, and I thought about the thousands of homeless Vietnamese people who will still be adrift in their country long after the bombs stop falling and the soldiers withdraw. I also thought that Dunas was making me feel something about the tedium of a very long march or other repetitive task — about the way you conserve your energy and maintain your feelings at a very low intensity, and the way you occupy your mind with minute detail in order to keep from going crazy; the prisoner who counts the tiles in the floor of the cell, the assembly line worker who follows a patch of sunlight all day in its progress across the room.

January 1973

Bucolic Violence in Middle America

STOREY, AN AMERICAN NARRATIVE starts out as an elegiac memoir of small-town America and ends in violence. Yet the dancer, narrator, and musician who perform it are detached, dispassionate. There's something terse and literary about this, and also something tough and rednecked. Hemingway captured it, that typically American combination of grim morality and emotion denied.

In a bare white loft with a rotted wooden floor, the audience is seated on a church-basement bench that's too high for a small person's legs to rest on the ground, and has the brick wall for a back. The performers, wearing plain wash clothes, enter and station themselves: John Smead goes to one side of the long shallow space where his musical instruments have been set up, Arleen Schloss sits in a chair at the opposite side, and dancer William Dunas stands behind her chair looking out over the space that will be his territory for the next hour.

Smead starts to play some countrified chords on a guitar and harmonica while Schloss begins the story. "I remember the autumn morning when I returned to our home. I passed the butcher's wife on her way to church." Dunas walks slowly across the space making small circles with his arms by rotating his shoulder joints. He takes positions that look like preparations for ballet steps. He walks along a diagonal, plié, relevé, plié, relevé. He hops in place. He runs with tiny steps.

Smead continues his Dylanesque music while Dunas' steps get gradually more fussy, cover more space, and Schloss remembers an incident from "when I was alive and very young." After a long time, what with all the detail of reminiscence, we learn that on the same Sunday that her grandmother was dying, the girl saw a bank robber escaping, pursued by a dog.

The story grows more bizarre and Smead switches to a snare

drum, making a constant roll with sticks, getting louder and softer like a circus fanfare. Schloss tells how she announced the robbery to her father as people came out of church. Incensed that their money has been stolen, the town citizens turn into a mob and set out to find the one member of the community who wasn't in church. They stone him to death. Schloss, returning home where the preacher is saying prayers for her grandmother, notices that his coat is ripped where she had seen the dog bite the robber. When she tries to accuse him, she's hanged for a witch.

As this macabre event unfolds, Dunas dances faster and more urgently, taking fewer breathers, and Smead begins playing an autoharp with a violin bow, scraping across the strings to make a thin, whiny sound that turns into squawks and yowls and finally into sobs. By the time Schloss says flatly, "I died," Smead has become silent, and Dunas, off to the side, is coming slowly forward moving his arms through a steady but exhausted port de bras in the diminishing glow from a spotlight.

Dunas has been doing these collaborative works with Smead, lighting designer Edward Effron, and various speakers who recite Dunas' scripts, for several seasons now. All the components contribute to the impact of each piece, and none is communicative in the usual modern dance descriptive-expressive sense. Each performer works with great control and intensity to produce a changing coloration. As Schloss's story becomes more vicious, the quality of Smead's sound also gets harsher and Dunas' dancing reaches punishing limits of endurance. But none of them become totally involved or identified with the horror of it.

Dunas uses a presentational ballet vocabulary with embellishments and variations. He keeps moving for the entire length of the piece, doing small batches of steps — little step-hops in circles, shifting from foot to foot very fast in place, turning or hitching around in a circle with one heel dragging, pacing slowly at the side to rest. Except for a couple of signature themes, no phrase is exactly like any other. His arms are constantly in motion, sketching formal designs around his upper body.

You could enjoy it like any pure-dance solo except it's all

understated, underdone, unfinished-looking. Dunas is a big man who always works below his maximum force. Sometimes he looks almost delicate. His jumps are held close to the ground, his grand jetés hardly travel. He gets a lot of his propulsion from his powerful hips and legs, but the drive that initiates his leg action never spreads to his upper body, which is held straight and facing forward.

His dancing always conveys to me a fanatic determination to do more, to last longer than anyone humanly can, together with a holding back from complete commitment, an implied fear of unleashing his full strength. I think Dunas is making his dancing into a metaphor, into another of the American rituals for containment of aggression — like sports, truck driving, parades, beauty contests, and spelling bees.

May 22, 1975

Watching the Words Go By

WE'RE SO CAUGHT UP with the nonverbal these days that we often want to discount words altogether. I do anyway, whenever words are offered as part of a dance. I listen to them as music or static — background or interference — but seldom as information that I need to see the dance with. During Kenneth King's November series it occurred to me that maybe there are only great words and all the rest of the words. Maybe it gets down to that.

Kenneth King's *High Noon*, billed as "a portrait-play based on the writings and life of the great Prophet-Philosopher Friedrich Nietzsche," was almost all talking and no moving. *Time Capsule*, a "theatre event and reading," had one man dancing

live and one man dancing on film almost continuously while
another man talked. I found the Nietzsche piece thoroughly
absorbing; the other was like a broken radio from which you
can decipher intelligible ideas every once in a while out of the
buzz.

High Noon is a staged monologue of Nietzscheana, chosen
and slung together by King, who reveres the great German
thinker as a cornerstone of modern theater. Using the voice of
Pontease Tyak, one of his own fictitious alter egos, and other
vocal disguises, King meditates, reasons, and rages at the world
for an hour and a half.

It all takes place in a tiny dim space designed to look like the
boarding-house room, or one of the rooms, in which Nietzsche
spent a good part of his life. Kenneth King seems to have an
innate kinship with this reclusive genius, who invented a make-
believe society and then delivered messages to it that he didn't
expect the real world to understand for a hundred years.

As the play begins King/Nietzsche/Tyak/Zarathustra, in dark
glasses, long gray hair and beard, ratty black overcoat and cap,
is sitting all bundled up in a squeaky armchair. A cold light is
coming in the window, and you get the impression he's awak-
ened at dawn and can't get back to sleep, or maybe he doesn't
ever sleep, just mulls over his thoughts and dozes.

In a heavy accent that might be Russian or Middle European, he tries out aphorisms, argues with himself, defines the
"Overman" who will inherit the world when the present race of
men has destroyed itself. "Not around the makers of new noise
but new values does the world evolve." This Overman will be a
dancer and a cynic — "The gods enjoy mockery." He will "see
things through a hundred eyes," and will understand that "every profound spirit needs a mask."

As he debates these momentous ideas, King walks up and
down in his cubicle, writes at a stand-up desk with a quill pen,
mixes medicines that he rarely drinks, looks unseeing out the
window. Gradually, odd things materialize out of this literal
setting, the deranged, beautiful visions of someone who has
been confined for a long time.

Talking about masks and deceptions, he begins pulling out
the hairs of his beard and slowly transforms himself into a

younger — but still possessed — hermit. In a burst of anger about "the American lust for gold," he throws back a curtain you didn't know was there, and reveals a huge, fake, fat bird, a cock or a turkey, hanging by its neck in a cell flooded with a sickly yellow light.

Toward the end, still ranting, he pulls something like a skull out of an open trunk, hangs it on a coat rack, and begins constructing a dummy that looks a little bit like himself — hat, silver shades, his overcoat, a length of white chiffon that he arranges across the head, shoulders, and chest where the gray hair might be. When it's done he seems to feel himself dying — he isn't really, it's just another panicky moment. He drapes himself on the dummy-Overman for a minute and sobs, "I am Dionysus the crucified." Then he climbs back onto his couch and as the lights go out he repeats the line in King's own voice.

Time Capsule is a kind of continuation of *High Noon*, or at least an exploration in King's own stuttering, punning words of some of the same ideas. King, who enters dressed like his Overman dummy, stands or sits near a school desk and reads from his notebook while Arnold Horton turns in the foreground at fluctuating speeds. Much of the time there's also a film being shown — spliced-together sequences photographed with different lenses and filters at different times, of King dancing in different clothes, in a room where the furniture changes.

Certain things happen in the piece — King changes position, goes away, comes back — but eventually I could only sense the flow of it, a rhythm that poured out of his words and his filmed dancing, connecting the changes of tempo and outward form, reassuring, timeless. After a time, another Overman-figure climbs out of the trap in the floor where King first appeared, this one dressed as an Arab oilman. Does King mean this is where evolution ends, or is it just another stage in the Nietzschean progression?

November 21, 1974

Did Anybody See My Monster Dress?

ONE DAY LAST FALL the Grand Union invited most of the New York dance critics who are interested in the avant-garde to a rap session about criticizing the Grand Union. To begin, one member of the Grand Union said he was disappointed because the critics never wrote about how revolutionary the Grand Union is. He turned for corroboration to another member of the Grand Union. She said she didn't think the Grand Union was particularly revolutionary.

I felt a lot better after that.

The essence of the Grand Union's work is its improvisational technique. One performance is amazingly unlike any other performance. The parts of any one performance may not relate thematically to each other. What you're seeing is an interaction among six people that just flows out and disappears. The point is not to stop it or repeat it or rework it. Strange that the people who do it are so concerned with recording it.

What comes across most consistently to me about the work is the personal styles of the individual performers. Without prearrangement — I can't imagine how they rehearse — six people have agreed to come together and live a part of their lives in public. Even though they've worked together for years, any one of them can affect the course of this life, and eventually the audience begins to see the particular role each one is playing in the relationship.

Steve Paxton is like the conscience of the group, and also a subliminal prime mover. On the Saturday night of their recent series at La Mama, Paxton hovered behind David Gordon, who was playing a game of I'll-scratch-your-tummy-if-you-scratch-my-thigh with Trisha Brown and Barbara Dilley. Shadowing Gordon like a Kabuki stage manager, Paxton quietly warned him not to get excited, to remember they had another performance to do the next day.

Paxton often seems to stay outside the jollier games, joining up with participants, after they've finished, to talk things over confidentially — except what he's talking about might be some totally different subject — movie sound tracks for instance. There's a very strong drive for domination in Paxton which seems short-circuited a lot of the time. It bursts out in lifting/carrying/throwing duets with Doug Dunn, in his dogged conducting of Nancy Lewis and the group in an interminable song without a tune. When you guys *When you guys* Meet you guys *Meet you guys* . . .

Nancy Lewis is a perfect foil. She plays the ingénue — the dumb, attractive female. At one point she stood for ages on the stage at one end of the space, with a blanket thrown over her head. Hearing Dilley tell Paxton, "I get confused," she piped up, "I do too. Am I doing anything important?" Lewis is also the possessor of the quickest imagination. She can become a sylph or a monster or a Grecian shepherdess just like that, can vocalize like a Moroccan at prayer.

It was Lewis who saw the possibilities of all three women doing a hilarious hand dance with a follow spot, and Lewis who initiates episodes of sexual innuendo. Walking arm in arm with Dunn she asked, "Is this your first time?" "Never you mind," he replied. Gordon, scratching Dilley's shoulder, picked up the idea. "How do you like this one?" he said, punching Dilley in the stomach. "That was terrific," said Brown. "That's my favorite so far," she said as Dilley sagged to the floor in her arms.

Brown and Dunn seem to like working on movement ideas, alone or with others, better than they like skits. Dunn did a long solo standing still, moving only his mouth — later he added the eyebrows — during the women's dance with the follow spot; and Brown often spends long periods of time sitting still in a prominent place, as if she mildly disapproved of the surrounding zaniness.

Dilley also likes physical things, and seems slightly self-conscious about taking an acting role. But she'll fall in with any risky plan. Gordon and Brown at one point had hefted her and

Paxton like bags of groceries in front of them. "We'll throw Steve and Barbara in the air. They'll clasp bodies in the air, change places, and come down in our arms again," explained Gordon. Dilley looked prepared to do just that.

David Gordon does a lot of the talking, masterminding, cracking jokes, and commenting on how things are going. He seems to want to control events, but he gives in when the events take over. Power struggles are subtle with the Grand Union, and at this performance there were no casualties.

After a long sequence when everyone did a kinky-looking solo — perhaps Paxton touched off this one — Brown and Dunn found themselves standing close together, very straight and serious like the couple in "American Gothic," facing the others, who stood about ten feet away in a tight group. After a long silence, Brown said, "CAN WE STOP?" Gordon tried once to have the last word but she held her ground. "I just want to stop and go home," she said in a tired voice. So they stopped.

March 27, 1975

Brown Studies

TRISHA BROWN'S CONCERT at Brooklyn Academy was too short. And also too long. Looking at her work, my time sense keeps shifting. After a piece has been going on for a while, I find myself doing things I do when a dance gets really monotonous, then that helps me discover more of what's happening in the dance, then it gets really interesting, and suddenly it ends.

Brown takes all kinds of liberties with the approved ways of making dances — how long they should last, how the performers are supposed to appear to the audience, and how they're to state their business. Two of her works were unthinkably short — not more than five minutes each, I'd say. Two were quite long. One didn't seem to be a piece at all, but a preliminary to a piece that wasn't ever shown. But what affects time more than any of these tangible things is the way Brown moves, makes movement and movement structures.

Working from the avant-gardist ideas of the early 1960s, Brown wanted to find more basic ways to move than the traditional expressive or decorative modes of modern dance and ballet. She and her dancers work with a flexible, unstretched, unstressed body. No one part of the body is trained or emphasized at the expense of the others; no movement is meant to look better following any other particular movement or is grouped with others to form a phrase. It all just flows easily from here to there.

Brown also wanted to find ways of *using* movement, which set her apart from some of her contemporaries. Everything I've seen of hers has a structure, a job to be accomplished, or a problem to be solved. So there's this odd contradiction in watching her; the movement is even, modular, not loaded, but the sum total of these all-alike movement occurrences is very important. The movements may not be fabulously interesting in themselves, but each one is a clue, and once you start discovering the pattern in which they're arranged, they become satisfying in the ways all aesthetic structures are.

The two short works at Brooklyn were 4321234 and *Solo Olos*. In 4321234 four women spaced themselves over the floor so that by walking four steps, turning in a certain direction, three steps, turning, and so forth, they crossed the space and ended up on the opposite side from where they began, but in the same formation. In an interview last week Trisha Brown explained the idea behind *Solo Olos* — a kind of sketch for a bigger dance to come — but I hadn't read those remarks before the concert and there wasn't enough of the dance to grasp it. Most of all I noticed how perfectly aligned Brown's body is, so that when she moves in a direction she goes straight there with everything she has — no waverings or unintentional detours.

Sticks, on the other hand, was one big detour. Five women lay foot-to-head in a line. Each one held a long pole above her body, touching the pole of the woman in front and in back of her. The object was to make a complete revolution over the pole without breaking the connection. I'd heard this piece described before, but never imagined how laborious it turned out to be, just sliding to the side, getting up on one knee, swinging the knee over the pole, folding down and sliding under again. Calling warnings and instructions to one another like construction workers guiding a giant crane, the women had to make a constant series of adjustments, and their progress in short, careful spurts was so broken that they didn't seem to be moving at all.

Locus, first shown in Brown's studio last spring, offers the dancers a large choice of direction and distance within which they can perform a set sequence of movements. What they do is quite simple in a dancing sense — the torso is kept quiet and most of the movement has to do with folding or unfolding of arms and legs, or rotating a limb or the head or the hips. Only one thing happens at a time, then the next and the next. The body is relaxed, the intensity low. But, perhaps because each movement is given equal importance, there seems to be a great deal of design that's getting created and erased very quickly.

They can also begin this sequence at different points. So, although they begin in unison, the dance never looks like a unison dance because everyone is facing a different way. Later, they're not even doing the same movements together, but their body shapes and progressions keep echoing off each other like chimes.

At one point my eyes decided to go a bit out of focus, and instead of seeing individual configurations, I saw the design of the whole dancing-space changing, like the stage in a big ballet ensemble. Maybe because of the movements Brown chose or because each dancer was working within her own imaginary cube, they often seemed to be fortuitously arranging themselves into harmonious sets of diagonals or folded and unfolded body parts. Toward the end, they began falling into and out of unison with one other person, and this added to my impression of formal choreography.

Brown's new piece, *Pyramid,* had Elizabeth Garren, Wendy Perron, Judith Ragir, and Mona Sulzman working to a metronome. Each dancer had made her own, Brownish movement sequence, but especially with the metronome going you could see how hard it was for them to avoid phrasing. A running step would automatically want to go faster, then slower. A gesture of touching the shoulder would be followed by an instant of stillness.

I hadn't read beforehand how this dance was made either: by a complicated process that they worked out themselves during the dance, the women added and subtracted parts of their sequences until they were all down to the one movement with which they began, and that was the end of the dance. But I was beginning to catch on anyway. Because the sequences are repeated often, you begin to learn Brown's dances; you see someone doing something familiar, and then you can stick with that person through the whole round until she gets back to the beginning. That's how you find out what's changing. In another half an hour I would have had it.

January 15, 1976

Dunn Reposing

DOUGLAS DUNN makes you think about polarities. About emptiness and clutter. Life and death. Work and idleness. Seeing and being seen. He makes you wonder for a minute which is which.

Dunn's Performance Exhibit 101 ended a two-week run recently at his loft on Broadway. Imagine turning your home into a museum and putting yourself on exhibit every day for four hours, and you get some idea of the extremity of the man's conceptions.

Entering the loft, you find the entire space has been shelved in with rough two-by-four construction, very straight and neat and uniform, and also dark and foreboding. First I look through it — one set of spaces is just at my eye level — a vista so extended, as if through a series of mail chutes, that I can't see the end of it even though I know the other wall isn't more than thirty feet away.

I start to move through what seems to be a corridor in a maze. But it's not really a maze, it's a very clear pathway leading around a central section of the room. Alcoves and side chambers open off from the main passage, but they're all blocked by waist-high shelves and crossbars supporting higher parts of the structure.

As in a dense forest, I can't see more than a few inches in any direction without my view being interrupted by another piece of scenery. But the feeling of the place is too man-made. It's more like a warehouse for outlandish packages all the same size. Or a morgue.

Just as I get into the middle of the room — it seems as if I've been traveling for days to reach the interior — I glance through the interstices up above and see a man's head resting on something like a hunk of wood covered with cloth. The sight is startling, shocking even. Every straight sandy-colored hair combed back against the head seems to stand out in relief. I hadn't realized how bare the place was of human relics.

It's Doug Dunn's head I see right away, and after I've made my way around to a few other vantage points, I see it's attached as usual to his body, which is lying flat out like a corpse on the very top of the center of the construction under a spotlight.

Well, I know it's the real Doug Dunn but I keep checking to make sure. Peering up from the right of him, I see that a tiny stream of sweat has trickled down through his make-up from the corner of one eye. His eyes are closed. I climb up to his level from way across the room — I haven't got the courage to move closer — and I see his chest moving up and down slightly.

Asleep then. Can a person control his sleep so he doesn't change position in four hours? Alpha wave? Trance? Perhaps he's just thinking quietly. Thinking about me, or aware of my presence anyway, since I'm the only one in there with his body.

The room is restful. I like it, and I want to stay there a long time. It seems as if I could just wipe all the minutiae from my mind, and I stay poised on the crossbars or sitting in the alcoves for long times without moving. But just as he's filled an empty space with insistent pieces of lumber, Dunn fills my mind with ideas a minute after he's allowed me to make it a blank.

Maybe I'm on exhibit. I begin to wonder about this when someone else comes in. She carefully avoids looking at me as she makes her way through the cavern, but we both take account of each other. She sits for a long time on the top shelf, and I down below, far away. I'm hiding. I don't want her to find me, but I want to see what she does. What is she thinking about?

The place is so still that every change in the air causes reverberations. The other woman breathes irregularly, setting off a chain reaction. I stir, she changes position, then comes down and goes stealthily past me and out.

I'm curled up in this tiny place feeling very exposed, while Doug Dunn lies out in the open, vulnerable, revealing nothing. I'm getting uneasy. It's time to go.

Doug Dunn hasn't moved at all.

October 24, 1974

ACKNOWLEDG-
MENTS

INDEX

Acknowledgments

Index